An Uncommon Life

An Uncommon Life
Thomas J. DeKornfeld, M.D.

Corvina

Text and images © Thomas J. DeKornfeld, 2015

Layout and cover design: Balázs Csöllei

Published in Hungary in 2015 by Corvina Books Ltd.

Dankó utca 4-8, H-1086 Budapest, Hungary
E-mail: corvina@lira.hu
Website: www.corvinakiado.hu

Distributed by Central European University Press an imprint
of the Central European University Limited Liability Company
Nádor utca 11, H-1051 Budapest, Hungary
Tel: +36 1 327 3138 or 327 3000
Fax: +36 1 327 3183
E-mail: ceupress@press.ceu.edu
Website: www.ceupress.com

224 West 57th Street, New York NY 10019, USA
Tel: +1 212 547 6932
Fax: +1 646 557 2416
E-mail: meszarosa@press.ceu.edu

All rights reserved. No part of this publication may be reproduced, stored in a retrieval system, or transmitted, in any form or by any means, without the permission of the Publisher.

ISBN 978 963 1 362565

Library of Congress Control Number: 2015935360

Printed in Hungary

Contents

	Introduction	7
Chapter one	Zsigmond	9
Chapter two	Manfréd	25
Chapter three	The Móric Kornfeld Family	53
Chapter four	Summertime	69
Chapter five	Derekegyháza	89
Chapter six	Growing up	97
Chapter seven	March Nineteenth, 1944	125
Chapter eight	Portugal	149
Chapter nine	American Adventure	165
	Glossary	253
	Biographical Sketches	255

...nothing less than the total destruction
and extinction of an entire way of life...

Sándor Márai, *Memoir of Hungary 1944–1948*

Introduction

This is the story of a young man's life before, during and after the catastrophe of March, 1944. The youngest child and second son of a prominent family he tells of a way of life that will never be experienced again.

My mother said that if you didn't live before 1914 you don't know what the good life really was. For about fifty years, Hungary had been at peace. The population was growing; prosperity was not limited to the upper classes. Budapest was ever more beautiful. The coffee houses were thriving; music, art and literature were in a period of great vigor.

The advent of the First World War brought changes that would tear the country apart. During the twenties and thirties Hungary was coping with the loss of a huge portion of its land and millions of its people. There was tension in the air about the growing strength of Germany. By the mid-thirties people were beginning to talk about their fear of a German expansion and anti-Semitic legislation was being introduced. The outbreak of the Second World War on September first, 1939, was a turning point from which there was no return. Much of my story takes place during the late twenties, thirties and early forties. With my family's immense financial resources and what seemed like our impregnable social status, I thought that we had little to worry about. In a sense I could view world affairs as something that existed outside of our domain. I was wrong. This work was written primarily for my children and grandchildren so that they would have a better understanding of their family. In writing it in some parts I relied heavily on the work of Ágnes Széchenyi to whom I wish to extend my warmest appreciation. I am also indebted to Professor Peter Pastor and to László Kúnos for their advice and encouragement. First and foremost, however, I want to express my deep and most grateful appreciation to my wife, Helen Dilworth DeKornfeld, without whose stimulation, many hours of work and unfailing support this book would never have been written and certainly would not be anywhere this complete.

Chapter one

Zsigmond

My paternal grandfather, Zsigmond Kornfeld, was born in 1852 in a small town called Jenikau (Jenikov) in Bohemia which is now the Czech Republic. His father leased a small distillery where he made fruit brandy. About fifteen years after Zsigmond was born the business failed which meant that the boy's formal education came to an end. He was in the sixth year of the secondary school; graduation was two years away.

I know next to nothing about his family. He had some brothers who became professional men – doctors, lawyers – but I don't know anything about them. I assume that Raphael Kornfeld who lives in Israel is the descendant of one of them. The family was Jewish of a fairly orthodox persuasion and there was a rabbi, Reb Aaron Jenikau, in the family who was Zsigmond's uncle. The rabbi was a highly respected person in the community. There is an appealing story that once, on a hot summer day, he was walking toward his home from a neighboring village when a member of his flock met him and said, "Rabbi, it is much too hot for an old man like you to walk all that way. Why don't you hire a carriage, it costs only 2 crowns and you can well afford it". The rabbi smiled and said, "Yes, I can afford 2 crowns and that is the reason why I gave them to a poor man who needed them much more than I".

Upon leaving school Zsigmond went to Prague, the capital of Bohemia, where he started to work for the M. Thorsch & Son Bank as a clerk. He evidently did well and moved on to work for the Wahrmann Bank which had extensive international interests. In 1870 he was sent to Paris and was there during the time of the Franco-Prussian war and the Commune. Paris was in chaos. He must have seen some terrible things because until the end of his life he never talked about it.

Returning to Prague, after two years, his career progressed rapidly and by the time he was twenty-four years old he was first vice president and then president of the Prague Bankers' Association. Shortly thereafter he became a director of the Prague branch of the Rothschild Credit Bank. In December, 1877, Baron Albert Rothschild called him to Vienna and asked him if he would go to Budapest and see what he could do to salvage the Hungarian General Bank of Credit, a Rothschild affiliate, which was in financial difficulties.

On March twelfth, 1878, Zsigmond arrived in Budapest wearing pince-nez and a beard. He did not have much money and did not know a word of Hungarian. However, his job involved him immediately with the problems of the bank. Soon becoming a member of the board of directors he took control for the Rothschilds. He was extraordinarily successful and within a year he made an offer to the Hungarian government to convert the outstanding debts of the country into an annuity loan. It was due almost entirely to his efforts that within a few months the government was able to sell three hundred thirteen million forint worth of gold-backed annuities on the German, Dutch and French markets. Only one year later he sold 6% gold-backed annuities with a nominal value of 400 million forints.

At about this time his wife and new-born son, György, joined him and, with his wife's agreement, he decided to remain in Hungary and make his home in Budapest. He started to study Hungarian with Professor Ármin Balog who became his friend and remained a friend of the family until his death many years later. I don't know where the family first lived in Budapest but about 1890 Zsigmond bought a large house at Bajza utca 32. He and the family lived on the first floor. The second floor was rented out and the third floor became the home of professor Balog and his wife and son.

The apartment, as I knew it when I was growing up, was very large and occupied the entire first floor of the building. In addition to a number of bedrooms there was a large sitting room, a large salon, a smaller library and a very large dining room that could easily accommodate twenty-five people around a long oval table. The furniture was generally Biedermeier of good quality and was impeccably maintained. When there were no guests most of the pieces were protected by dust covers which were removed only when Grandmother expected company. In one corner of the living room there was a card table with four armchairs where she and her elderly lady friends took tea and played whist. In both the living room and the salon there were small tables with tasteful displays of pieces of silver and glass but without a sense of clutter. As a small child I felt that I was in a museum and not in a place where people really lived.

Sometime in the early 1890's Kornfeld bought a one thousand acre property called Rakovic in what was at that time Bohemia. There was a very nice early nineteenth-century house and a large garden with a pond. The family spent the summers there and Grandfather commuted by train from Budapest to the city of Pöstyén, known as Pistian in Czech, which was only about ten miles from Rakovic. Once when Grandfather got onto the train in Budapest to return to his country home the conductor, who knew him from his weekly trips, told him that he had the book my grandfather had left on the train the previous week. When Grandfather asked the conductor how he knew that the book was his, the man said, "Sir, you are the only gentleman on this train who reads Latin". The book was Thomas à Kempis' *The Imitation of Christ,* an intensely theological text describing the Roman Catholic ideal of behavior. In Rakovic he had a synagogue built for the Jewish community living in the area. He was fairly active in the Jewish affairs in Budapest as well, even though he and his family were not particularly religious, did not attend the synagogue or keep the dietary regulations.

Zsigmond became a true Hungarian. He converted the Bank into a strictly Hungarian institution, left the Rothschild's employ and even, some years later, got into a controversy with them about Hungary's economic and intellectual role in the Monarchy. That was one of the many fights that he won. He became a leader in Hungarian economic affairs and established excellent relationships with important circles in both government and business. Over time he became very active in a wide range of financial projects. Being a member of the largest bank in Hungary at that time gave him a position of considerable power in the financial world of the day. The president of the Bank was Marquis Ede Pallavicini whom Zsigmond succeeded in 1895.

His numerous successful business ventures included establishment of an oil refining and marketing company in Fiume of which he became the president. Also in Fiume he purchased a rice mill and turned it into a corporation with shares of stock held by the family. He founded a mining company in Bosnia as well as the Transylvania Petroleum Company. He became interested in transportation and established the Budapest–Pécs Railway Co., the Electric and Transportation Company and the Hungarian River and Maritime Transportation Company of which he became the president. In 1887 he had the Bank take control of the Hungarian Metal and Lamp Co. and did the same a year later for the Danubius Shipyard. This latter was then joined with the Ganz Engineering and Metalwork Company, becoming at the time the largest industrial organization in Hungary under the name of Ganz-Danubius.

Perhaps Zsigmond's most important contribution to the Hungarian economy was the expansion and restructuring of the Budapest Commodity and Stock Exchange becoming president of in 1899. Prior to that time all stock transactions had been handled by the Austrian stock exchange in Vienna. As the first president of the Stock Exchange, he changed the language used to Hungarian from German – an unprecedented step. After his death a bronze bust of him was erected in front of the stock exchange building.

Grandfather also became active in Hungarian cultural affairs. He bought the Franklin Publishing Company which had published, among other things, a very popular series of books about the interpretation of dreams. At the first meeting of the Franklin Board of Directors, he stated that this had to stop. "One must never delude the people!" he said. Under his leadership the Franklin Publishing Company became one of the most highly respected publishing houses in Hungary.

The following is a quotation from a distinguished Hungarian author and editor, Zsigmond Móricz, who wrote a review of the biography of Zsigmond Kornfeld written by journalist József Radnóti.

> "The life and career of Zsigmond Kornfeld draws attention to several important aspects.
> First and foremost to the miracle of talent triumphant. How many other twenty-six-year-old men lived in 1878? How is it possible that none of them showed the ability that he had? How was it possible for him to assume his place among the leading elements in a foreign land, easily and almost playfully, at an age when men generally are but hesitant beginners?
>
> Genius has no barriers. Zsigmond Kornfeld, speaking a foreign language, having a foreign culture and a foreign perspective should have seen nothing but hurdles and difficulties hemming him in on all sides and

yet he immediately found his place in a thousand-year-old structure and his soul penetrated through impassable substances seemingly like atomic radiation. The second miracle is character. Every feature listed by his biographer indicates a crystalline character, a moral and harmonious being and an active, decent human soul. Precisely as it should be in those destined for a leading role.

His biographer writes: 'He chose the simplest but most difficult path for himself. He always trod the straight road. This came honestly and from deep within him. Because he was hard he seemed ruthless, because he was rigid he seemed to be a poseur even though he always stood on a pedestal of total human and business integrity. That he considered binding particularly on himself. He did not wish to be popular. He believed in people and he liked them but cared little for their opinion because he was fully confident in his own abilities, in the purity of his intentions and in the fairness of his judgment. He did not need anybody but was always willing to help those who needed assistance. He was very generous with advice, financial aid and moral support.

He was a vital collection of the best human traits. The most contradictory values and characteristics were assembled in his fragile body and it also held the strongest spirit. He lived, thought and acted according to the most strictly defined moral rules. He erected a special altar in his heart for purity, righteousness and justice. There was a strong and purposeful endeavor in him toward perfect justice. He claimed that one had to live and act so as to never have to regret anything. He set the most rigid rules for himself and he always lived up to them. He could not be forgiving to those in whom he found a lack of honesty or good intentions. Ignorance angered him, immorality offended him and he could hate evil although he kept strong emotions as far from himself as possible.

He was a good man in the best and noblest sense of the word although he never wanted others to view him in that way. He was not interested in public opinion and always acted according to his own dictates. He did not seek to share the opinions of others and always looked for harmony within himself. He valued intellectual activity, the outward reach of the soul and the creative force of the brain above everything else.'

I copied this characterization because I was captivated by the image of the description. In our era amorality, not immorality, and thought processes ignoring moral perspectives have become so powerfully prevalent that it is elevating if a biographer dares to pen such lines about his subject, particularly a banker."

About 1903 Grandfather was instrumental in arranging a very large loan to Imperial Russia. After it was all arranged the Russian ambassador in Budapest came to see him and told him the Tsar had awarded him a very important Russian decoration. Zsigmond answered, "I am a banker who did this on request of his government. Bankers are not obliged to, and generally don't, intellectually assess, morally evaluate or philosophically adjust to the public good those great financial transactions that they have the opportunity to perform. I accept your expression of thanks but I will not accept the decoration. I am a Jew and in your country Jews are being persecuted and murdered. I cannot accept a Russian decoration." It is impressive that he said this even though he was not a practicing Jew.

In addition to his other talents, Kornfeld was a gifted speaker in both his native language, German and in his adopted language, Hungarian. The two most widely quoted speeches were first, the one in Hungarian, delivered in 1887 to the Economic Committee of the Hungarian Academy of Sciences on the problems of the salt mining industry and the later one in German delivered in 1906 to the meeting of the Central European Economic Association in Vienna about the history, recent state and future of the economy of Central Europe.

Some months before Kornfeld's death the Prime Minister, Sándor Wekerle, came to see him saying that the government had decided to offer him an honorary Hungarian citizenship. Grandfather replied that he had received the Hungarian citizenship in the usual way several years before. Some weeks later the Prime Minister returned and said that the Emperor had awarded him a Barony and that he hoped that it would be accepted. After some hesitation Grandfather said that for the benefit of his family he would accept it. In fact the award was made just a few weeks before his death. My father and Uncle Pál, dressed in their morning coats and striped pants and wearing shiny top hats, went to Vienna to thank the Emperor. In continental Europe titles of nobility descended to all male and female members of the family in all successive generations. Hence, Father and Uncle Pál were barons, my mother was a baroness. My siblings and I inherited the title also. Grandfather's many honors included the Iron Cross Order Class III in 1890, the Iron Cross Order Class II in 1893, the appointment to the Hungarian Upper House of Parliament in 1901, and the Barony in 1909. Because of his absolute integrity and unshakable honesty he was esteemed and respected by members of the highest Hungarian aristocracy. Count Nándor Zichy, who was a member of parliament with him, once made the comment that Zsigmond Kornfeld was the first person who shook his long-held belief that anti-Semitism was both legitimate and just.

In 1909 he was close to death from complete renal failure. Father, who was still living at home at that time, went in to see him in the morning and said, "Papa you look so well today". Zsigmond knew that this was not true and responded, "Son, one should not carry politeness to the point of frivolity". On March twenty-fourth of that year he passed away at the age of fifty-seven. Kornfeld's death was considered a major event. The obituary by journalist Jenő Rákosi reads in part,"...our economic life has suffered a most serious blow with the death of this outstanding man. An extraordinarily creative and administrative force has ceased to exist in this most sensitive area, the world of finance..."

As a young man visiting in Vienna Zsigmond had become acquainted with the Frankfurters, a well-to-do family with several children one of whom was Barbara, nicknamed Betty, who was born in 1855. The young couple fell in love and she agreed to marry him in spite of some concern on the part of her parents who felt that she could do better than this young man, who came from nowhere, was socially unknown and whose family had nothing. Betty was a fairly strong-willed young woman and eventually prevailed and received her parents' blessing. The two were married and lived happily until he died.

The Frankfurters were highly respected in the Viennese Jewish community. One member of the family was a physician. In those days physicians did not have the incomes they have today and Dr. Frankfurter had a large family. The only thing I know about him is a family anecdote. In an effort to save money he told his children that when they buttered their bread they should always butter the narrower side because that was just as much "bread and butter" than if they had buttered the larger side and this way they were saving some butter. One of Betty's siblings was Clothilde whom I was taken to visit a couple of times in Vienna when I was a small child.

I remember how bored I was and how I wished that the visit would come to an end. It is quite possible that the Associate Justice of the U.S. Supreme Court, Felix Frankfurter, could have been a distant relative. His family lived in Vienna in the late nineteenth century and emigrated when the boy was twelve in 1894.

Grandmother Kornfeld, the only grandparent I ever knew, was a rather formidable old lady. She had very strict ideas about behavior and I was always very shy when I was with her. Once when I picked up some piece of porcelain or pottery she had in the living room she said, "Child, why don't you imagine that you have already dropped and broken it and set it down". Needless to say, I did. My siblings and I went to her for lunch every Thursday when my father's "Gentlemen's lunch" was held at our house. The lunches in the Bajza utca were very formal events. We sat at the table with Grandmother at the head, spoke when we were addressed and ate what we had on the plate. The lunches were enormous: soup, a meat course with several side dishes including such things as hot dogs and scrambled eggs, vegetables and salad, followed by a dessert and fruit. The dishes were served on silver platters or serving dishes and we were to help ourselves. We could take as much or as little as we wanted but what we took we had to eat. After a few years when I was about ten, my siblings no longer went and I had to go to the Thursday lunches by myself. Once I forgot to go until I was reminded by my mother. I ran all the way but got there about fifteen minutes late. It was obvious that my grandmother was not pleased and the occasion was not pleasant and relaxed. Service, however, was always excellent and Grandmother had a strict rule that all the silverware used on the platters had to be laid out in line on the sideboard. The story has it that a maid was fired because, for the second time, she had to open a drawer to take out an additional piece of silverware.

Grandmother had a companion, Fräulein Emma, who was with her for many years. The three of us used to go to the movies about two or three times in the winter and these were also very formal and ceremonious occasions. There were two requirements: the movie had to be suitable for my tender age and the cinema had to have a box for my grandmother to sit in. When we started out from the Bajza utca, I was carrying her footstool and a blanket. Fräulein Emma carried a shawl. When the chauffeur deposited us at the cinema it was my duty to buy the tickets and then escort the ladies to a box. Grandmother sat down, I opened the footstool and placed it under her feet. Fräulein Emma placed the blanket over her knees and the shawl over her shoulders. Then we watched the movie.

My grandmother Kornfeld's 80th birthday was a major family event. It involved considerable planning and lengthy preparation. There was to be a performance by each of the grandchildren, an afternoon tea for her old friends and a formal family dinner. This was all to take place in the Kornfeld apartment in the Bajza utca where my father and his siblings grew up. For the birthday celebration, it was decided that, instead of performing some kind of play, each grandchild would recite a poem in honor of the occasion. My grandmother had been educated by tutors and was raised in a very learned family. She both knew and liked German, English and French classic literature. She could recite Goethe and Schiller by the hour. I had to memorize four stanzas of a Goethe poem whose title now escapes me. I do vividly remember, however, how frightened I was of forgetting my lines.

When the great day came my parents, my siblings and I, all in our best Sunday clothes, walked over to Grandmother's house at about four o'clock. The old lady received us in the salon where she was seated in a large chair surrounded by flowers and gifts. After the initial greetings and affectionate embraces we settled down for the performance. Fortunately the recitals started with me; all went well and I got through my part without any glitches. Then my brother, sisters and cousins recited but I was so happy that my turn was over that I paid little if any attention to the other performances. We then had tea with little cakes and cookies and some old lady friends of my grandmother came to wish her well. The dinner, starting at eight, was a very formal occasion with several servants in livery who brought in a series of dishes. Being the youngest by several years I sat at the end of the table and spoke only when I was spoken to. My father made a short speech at the end of the dinner and champagne was served for a formal toast. My grandmother was a very strict old lady and I stood in very great awe of her. I knew she loved me and I did love her albeit our relationship was a very formal one and I always had to be on my very best behavior when I was with her. Her 80th birthday was indeed a festive occasion but I was very glad when it was finally over and we could go home.

Toward the end of her life Grandmother developed what would be called Alzheimer's disease today. She became very forgetful and somewhat confused. For many years in the summer she spent four weeks at the Svábhegy Sanatorium, naturally always in the same set of rooms. The summer when she turned eighty she was driven up to the Sanatorium and was taken to her suite as always. She looked around and said that these were not her rooms and she did not wish to stay. The director took her to his office, apologized profusely for the terrible mistake and begged her not to leave saying that her own place was waiting. They went back upstairs to the same suite as before but now Grandmother said that these were indeed her usual rooms and hoped that such a mistake would not be made again. She died about eighteen months later possibly with a little assistance from her physician.

My Kornfeld grandparents had five children. The oldest, György, was born in Vienna in 1878. The next one, the only daughter, Mária who was called Mici was born in 1880. Then came my father, Móric, born in 1882. He was followed by Pál in 1884 and Ferenc, 1897.

György was a very bright and industrious young man who did very well in school. While at the University he fell in love with a young woman whom his parents considered unsuitable. I don't know what the problem was but it must have been resolved because after a while Zsigmond agreed to the marriage and told György that he would give the young woman the same dowry he would give to his own daughter. However he advised him to finish his legal education first. I would have thought that after all of this everyone would be happy. But shortly after Grandfather gave his permission for the marriage, György committed suicide. Sitting on a bench on the Margit Island, he shot himself in the head. Later a guard passed by and thought that the man was sleeping. When he touched György on the shoulder the body toppled over. He had left no note, no message, no reason for this drastic action. The tragedy was devastating for his parents and affected them for the rest of their lives.

The second child, Mici, was a most attractive woman whom I got to know much better as an adult than as a child. She married Móric Domony who was an attorney but went into business. He succeeded my grandfather in the presidency of the MFTR, the Hungarian River and Ocean Navigation Company. A very pleasant and talented man he developed major advances in creating an effective and very lucrative Danubian transportation system. There was little contact between the Domonys and my family other than at formal occasions such as birthdays and Christmas.

Aunt Mici developed pulmonary tuberculosis at a fairly early age and spent considerable time in Davos, Switzerland, in a sanatorium receiving what little treatment was available at that time. I was taken to visit her a few times as a child and may have been infected. The disease did not develop in me and the only effect was that I have several scars on my lungs which have regularly confounded radiologists whenever I have a chest X-ray. An intensely devoted Catholic, Aunt Mici was very active in Church affairs. She died in 1939. Her husband was killed by the Arrow Cross thugs in 1944. Allegedly he was thrown into the Danube in the middle of winter together with a number of other people. The story has it that when the Arrow Cross men asked him what he had done for a living he told them that he had been the president of the Danube and Oceanic Navigation Company. They laughed and said, "Well, then perhaps you would like to take a little swim in your river", and threw him in among the ice floes.

The couple had two sons. The older one, Péter, was one of the brightest people I have ever known. Although he was twenty years older than I we were good friends. He was a very successful attorney in Hungary and when he came to the U.S. after the war he passed the Bar Exam and practiced in New York. He married a very attractive young woman, Eszter Gross, the daughter of the Professor of Ophthalmology at the University in Budapest. They spent some time each summer in Ireg and Eszter was the first woman guest to wear slacks, much to my father's dismay. She died tragically in New York in a fire that was started by her smoking in bed. Péter managed to get out but she could not. Later on I saw Péter whenever I was in New York and we usually had lunch together.

The other son, János, was also very bright and was successful in business. After the war he managed to get to Austria and spent the rest of his life in Vienna with his wife who was a physical therapist. He used to spend some time in Ireg each summer and there he taught me to play bridge at which he was a master. Once when I was traveling in Europe I stopped in Vienna primarily to see him. Since his wife had a patient coming, János and I went to one of the lovely Vienna coffee houses and engaged in learned conversation. We also visited museums together and had a most pleasant time. He died a year or two later. Neither Péter nor János had any children.

The next member of my father's family was my uncle Pál. He was very bright and had a good education with a doctorate in economics. He started his career at the Hungarian General Bank of Credit, following his father, Zsigmond. He married Olga Neumann and they had one daughter, Mária, known as Stupszi. Olga's family was well-to-do, respected and related by marriage to the Weiss Manfréd family. Sadly, Olga was emotionally unstable and the marriage was dissolved after several years. Stupszi was raised by her Neumann grandparents. It became apparent that Pál was gay and after some minor scandals and fairly substantial gambling losses he was forced to resign from the Bank. He moved to Paris and made a living there representing some Hungarian interests. During the war he was arrested and placed in a French concentration camp but survived and eventually settled in Vienna where he died several years later. During the last couple of months of his terminal illness, my sister Mária was with him and took care of him. I did not know him very well but as a youngster I did see him from time to time and liked him. Stupszi survived the war and the Russian siege, married a man named Tibor Zahorán and eventually immigrated to Canada. The marriage did not last and Stupszi lived alone for a number of years in Montreal. My sisters were in touch with her and, I believe, supported her until she died around 2002. She used to spend some time in Ireg so that I knew her quite well and liked her. The last time I saw her was in 1943.

The youngest of my father's siblings was Ferenc who was born in 1897 and was thus fifteen years my father's junior. He was highly intelligent, very well read and had a doctorate in chemical engineering from a very good German university. Unfortunately he also had some emotional problems of which an addiction to gambling was only one. He married a very nice German woman whose name was Stella but the marriage did not last. There were no children. Ferenc made some kind of living in Budapest and we saw him from time to time at our home on Lendvay utca. I liked him very much. Unfortunately his gambling increased and he lost a very large sum of money for which my father assumed the responsibility. Subsequently Ferenc moved to Tehran where he was the representative of some Hungarian chemical companies. While there he met and married a young Hungarian woman, Teréz. Like so many young and attractive Hungarian girls at the time, she made a living as an entertainer in various nightclubs and other establishments in the Near East. The couple returned to Hungary but my parents disapproved of the marriage so strongly that they never allowed them to come to the house and I never met Teréz. She and Ferenc had a son, Pál, whose nickname was Palkó. He was raised by his mother after Ferenc was killed by the Germans in 1944. I don't know when Teréz died but Palkó, who was trained as an engineer, is still living in Budapest at this writing. My sisters used to see him whenever they were there. I met him only once, at the time my father's book, *From Trianon to Trianon*, was published in 2006.

Chapter Two

Manfréd

My maternal grandfather, Manfréd Weiss, was born in Budapest on April 11, 1857. His grandfather, Baruch, had made tobacco pipe bowls in a village somewhere in Bohemia. He moved to Hungary where he started a small produce business and where his son, Adolf Weiss, was born in 1807. As an adult Adolf was in the produce business and also started the large scale production of plum jam which is called *lekvár* in Hungarian and was known as *povidle* locally and from which Adolf got the nickname of *"Povidle"* Weiss. He had six children of whom Manfréd was the youngest. I knew two of the children, Helen Neuman and Jenni Eissler.

Adolf's wife, Eva, Manfréd's mother, was born a Kanitz. Sadly, she died quite young in a cholera epidemic. One of her brothers, Felix Philipp Kanitz, was a noted Balkan explorer. He entered the University of Vienna in 1846 and settled in that city in 1856. His life work focused on the study of the South Slavs and he was the author of numerous books which, as a fine artist, he illustrated himself.

One of Dr. Kanitz's books about his explorations came into my hands quite unexpectedly when I was about eighteen and learned that in the large house on the Lipót körút which Manfréd had owned, there were a number of books that had come from my grandfather Kornfeld's library in the Bajza utca. Most of them were German and French classics as well as English novels of the nineteenth century. But there were also some more unusual ones like the Kanitz book which I immediately took home and read with great interest.

At the time of Manfréd's childhood Pest and Buda were still German-speaking and his parents never learned Hungarian. Manfréd was educated at a German middle and high school and completed the course at the Commercial Academy in 1873. Upon graduation he was sent to Hamburg where he was apprenticed to a grocery wholesaler. There he started his career by going to work at seven o'clock in the morning and sweeping the sidewalk in front of the store. He moved up rapidly and within two or three years became one of the managers of the company. He returned to Hungary in 1877 because his father had become seriously ill.

Adolf Weiss died in 1878 whereupon Manfréd joined his older brother Berthold who had become successful in the produce business. Continuing in Adolf's plum jam *(povidle)* business, they applied for a license to can meats in 1882. This became the First Hungarian Packing Plant *(A Weiss Berthold és Manfréd Első Magyar Konzervgyár)*. The license was awarded on December twenty eighth, 1882, and the plant was established on the Lövölde tér in Budapest. They selected the name "Globus" for their trademark and early in 1893 Manfréd sent a sample of the meat they had canned to the Ministry of War in Vienna. Initially limited to processing meat, the Packing Plant slowly grew and was soon combined with a slaughterhouse. Shortly thereafter the brothers enlarged the plant by establishing a machine shop to manufacture the cans in which the meat was to be packed. They also developed a system to solder the tins and install the tops and bottoms. The thin metal from which the cans were made was dipped into melted lead to keep it from rusting. By today's standards this would seem to be a very dangerous thing to do, but no evidence of lead poisoning was ever identified among the military personnel who consumed the contents of the cans. The entire output of the plant was taken by the military organizations of the Monarchy.

Once the operations of the meat packing and shipping were running smoothly the packing plant, which had seasonal lows, was also used as a site to work on munitions. Initially this consisted of dismantling old, out-of-date ammunition and using the powder to fill a new and different type. Because of the hazards of working with explosive substances in a facility that was primarily a food packing plant the brothers sought another area not too far away which was not surrounded by houses.

The largest island in the Hungarian part of the Danube is called Csepel. It is approximately thirty miles long and about five miles wide. There are several small villages on the island and two or three medium-sized towns of which Csepel is the largest, located at the northern tip. Most of the central and southern parts are agricultural and, at the southern end, near the town of Ráckeve, there was a sizable estate which once belonged to the Prince de Savoie. The very lovely chateau, built in the mid-1700s, is still standing and is now a hotel-restaurant where my wife and I and two Hungarian friends had a very pleasant lunch in 2008. Curiously enough this island was the first place settled by the Hungarian conquerors at the end of the ninth century when the head of the Hungarian tribes, Árpád, established his headquarters there. The island was named for his groom whose name was Csepel.

On December twelve, 1892, the brothers leased from the village of Csepel a five-acre plot known as the János grazing ground on the northern end of the island. Here the new factory was built on a sandy, level stretch with little vegetation and no buildings. The location was ideal with access to the Danube for the river transport of merchandise. About a thirty-five minute carriage ride from the Weiss home on the Andrássy út, it was not too far from the cannery. The farmers on the island, used to seasonal work, were very pleased to have steady employment under reasonable conditions. Part of the Csepel property became the area where the factory buildings were erected and one part eventually became the Csepel Free Port.

When the decision was made to build, the brothers were on firm financial footing – they were active in a variety of banking and industrial activities and had made important contacts in government and business. On January twelfth, 1893, the government granted the brothers a license to start a manufacturing plant at the site. Work began shortly after the erection of several small wooden frame buildings with an initial workforce of about thirty-five men and over one hundred women. Work increased quite rapidly and in 1896 the brothers bought the land on which by now there were about twenty buildings and a workforce of more than four hundred. Most of the work at this time was still the repair and recharging of artillery shells.

A major step was taken in 1896 when Manfréd bought out Berthold and took over control of the works. Berthold had wished to enter politics and had managed to get elected to the lower chamber of Parliament. A family anecdote had it that shortly after he entered Parliament he addressed, with his very thick German accent, a question to one of the ministers. That gentleman began his response by saying, "In answer to the honorable gentleman who speaks our beautiful language so abominably badly..." In any event, a contract was drawn up according to which Manfréd was going to pay Berthold and his family a certain large sum annually without any time restriction. These payments were actually continued into the 1920s when Manfréd's son, Alfonz, finally decided to end the custom. Prior to Berthold's leaving the firm the two brothers had been engaged in major real estate investments both in the city of Budapest and also in the surrounding suburbs.

Shortly after Manfréd became the sole owner of Csepel, the Emperor, in recognition for his services to the country, awarded him the patent of nobility. He took the predicate of Csepel and was entitled to use the name of Csepeli Weiss Manfréd, in Hungarian or Manfred von Weiss, in German or Manfred Weiss de Csepel in French. In 1918 King Charles awarded him the Barony. Manfréd was very proud of being a Hungarian and was truly a patriot. One of his proudest moments came when he, in full Hungarian traditional garb with a sword at his side, marched in the coronation parade of King Charles from the castle in Buda to the Mátyás church. His mother-in-law wrote him a letter saying, "When today I saw you among the noblest of the land marching so firmly and handsomely I was filled with the most justified pride. What you are you created yourself. It came from your own strength, your tireless diligence, your most serious endeavor and your most significant genius."

Under Manfréd's skillful and industrious leadership the business grew rapidly and developed into the largest military supply manufactory in Hungary with ammunition, while not the only product, being the major item. The Weiss Manfréd factory, which was generally referred to as the WM Works, regularly added new areas of activity. In 1896 it started producing the copper needed for the brass shells in its new copper smelting section. That was followed by the construction of a large smithy, a water tower, a large central boiler-house and numerous storage buildings. In 1901 the WM Works started making camp kitchens, baking ovens, food containers and numerous other items for the military. In 1904 the factory in Csepel became the principal site for the entire Weiss Manfréd business complex and the administrative offices were moved there from the city of Budapest.

By the fall of 1907 a metal pipe and bar workshop was built and, a first in Hungary, motor vehicles were constructed for the army. When it was realized how much steel was being used in the various manufacturing processes the decision was made to establish a steel production unit. Initially two blast furnaces were built and a third one was added during the First World War. In addition to the blast furnaces there was a rolling mill to process the steel and a separate building to make sheet and wire. The demand for cast iron products increased so much that a foundry was built to provide the molten iron for castings of all sorts. Next came a non-ferrous metal foundry with its workshops.

The First World War broke out in August, 1914, leading to an enormous increase in the activities at Csepel. Under pressure from the military for additional production, Manfréd introduced the three-shift workday – a major innovation at that time. In addition to munitions the factory also produced other heavy equipment for the army. When it became so large and prosperous, Manfréd decided to convert it into a corporation, with all of the shares held by the members of his family. In 1917 an insurance company estimated the value of Csepel to be around one hundred million crowns. Due to the expansion that took place during the war, the WM Works became one of the three largest military suppliers in the Monarchy with Skoda in Bohemia and Steyer in Austria being the other two.

Weiss had a very strong social conscience and was deeply concerned about the physical well-being of his workers. Starting before the war a training school for apprentices was opened, a recreational building was built and, outside the plant, a large nursery was set up for the benefit of working mothers. The factory also had a first-aid station which was an unusual structure in heavy industry in the first decade of the twentieth century. Other social innovations were a retirement program for employees and paid vacations for both office employees and factory workers. The town of Csepel grew in parallel with the factory and by 1910 its population had grown to about ten thousand. An electric street car line connected the town with Budapest and a freight railway line was built directly to the factory. During the war about thirty thousand men and women worked in the factory and the town again increased substantially.

Manfréd was very proud of Csepel and enjoyed taking distinguished visitors on a tour of the Works. These people included Crown Prince Charles, the future King and Emperor, Archduchess Augusta, Baron Alexander von Krobatin, the Minister of War of the Monarchy and numerous other high-ranking politicians.

Csepel was by no means his only industrial enterprise. He established a cloth factory, the first Hungarian textile company with plants in four cities, as well as one to produce yarns. He was active in the management of the Ganz-Danubius Shipping and Transportation Company, the rifle factory in Magyaróvár, a factory to produce hemp and a number of other industrial and commercial enterprises. He also served on the Board of the Hungarian Bank of Commerce and of several industrial and commercial enterprises.

In 1884 Manfréd married Maria Alice de Wahl. Alice, as she was known, was the daughter of Albert de Wahl, Kt. who was the director of The Hungarian Alföld–Fiume Railway Company. The de Wahl family originally came from Alsace and had settled in Hungary around the middle of the nineteenth century. Alice's parents, highly educated and cultured people, lived with Manfréd's new family in the lovely, large house on Andrássy út.

Albert de Wahl retired early from the railway company after it was nationalized. At that time railroads in most of Europe were owned and operated by the State. Like any good railway-man he was a slave to the clock and lived the years of his retirement according to a rigid daily routine. He always rose at the same time, insisted that lunch and dinner be served precisely at the same time and then retired at exactly ten thirty. This created a minor problem on New Year's Eve which was a family event. He solved the problem by setting the clocks ahead by two hours and thus the family celebrated the coming of the New Year at ten o'clock which allowed him to go to bed at his usual time.

My grandmother, Alice, was a very lovely woman, a good wife and mother who produced six children in a relatively very short time. There was Elza in 1885, Jenő in 1887, my mother, Marianne in 1888, Alfonz in 1890, Daisy in 1895 and Edith in 1899. Manfréd and Alice were loving but very strict parents. They recognized that children do best with consistent discipline – fair and firm. Schooling began at home with Alice establishing a fairly rigid daily schedule with times for study and times for recreation. Musical evenings were enjoyed weekly with Grandfather Manfréd playing the violin and Grandmother Alice playing the piano. The family attended the National Theater, the Opera and the Philharmonic. They also enjoyed visiting museums both at home and when traveling. Frequently there were guests and sometimes there was for dinner the wonderful fish called *fogas* from Lake Balaton. Family lunches and dinners were of considerable size. They started out with soup, followed by a first course, then a meat and vegetable course and finally a dessert. Manfréd frequently had a glass of red wine but everybody else at the table drank only water.

In the afternoon Manfréd went to the office in the city or attended business meetings with government agencies and other industrial and leading mercantile organizations. He was also quite active in the National Association of Manufacturers (GYOSZ), which was headed by Ferenc Chorin, Sr. He returned home about six p.m. and dinner was served at seven thirty. It consisted of the same series of dishes as lunch and, considering that only the richest ingredients were used, it is incomprehensible to me that they did not all weigh three hundred pounds. In fact, while Manfréd was only very moderately overweight, the children were all very slender. He slept poorly and kept a notebook at the bedside table in which he frequently entered thoughts and plans about things to do the next day.

The family life on Andrássy út was quite harmonious but there was no question that Manfréd was in charge. The poor man suffered from frequent headaches which his wife treated with cold compresses. At these times the children had to be absolutely quiet. He also took headache remedies fairly often and carried some in his purse all the time. Once he had a mild concussion when his carriage turned over on the way to Csepel and he had to keep to his bed for a few days. Manfréd and Maria Alice's birthdays were major family events. The children recited poems and presented little plays or played music. For them it was an annual event but when I grew up the pageantry in my family was fortunately limited to decade birthdays.

Sadly, Alice died from pernicious anemia in January, 1904, at age thirty-nine. There were no treatments for this disease at the time and a variety of "experimental" therapies were inflicted on my poor grandmother without any benefit. Upon her death my aunt Elza, at age nineteen, took over the role of the lady of the house, but after her marriage, my mother replaced her and remained in that position until her own marriage in 1913.

Although he loved his adult sons dearly, Manfréd's relationship with them was sometimes difficult. Jenő was clearly a brilliant engineer and was instrumental in developing excellent procedures and processes at Csepel. Alfonz had had an excellent education and had business expertise, but Manfréd did not take him into his confidence until the purchase of the Derekegyháza estate in 1914 when he asked his son to take charge of the negotiations. One of Manfréd's legacies to his children was the desire to keep the family relationship strong.

Even in his will he advised them to "Always act one for all and all for one in pleasure and sadness, which latter may God keep away from you always".

In honor of his late wife Manfréd established two major institutions: the Maria Alice Hospital for Women and Children, an obstetrics and neonatal hospital, which was still active in 1944. So far as I know it is still in existence as this is written. The other hospital Manfréd established was for the terminally ill. I do not know how long that hospital functioned, because while my mother was quite active in the Maria Alice Hospital, the other one was never discussed. The two hospitals were closely associated with the Jewish community in Budapest. Manfréd, however, made it a major item in their charters that no patient requiring care could be turned away on the basis of race, religion or national origin.

Grandfather also believed that it was important for the leaders of industry, commerce and society to gather socially in a pleasant environment. Thus he initiated the establishment of the Union Club. Faithful members were, among many others, Sándor Popovich, the President of the Hungarian National Bank, Gusztáv Grátz, the future Minister of Commerce and of Foreign Affairs, Vilmos Ormódy, the head of the First Hungarian Insurance Company and Ferenc Heinrich, the Minister of Commerce. His circle of friends included the Ministers Samu Hazai, József Szterényi, János Teleszky, the founder of the Hungarian sugar industry, Sándor Hatvany-Deutsch and the distinguished professor of medicine Baron Sándor Korányi.

After Manfréd's death in 1922 the industrial empire continued to grow under the leadership of his sons and sons-in-law. While it still manufactured some supplies for the military it also branched out into commercial production of civilian products. Automobiles, motorcycles and bicycles became major items and the manufacture of seamless steel tubes became one of the most important products. Even manhole covers, having the WM logo, were manufactured. They were still to be found on the streets of Budapest in 1998. Concern for the employees also continued. A very fine hospital was built on the factory grounds and workers and their families were provided free medical care. Toward the end of the 1930s the WM Works began building airplanes and, during the Second World War, this became a major part of the productive capacity. After the German occupation on March nineteenth, 1944, the WM Works was largely under the supervision of Hungarian and German military officers.

Manfréd's brother-in-law, Oscar de Wahl, was an interesting personality. He was a very good-looking young man with impeccable manners. He was also quite cynical with an excellent sense of humor. He spoke Hungarian, German and French fluently and apparently also had a good knowledge of English. Manfréd relied on him heavily for all negotiations outside of the Monarchy and he represented the Company in a number of transactions. Perhaps his most famous case involved a major negotiation with Russia involving a huge order for military rifle ammunition. Oscar negotiated with the Russian Archduke who told him that he had awarded the order to the WM Works. Oscar joyously cabled the news to Budapest where Manfréd immediately started to make arrangements for the manufacture of the 100 million pieces of ammunition. A few days later, Oscar, still in St. Petersburg, was told that he did not get the order. He found out that the Hungarian military attaché at the embassy, one Prince Francis Hohenlohe, had approached the Archduke at a party and told him that the WM Company was Jewish and that he hoped that the Tsarist Empire would not give such a large order to Jews. Oscar asked to see the Archduke again and told him that he was devastated by the news and that, in fact, preparations for meeting the order were already under way in Csepel. The

Archduke said that Oscar did not have a written contract and thus had no reason to start the production. Oscar told him that if he himself had negotiated with a Polish Jew this would have been the situation but that he believed that the word of a Russian Archduke was equivalent to written contract and he never doubted for a second that it would be met. The Archduke thought about it for a moment and said, "You are right". The contract was duly signed and Oscar returned to Budapest, the conquering hero.

Another anecdote about Oscar was that he decided to have his children baptized but was not quite sure how to tell Manfréd who would have been strongly opposed. So, sometime later when Manfréd was going to Vienna, Oscar accompanied him to the railway station. Manfréd was standing at the window of his carriage with Oscar talking to him from the platform. When the train started out Oscar was trotting along and said, "Oh, by the way, Manfréd, I had the children baptized". This then avoided any discussion and when Manfréd returned he had resigned himself to the event.

Many years later, in the late thirties and early forties, Prince Hohenlohe was a regular guest in Derekegyháza, the Weiss family country estate, for the winter hunts. I remember him well at the New Year's Eve parties when he wore a dark green dinner jacket. He seemed to be a very nice and friendly elderly gentleman a long way from the young anti-Semite military attaché in St. Petersburg.

At the end of the war in 1918 the Monarchy collapsed and the Károlyi government was succeeded in 1919 by the Béla Kun Hungarian Soviet Republic. Weiss was devastated. The Soviet Regime meant the end of his life's work. It was for him a personal catastrophe. By the logic of Communist thought Manfréd obviously became "an enemy of the people". He even attempted suicide by taking a large amount of hypnotic drugs but was pulled back from death or serious neurological damage by good medical care. Taken to Vienna he recovered and only returned to Budapest after the collapse of the Communist regime and the Horthy takeover. He became active again in the rebuilding of Csepel which had been looted by the Romanian occupation forces. Some time in about 1920 he may have had a mild stroke. But in mid-1922 he suffered one much worse. He recovered only partially and died on December twenty four. This was such an emotionally traumatic event in the life of his children that my mother, for instance, wore full black mourning clothes for a whole year.

Undoubtedly the man was a genius. While he started from a moderately solid lower middle class background and had considerable family support, he created a major industrial organization that became the largest such structure in Hungary. But it was not just limited to Csepel. Included were several other manufacturing establishments, such as the Globus Cannery, the Hungarian Fabric Factory and the Rifle Factory in Magyaróvár. He also had considerable financial interests in a variety of other industrial organizations.

His private life was dominated by his work. The only times away from work were in the summer when the family went for a two- or three-week vacation. These trips were spent in a variety of resorts in Austria, in Bohemia, in the Netherlands and in Switzerland. He frequently spent a week in St. Moritz in the Swiss Engadin where he engaged in the popular practice of the day of bathing in supposedly beneficial mineral waters. The owner of the hotel in St. Moritz, who knew him well after several yearly visits, told him that in 1908 he was planning to open a new and very beautiful Hotel, the Waldhaus, in Sils Maria about ten miles away. He said that he would be pleased if Manfréd and his family would be his guests there the following summer. Thus Manfréd took his sister, Jenni, my mother, and Uncle Jenő. The place was magnificent and my mother fell in love with walking and hiking, especially in the Fex Valley. The family returned to Sils in subsequent summers. In 2007 my wife and I stayed at the Waldhaus for a few days. The manager, who was the grandson of the first owner, recognized my name and showed us the guest list from 1908. On it were listed Manfréd and the members of his family.

The oldest child, Elza, was born in 1885. She was a pert and lively child, curious about everything, a habit she maintained to the end of her life almost 100 years later. Healthy and active, she hated all sorts of caterpillars and worms which, of course, gave her brother Jenő a splendid opportunity to chase her around the garden with a caterpillar in his hand. Elza had no formal education but there were tutors who came to the house and there was also a British nanny, Miss Morrison, who not only taught her and her siblings English, but also English literature and good manners. When her mother died Elza, at age nineteen, became the lady of the house. Shortly thereafter she met and fell in love with Alfréd Mauthner, the son of Ödön Mauthner, the owner of a seed company which was active in both marketing and producing a large variety of agricultural and garden seeds. At a somewhat later time the Mauthner seed company became active in experimental work and produced a number of hybrid varieties which were important in improving the productivity and hardihood of agricultural products and the beauty and variety of flowers. Manfréd was initially opposed to this marriage because Alfréd had already converted to Catholicism, but he eventually agreed on his own terms: Alfréd had to promise that the wedding would be performed according to Jewish ritual and that the children would be raised in the Jewish tradition.

It was a very happy marriage. Elza apparently enjoyed very much having babies, all seven of them, and loved to breast feed. The story has it that she suckled them until they were old enough to bring her the chair to sit in. She and Alfréd were the host and hostess at Derekegyháza, the Weiss family country estate, and spent a considerable part of the year there. The marriage came to a tragic end when Alfréd died of cancer in 1933 at age fifty-six. After Alfréd's death Elza wore nothing but black. She had a number of black dresses and suits which all looked alike to me and were all rather dowdy. She was bent over and always carried two large black handbags. Later in life she looked very much like a witch from a Hans Christian Andersen story. She was insatiably curious and spent many hours in museums all over Europe. Traveling with her was an experience and a very fatiguing one at that. We had to stop everywhere and look at everything. She played the poor old lady role to perfection and used it to get into places that were not open to the general public. On one occasion she talked a Swiss Guard into letting her into the part of the Vatican where the Pope resided and it was only the appearance of an Officer that promptly put an end to the visit. Elza read widely and had an excellent and very large collection of books on art and history. She also had an important collection of old laces. Possessing an excellent sense of humor, she never took herself seriously. I liked her very much and enjoyed her company. Elza, at age ninety-four, died quietly in 1979.

Alfréd and Elza's seven children were Ferenc (Öcsi), Mária (Baby), Anna, Krisztina (Mopi), János (Hanzi), István (Pisti) and Gabriella (Memi). It is an old and honorable Hungarian tradition for children to have nicknames.

Ferenc was born in 1909. After extensive training at Hungarian and German universities he followed his father's career in the seed business and was considered by many to be a leader in the field. He was an unusual person with a few small quirks and some very bright ideas. Blessed with an excellent sense of humor he was pleasant to be with and even though I rarely saw him I liked him. He stayed in Portugal after the German invasion of Hungary in 1944 and eventually married a Portuguese lady with whom he had a daughter. Ferenc died in 1993.

Maria Alice, born in 1908, was known to one and all as Baby. She was a particularly nice woman whom I got to know at all well only as an adult when we visited in Zurich where she lived after the war. Her husband, Dr. Ferenc Borbély, was an outstanding general practitioner with great interest in pharmacologic research. He was our family physician both before and after his marriage to Baby and he took care of me when I had a severe case of pneumonia at age thirteen. Dr. Borbély also became the medical director of the hospital in Csepel and did much to improve the medical care provided to the workers at the factory and the residents of the town. He and Baby had several sons and a daughter. The only one I knew at all well was the oldest one, Sándor, who had a distinguished scientific career and who spent some time in the U.S., where he came to see me in Ann Arbor on a couple of occasions. Baby died in 1989.

Anna, born in 1912, was the least academically inclined in the family. She was a very pleasant person; however she never married and, sadly, died in 1971 of cancer.

Krisztina, known to all her friends as Mopi, was born in 1915. She was a very bright person with an excellent sense of humor. My sister Hanna's best friend, they frequently went skiing together. Once when they came back from a week of skiing in the Austrian mountains they were so darkly suntanned that they overheard a woman at the railway station say, "Look, those two must be from India or Africa". Mopi married Herbert Margaretha, the son of a very distinguished Viennese family and they had several children whom I have never met. Mopi, like almost all the Mauthners, died of cancer at sixty-six in 1983.

János, known as Hanzi, was the next in line, born in 1917. He was bright but totally irresponsible and was known for pulling practical jokes and doing foolish tricks. He engaged in a variety of jobs never keeping one for any length of time.

For all that, he was a grandmaster at bridge which more than demonstrates his basic intelligence. Utterly fearless, during the German occupation of Hungary, he was very active in helping Jews to get to safe houses. He was one of the family members who stayed in Vienna as hostage when the rest of us went to Portugal or Switzerland. He married late in life and died in 1994 of cancer.

István, known as Pisti, was born in 1921. He was reasonably bright but as a young fellow he had a mean streak and he and I thoroughly disliked each other. He was sent to Switzerland in 1938 to study in Zurich and he was there in 1944 when the Germans occupied Hungary. Spending the rest of his life in Zurich, he established a medical supplies and equipment brokerage that was quite successful. As adults Pisti and I became friends and my first wife and I visited him and his Swiss wife on two occasions. Pisti died of cancer in his sixties in 1986.

The youngest Mauthner child, Gabriella, known as Memi, was born in 1923. She was the only one who lived to a ripe old age and fortunately did not die of cancer. She spent most of her life in the United States working for many years in New York for several organizations which offered help to immigrant Hungarians particularly after 1956. She was jokingly referred to as a "professional Hungarian". We were good friends and I was sorry when she died in the autumn of 2010 at the age of eighty-seven.

The Mauthners lived in a large house at 13 Lendvay utca directly behind the Manfréd Weiss house and separated from it by a large garden. Actually this house was rebuilt and enlarged by Manfréd when Elza and Alfréd were married. The Mauthners also owned a villa on Budakeszi út in the Buda hills, which was the site of the signing of the contract between the Germans and the family in 1944.

Jenő, the second child of Manfréd and Alice, was born in 1887 in Budapest and died in 1983 in Munich. He was a very active and mischievous youngster who grew up to become a brilliant engineer. The holder of several patents, he made major contributions to the manufacture of seamless steel tubes in his father's factory in Csepel. He also designed an irrigation project at the family estate in Derekegyháza which was the first of its kind in the country. In his late teens he developed several emotional problems one of which was agoraphobia. Due to the stress he experienced when in crowds his family had him driven to and from his classes at the University. All of his symptoms were alleviated after his marriage to Annie von Geitler, the daughter of a prominent German family living in Prague. Aunt Annie was a very lovely and extremely nice woman whom everybody liked. She also kept an excellent home for Jenő and for their children and having an opportunity to have a meal with them was always a great pleasure. I liked her very much and was sad when she died after a long and very courageous battle with leukemia in 1961 at age sixty-three. Jenő and his family moved to the U.S. sometime in the spring of 1947. Uncle Jenő and I got along very well and I thought very highly of him for his many accomplishments. Having once been trapped in an elevator when he was a young man he found the prospect of riding in one overwhelming. This was not much of a problem in Portugal or Switzerland, but once when he came to New York it was. One special memory of mine is about the time in New York when he had an appointment to see an attorney who was working on some immigration problem. The office was on the sixteenth floor in downtown New York. I happened to be in the city at the time and when Uncle Jenő told me about the appointment I offered to go with him. We went downtown by taxi and when we entered the lobby of the office building I took him by the arm and led him to the nearest elevator. We rode up and at the end of the meeting we rode down again. He thanked me very much and, so far as I know that was the last time that he used an elevator. Their very nice apartment was on Park Avenue and on the second floor. He and Aunt Annie always used the stairs. I was so glad to be able to be there for him.

There were three children: György, whose nickname is Pic (Pits) Alice and Annie. Alice, one day older than I, was a very pretty girl. She was not intellectually oriented but had an excellent sense of humor and was very pleasant company. She never held a job for any length of time and did not like New York. She eventually married Lajos Cséry, a bright and very handsome man with whom she had one son. After the death of her mother they moved to Munich. Uncle Jenő and Annie also moved to Munich, where they rented a very pleasant house in which Annie and Lajos are still living. Alice, tragically, had a brain tumor and died at home after a lengthy hospital stay in 2009 at age eighty-five.

Pic was also not interested in intellectual and scholarly activities. At the time of the Korean War he would have been eligible for the draft but his parents insisted that he leave the U.S. He moved first to Argentina where he was employed in some mercantile capacity. Eventually he moved to Switzerland, to Zurich, where he is still living as this is written. The only time when he and I spent any time together was in the U.S. when he joined my parents and me on our first car trip to Canada. I saw Pic in Zürich in 2009 when my second wife and I visited him and met his lovely wife Hédi, a very pleasant lady.

The youngest of the Jenő Weiss family, Annie, was and is a very lovely woman. She has always been excellent company with her marvelous sense of humor. She is a dear, dear person. She never married.

Manfréd and Alice's third child was my mother, Marianne. Born in 1888, she was a beautiful and bright little girl. She grew up with a love of art and music and always enjoyed attending symphony concerts and the opera. Her special love was visiting museums. Athletic for a girl in those days, she enjoyed horseback riding, tennis, walking and hiking, and was a remarkably good shot. Among her best trophies was a pair of large and very ugly birds called bustards which were stuffed and stood in the foyer in the chateau at Ireg. She was also a fine golfer which was most unusual at the time. As an early teen she suffered a cut on her right hand which turned into what was probably a staph infection. For a period of time it looked as though she might lose two fingers on that hand. Never to be stopped by anything, she proceeded with golf using a left-handed set. Swimming was another of her great enjoyments and when we went to Westend, in Belgium, in the summer she happily waded and swam in the cold sea. During the First World War Mother worked in a military hospital taking care of wounded soldiers. It must have been a harrowing experience because of the nature of the wounds and the limited amount that could be done medically.

When Grandmother Weiss died, in 1904, her oldest daughter, Elza, took over as her father's hostess and as substitute mother for her brothers and sisters. After Elza's marriage, those jobs fell to Marianne. She adored her father and enjoyed being his hostess but her particular delight was to be able to help him in his work. He usually returned to the Andrássy út home for lunch. My mother related the story that during lunch the telephone was on the table between her father and herself and that it was her job to answer the calls, screen them and hand the instrument to Manfréd only if the matter was important. According to her recollections there were few lunches when there were not five or six calls. Marianne was an excellent mother to her sibs, even to her older brother, Jenő. When I was growing up my brother and sisters and I often chided her saying that she loved them more than she loved us.

Alfonz was born in 1890. Tragically he was only fourteen when his mother died. He was a quiet child with some emotional problems as a youngster which included having a stammer whenever he felt slightly stressed. His grandmother, who helped to raise him, referred to him as, "my little idiot", a phrase which sounds dreadful in English but when spoken in German it was endearing. His problems seemed to disappear and he finished the gimnázium successfully. Eventually he went to Cambridge and studied there for two years but I am not certain that he received a degree. He worked for his father at Csepel and during the First World War he served with distinction in Russia in a cavalry regiment as a junior officer. After the war he became active again in Csepel and met and fell in love with Erzsébet (Erzsi) Herzog, the daughter of Mór Herzog. The Herzogs were a very prominent family and Mór was one of Hungary's major collectors of art. Having excellent taste he early recognized the value of the painter Greco who at that time was not regarded highly by the so-called experts and whose paintings could be purchased at surprisingly low prices. The Herzog collection included a number of Grecos and also numerous representatives of the best French impressionists.

Erzsi was a very bright young woman. At the time she met Alfonz she was studying medicine. Continuing her studies after their marriage, she graduated from the medical school in Pécs with distinction. She ultimately became a Freudian psychiatrist. I was fond of Erzsi and on the relatively few occasions that we met in Budapest we always got along very well. When the family came to this country and I was in New York for any reason, I enjoyed visiting her and telling her about my research. She was fascinated and always wanted to know all about it. Erzsi and Alfonz had four children. Gábor (Gabi), the oldest, was born in 1922 and was followed by Márta (Juci) in 1923, Mária (Marika) in 1927 and János (Jancsi) in 1929. Gábor worked with his father at Csepel after he graduated from the gimnázium but this came to an end with the German invasion. After a couple of years in Portugal, he and his parents and siblings moved to New York. He did not have a very happy life and died at age sixty-five.

Márta (Juci) was not only very attractive but also very bright, finishing her college education in the United States. She and I were the first ones of the family to come to the States, arriving here on December twenty-six, 1945. She married Ted Nierenberg, a very able and ambitious young man. The two of them worked together and became the U.S. representatives for the Dansk Company. Great success followed their hard work and the Dansk line of beautiful table ware and decorative objects became extremely popular in the nineteen-fifties and later. Juci and Ted lived with their four children on a beautiful estate in Armonk, N.Y. Sadly, Ted died in 2009.

Mária (Marika) was happily married to Richard Radcliff and lived on the West Coast. They also had four children.

János (Jancsi) was a very lively youngster. He was educated in the United States and worked as a stock broker in New York. He had an excellent career and was deservedly successful. In fact he managed the estate of my sisters and did very well by them. He and his wife Lenore (Lennie) have three children.

I had relatively few contacts with these cousins in Hungary. They lived on the Buda side of the Danube, quite a distance from us, and I really got to know them only when we lived together in Curia, in Portugal, after July 1944. Gábor, Márta and I became good friends. After we had come to the U.S. we again saw each other only rarely due to living at a great distance from each other and being busy with our lives and growing families.

Daisy, the next to youngest of Manfréd and Alice's children, was born in 1895. A pretty, gentle and well-behaved child, she grew up into a lovely and charming woman. She was courted by a number of suitors but she admired and loved Ferenc Chorin, Jr. even when he wanted to marry her older sister Marianne. When Marianne finally agreed to marry Móric Kornfeld, Ferenc Chorin became interested in Daisy and after a lengthy courtship married her in 1920.

The Chorin family had lived in Hungary for a long time. Grandfather Chorin was chief rabbi in Arad in the south-east of Hungary. His son, Ferenc, was a successful businessman whose major claim to fame was that he organized the National Association of Manufacturers (GYOSZ) and served as its first president for many years. According to family tradition he was a very strict and rigid individual who toward the end of his life developed what would be called today a form of Alzheimer's disease but in a paranoid form. Sadly, he was convinced that his family wanted to kill him by starving him to death. The family made arrangements such that, in the apartment where the old man was living, the kitchen was to be ready twenty-four hours every day to serve him a hot meal.

Ferenc Jr. was extraordinarily bright, graduating from both the *gimnázium* and the university *Magna Cum Laude*. He was also a most charming individual beloved by his family and friends. In his business activities he was forceful and commanding. He created a significant mining and manufacturing combine. Apparently he could be quite ruthless in resolving his business problems and was viewed by labor organizations as the archetypical capitalist exploiter. He was also quite active politically, was appointed to the Upper House of Parliament, and eventually was awarded the First Class Ministerial Counselor title which meant that he was addressed as Your Excellency. He was well liked by Regent Horthy who did him a number of favors at a time when this was no longer politically prudent. Ferenc respected and liked the Regent and, in fact, supported him financially when after the war Horthy and his family lived in exile in Portugal.

The Chorins lived in a very large and elegant home at 114 Andrássy út next to the old Weiss mansion at 116 Andrássy út. Uncle Feri had a very beautiful library including the fifty-volume Kehl edition of Voltaire's works, bound in leather, as well as many other books. It was an important collection and he was very generous and allowed me to borrow freely which I gratefully and diligently did.

The Chorins also had a lovely villa on the Svábhegy where they spent much of the summer and well into the fall. It was there that I spent several weeks each fall for several years. This was a very pleasant time for me. I was very fond of my cousins and I both respected and loved Uncle Ferenc and Aunt Daisy. The old German nanny, Schwester Marianne, was also still there and she and I were the best of friends. Uncle Ferenc introduced me to golf and paid for my lessons as well as for playing. The golf course on the Svábhegy, not too far from their villa was fairly exclusive at that time and not used very much. I believe it was the only course in Hungary in the nineteen-thirties.

My cousins Erzsébet and Daisy attended a Catholic girls' school not far from the Piarist Gimnázium where I went to school. We were driven down from the Svábhegy every morning by the Chorins' chauffeur and were usually picked up at one o'clock, at the end of the school day. If I had a scout meeting or anything else going on after school I returned to the villa on my own, taking the street car to the cogwheel train terminal and riding it to the top of the Svábhegy. From there to the villa was less than a mile so that walking presented no problem at all.

The third Chorin child, Ferenc, was several years younger than Daisy. Aunt Daisy had a difficult pregnancy and a very prolonged and hard labor and delivery. She was attended by the professor of obstetrics who at one point ran out of the delivery room and asked Uncle Ferenc and my mother who were waiting outside whether he should save the mother or the baby. My mother became incensed and said that he should save both and if he did not know how she would get another obstetrician. What happened was that the forceps which had to be used to get the infant out were applied poorly and caused a significant skull fracture with some damage to the underlying brain.

I am not sure about the sequence of events but I do know that the baby was seen by Professor Olivecrona, the Swedish neurosurgeon, who was the father of modern neurosurgery and a most remarkable personality. I believe he performed some corrective surgery on the baby who then developed essentially normally but had a very large and slightly misshapen head. He also had some minor weaknesses on one side but was mentally alert and was able to attend school and graduate. In New York where the Chorin family lived after the war he started having severe headaches and was seen by experts at Columbia who found that he had a cerebral aneurysm. Surgery for this procedure was just being developed and it was recommended that Ferenc, who was in his early twenty's, should be scheduled for what was clearly a risky procedure. His parents decided against the operation and not too long thereafter the aneurysm ruptured and young Ferenc died in 1954. It was a major family tragedy.

Of all my cousins I was probably closest at that time to the two Chorin girls. We saw each other quite frequently while I saw my other cousins only rarely. When we grew older the Chorin girls and I met much less often but remained good friends and spent a great deal of time together when we were in Portugal.

The Chorins moved to the United States and lived for many years in a very large apartment at One Thousand, Park Avenue in New York City. Erzsébet, a very bright woman, worked with her father in his wide-spread business activities.

She married István Ráth and had a son, Ferenc. After Ráth died she married an old flame, László Mándy, who had been courting her for many years before her first marriage and who was one of the relatively few Hungarians who survived Auschwitz. He also died some years ago leaving Erzsébet alone.

Daisy married Rudolf von Strasser, the son of a very distinguished Austrian family. Living in Vienna in September, 1939, he became involved in the Austrian Freedom Movement and in July, 1940, he was arrested and after four years in detention was tried and sentenced to ten years hard labor. Eleven of his friends were executed.

Freed at the end of the war in May, 1945, he became a journalist in Salzburg and then in Vienna. After working for the Austrian Federal Chamber of Commerce he eventually settled in New York in 1953. He continued both his newspaper work and his commercial activities. He joined Kidder-Peabody in 1958 doing both broker's work and representing European companies.

The Strassers lived in Pelham, N.Y. until they moved to Vienna in 1991. They have two sons and one daughter. The older son, Rudolph owns and operates a very fine winery in the Napa Valley in California. The other son, Christopher, lives in New York and the daughter, Daisy III, lives with her family in Germany.

Over the years Rudi has assembled a most remarkable collection of both very early and more modern glass and has become a leading expert in the field. The author of a classic text on this most interesting subject he was a consultant to the famous Corning Glass company. Recently he has divided his collection and donated half of it to the Kunstkammer in Vienna and the other half to the Chateau Ambras collection near Innsbruck.

The last one of the Weiss family was my Aunt Edith, the youngest of Manfréd's six children, born in 1899. She had a good education and read widely. At a fairly early age she made a trip around the world and brought back a large collection of beautiful art work including a bronze Buddha that graced our dining room in Lendvay utca. She never married and devoted her life to worthy causes, first and foremost, to help persecuted Jews in Hungary during the late thirties and early forties until March, 1944. She was a petite and most attractive person – immensely active and quite forceful. In New York she lived with the Chorins but frequently came to Washington to be with my parents. She died of cancer in 1967 at age sixty-eight, the victim of medical negligence and gross incompetence.

It is regrettable that there is no scholarly biography of Manfréd Weiss even though he was a major factor in the development of Hungarian industry. I have spoken to several historians in Budapest on this matter and hope that some day the omission will be corrected.

Chapter Three

The Móric Kornfeld Family

As was noted above my father, Móric Kornfeld, was the second son of Zsigmond Kornfeld and his wife, Barbara. Born on December thirty, 1882, he had a happy but very strictly disciplined childhood which was not unusual at the time. An example is that he and his siblings had to lie at attention in their bed when one of the parents entered the room. They were trained to speak only when they were invited to do so.

Father had the standard primary and secondary education and then enrolled at the university to get a doctorate in economics. In his second year he fought a duel with sabers with another student who made a disparaging remark about the Jews at the university. Ferenc Chorin was my father's second and told me many years later that my father fought very well and actually inflicted a small cut on his opponent which ended the duel. Because of this his university record showed a censure mark because in Hungary dueling was frowned upon. When in the following year he went to the University of Leipzig to study under an eminent professor of economics, the dean of that university, on interviewing my father, asked him what the censure mark on his record was all about. When my father told him that it was because of a duel he had fought, the dean smiled, said, "well done" and promptly admitted him to the university. In Germany at that time dueling was almost a national sport and was considered a manifestation of manly virtues. Returning to Hungary a year later he continued his studies and eventually finished with a dual doctorate in economics and law.

Shortly thereafter he was given a position by the Ganz Manufacturing Company and he started his career there as a secretary to the president. His first job was to copy the president's scrawled handwriting to a legible form for mailing. When he finished the task he handed the letter to the president for signature and returned to his desk. About three minutes later the letter came flying back through the door between his office and the president's with a command to do it over again, this time "properly". Father had misplaced a comma. However his background and exceptional abilities led to rapid advancement in the company and within five or six years he became first the vice president and then the president of the company.

Around 1905 he started courting my mother, Marianne Weiss. After considerable reluctance she eventually agreed to marry him in 1913. He was a very attentive suitor: my mother had been sick with measles and, upon her recovery, my father and his good friend Ferenc Chorin who was also courting my mother, arranged for a ball at the Hotel Ritz. This apparently was late in the autumn so that in order to simulate a summer garden party live trees were installed in the ball room and a person was hired to imitate bird calls. It was a wonderful event and everyone had a lovely time. On another occasion Father and Miss Weiss were at some function together but she told him that her carriage was waiting for her and that she did not particularly want him to accompany her. He very politely assisted her into the carriage and bade her good night. As the horses were starting he jumped on the rear axle of the carriage and held on all the way to her home on Andrássy út. When the carriage stopped at the door he jumped off and ceremoniously opened the door for her to alight from the carriage. She later said that she did not know whether to laugh or be mad at him, but deep down she was touched and impressed.

The formal engagement must have taken place sometimes during the spring of 1913 and was celebrated by a beautiful party at Gerbaud, the famous patisserie, in the Városliget. This event was the talk of the town for some time. The wedding was held on June seventeenth, 1913, in the Weiss mansion on Andrássy út. A very festive occasion, there were many guests. My mother's father, Manfréd Weiss, gave the young couple, as a wedding gift, a country estate of six thousand acres in the village of Iregszemcse.

The couple left for their wedding trip to Spain with fourteen suitcases and trunks one of which was exclusively for my mother's hats. Father had reserved a sleeping compartment and had it decorated with dozens of white roses. When my mother saw it she had a fit and refused to enter until the flowers were removed. She appreciated the gesture but hated any special public display that drew attention to them. She was basically a very modest person who was profoundly opposed to all unnecessary public recognition. The trip was happy after this unfortunate start.

Our home in Budapest at 27 Lendvay utca, was rented by my parents on return from their honeymoon in 1913, strictly on a temporary basis while they were looking for a house to buy. In fact they never moved and were still living in the same apartment on March nineteenth, 1944, when the Germans invaded Hungary and my parents had to flee. Lendvay utca was a small street parallel to the Andrássy út, very close to the Heroes' square and the Museum of Fine Arts. It was also very close to the Zoo and to the pond in Városliget which in the winter was converted into a large ice skating ring. The house we lived in was fairly large with three storys and with a large basement area where we had our kitchen and servants' rooms. We did not own the house and only rented the first floor. One of the reasons why my mother was not anxious to move was that this apartment was very close to where four of her five siblings lived. The Mauthners were just down the street at number thirteen. Their house shared a back yard with the original Weiss house at 116 Andrássy út. This was the building where my mother grew up and was inhabited now by her brother Jenő with his family downstairs and her sister Edith who had the upstairs. Immediately next to it, at 114 Andrássy út lived her sister Daisy Chorin and her family.

Our apartment, really the first floor of the building, had a nice entranceway and a small coat room and lavatory off to one side. The entrance hall connected to a library-living room in the left corner of the apartment and also to a dining room which was quite large. Next to the library was a salon which was used only at Christmas time and when my mother's elderly lady friends came for tea. It was furnished with extremely valuable Empire furniture which was lovely to look at but very uncomfortable to use. There was also a Steinway grand piano which my mother enjoyed playing. Across the room was Father's cello.

At the other end of the house were five bedrooms: one for my brother, one for my two sisters and one for me. Next to my small room was my mother's bedroom and next to hers, my father's. Because he snored very loudly my parents slept in separate bedrooms. There were two bathrooms, one next to my father's room which was exclusively his, while the other bathroom served my mother and the rest of us. Both bathrooms had a tub but no shower. The bedrooms were furnished comfortably albeit fairly simply.

On the other end from the dining room was a butler's room and pantry which was connected to the kitchen below it by a dumb waiter. All the food that was served in the dining room, occasionally for as many as a dozen or so guests, had to be pulled up from the kitchen in the dumb waiter. Just past the pantry was another fairly sizable room with a small bedroom attached to it. This was first used by the French-Swiss mademoiselle who was with the family for a number of years when my sisters and brother were young. Mademoiselle was a tutor-cum-nanny for them. After she left, my mother's elderly maid stayed there and when she died it was converted into a sewing room and servants' sitting room.

The public areas – foyer, library, salon and dining room were furnished with quite valuable antiques including my father's enormously valuable collection of very early carved wooden statues which currently happen to be the ornament of a museum in Moscow. Among other things the dining room also had the beautiful large bronze sitting Buddha that Aunt Edith bought in China. Upon her return she presented the statue to my parents. At one end of the dining room there was a very large and beautiful Maria Theresia armoire in which the "good table silver" was kept. It may be of interest to mention that Mother had three sets of both china and sterling silver. There was the "every day" set, the "good set" that was used regularly when there were guests and the "special set" that was used only on very special occasions. In all of the years that I lived there I saw this set used only three or four times. There were also some very lovely paintings several of which were destroyed during the war. Some were looted but one actually came to be in the Museum of Fine Arts in Budapest as did one of the smaller wooden statues. We could have gotten them back but we decided to donate them to the museum because we felt that since they were Hungarian in origin they should remain in Hungary to be enjoyed by the visitors to the museum. At the present time the building where our apartment was, and which survived the war and the Russian siege, houses the French Embassy.

My parents entertained many guests, but Father's favorite party was the luncheon given every Thursday for his bachelor friends. Great good fun did they have joking and teasing. The quantity of food consumed was amazing. The only caveat was that if a member of the group married he was no longer welcome. Once one of the gentlemen decided to marry his housekeeper and was never invited again. Among the distinguished guests were Baron Samu Hazay, the former Hungarian minister of war during the First World War, Géza Szüllő, a high-ranking politician and leading member of his party in parliament, Elek Petrovich, the former director general of the Hungarian Museum of Fine Arts, Pál Bakonyi and Jenő Kőnig, both high officials in the Ministry of Commerce, János Meltzer a prominent attorney and my godfather, Zsiga Thaly, former deputy minister of education and two or three others. When I was a little boy, if I happened to be at home when Dr. Petrovich was visiting, my parents always urged me to show him my childish drawings and sketches. He would look them over very seriously and nod and say, "Very nice, yes, very nice".

Christmas was a major event. In Central European tradition it was not Santa Claus who brought the presents but the Child Jesus. When I was little I firmly believed in this and was always looking forward to meeting Him. I knew that Christmas Eve was approaching when a settee was moved out of the salon and I was told that I could not go in. The Christmas tree was large and beautifully decorated with tinsel, silver chains and glass ornaments. The lights were real candles in holders clipped on the small branches. There was always a large bucket filled with water in a corner of the room and the candles were lighted only on Christmas Eve for about thirty minutes and again on Epiphany, January sixth, for about ten minutes prior to the tree being stripped.

We had the presentation of gifts on Christmas Eve. Until I was a teenager I had to wait outside the salon until my mother rang a little bell which was the signal for me to go in. It really was a beautiful sight. The candles were burning brightly and the presents in lovely paper with ribbons and bows were under the tree in four groups for my three siblings and for me. We began with singing, *Silent Night, Holy Night* in German and wished each other a Merry Christmas. Finally I could sit down on the floor and start opening my presents. Even now, eighty years later, it is still a warm and lovely memory.

When I was ten I was allowed to accompany my family to Midnight Mass which in those days really was celebrated at midnight. That meant I got to bed at about 1:00 am which at that age was an exciting experience. On Christmas Day I could play with my new toys and enjoy my other presents. I also went ice skating and then we had a festive lunch usually consisting of ham with all of the trimmings. I don't remember what we had for dessert but I'm sure that it was something pretty fancy. Having been to Midnight Mass we did not go to church on Christmas Day. The following morning, December twenty-sixth, we went down to Derekegyháza where we spent a week with all of the rest of the family, returning home for the start of school in early January.

Easter was much less of an event. We had the whole week off from school and that, of course, was a grand time. When I was little we did have an egg hunt in the apartment or, when Easter was late, at Ireg outside the chateau. We went to church on Good Friday, Holy Saturday and Easter Sunday. Easter Monday was a major holiday and, traditionally, was the day the young men could visit their lady friends and sprinkle perfume on them in exchange for an Easter egg or a kiss as the case might be. This was such a pleasant custom and fun was had by all.

Our library consisted of a total of approximately ten thousand volumes in several languages. The classic literature of Greece, Rome, Italy, Great Britain, France, Germany and Hungary was represented and it also included a very special collection of early Hungarian books, the so-called Hungarica. Father started this collection at a relatively early age and quickly realized that he had a rare and practically unique collection. In 1913 a printed catalog of the collection was prepared by József Balogh, Professor Ármin Balog's son, under the title of *Index Librorum Hungaricorum Mauritii Baronis Kornfeld*. The *Index* listed two hundred twenty-seven books, alphabetically. Although the title of the *Index* was in Latin, the books were described in Hungarian. Very soon the Index was extended to include an additional forty-eight volumes. The *Index* is currently in the Manuscript Collection of the Hungarian National Széchényi Library.

Father continued to collect and by the outbreak of the Second World War the total grew to over five hundred volumes. The additional volumes were listed in handwriting in a personal copy of my father's which was recovered after the war and is now also in the Széchényi Library. According to this *Index* there were about five hundred volumes of early Hungarica of which about fourteen were unique: they were the only copies of early Hungarian printed material known to exist. During the Second World War all of the Hungarica were stored in the vaults of a major bank in order to save them from possible air raids. Many of the additional works in Father's library were also put into safekeeping with a major bookseller in Budapest who was his friend. Both the Germans and the Russians looted the vaults of the banks and all of my father's books disappeared. It was the general opinion that they were either destroyed or were hidden in some private collections. About one hundred copies appeared in 1948 in a sale of books in Budapest. They were nice works but not particularly valuable, and we do not know who had them or where they were found. However, a number of volumes were rare enough that they were purchased prior to the sale by the National Academy of Science. Some additional copies also appeared on the shelves of second-hand book stores in Budapest.

It became known in 2007 that a number of the most valuable Hungarica were preserved in the Russian State Library in Nizhniy Novgorod. About one hundred volumes are there including seven of the original unique ones. One of the seven had never been described and was for the first time illustrated and discussed in the excellent monograph by Dr. Judit Ecsedy, a senior official of the Széchényi Library. The monograph was published in 2011 and I have used it with the author's permission. The first of the seven by date (1544) is a word list in six parallel columns in Latin, Italian, French, Czech, Hungarian and German. The title of the book is in Latin first and then in Hungarian; in English it is *The Dictionary of Six Languages*. The third volume in this series was published in 1678 or 1679 and had the interesting title, *On the Devilish Ghosts*. The fourth volume had a title which might well be of interest to us today, *Spiritual Shield against All Wars*. The seventh book in this series was previously unknown. It was published around 1690 and was a book of prayers, *For Times of Misery*. A general comment about the Hungarica in Russia: the Hungarian government has been negotiating with the Russian government for the return of these books. To date the discussions have been unsuccessful.

Some years ago my siblings and I made an agreement with the National Széchényi Library that if Father's books were returned we would sell them to the Library at their valuation and turn the money back to them for the establishment of a Móric Kornfeld fellowship for the support of young Hungarian scholars. A similar agreement was made with the Museum of Fine Arts regarding the statues. On October twenty-ninth, 2001, I was awarded the "Pro Cultura Hungarica" medal and award. It was given by the Minister of Culture and Preservation of the National Heritage. As we found out later the recommendation was made jointly by Dr. Miklós Mojzer, the Executive Director of the Museum of Fine Arts and by

Dr. Géza Poprády, the Director General of the National Széchényi Library. They wanted to show appreciation for our agreement on Father's books and artwork.

The actual ceremony was an impressive and most pleasant event. We gathered in a reception room in the Ministry of Culture and we were surrounded by our Hungarian friends, Tibor Fabinyi and his wife, Vali, Ágnes Széchenyi and Joe Paulin. Dr. Mojzer and Dr. Poprády were there as were one or two other people from the museum and the library and some officials from the ministry. We sat around a long table with the minister at the head and my wife and I on his right. Dr. Mojzer, sitting across from me made a speech of introduction and spoke of Father's contributions to Hungarian culture. He also said a few very kind things about me. When he was done the minister spoke a few words and then presented me with the "Pro Cultura Hungarica" medal and with a very handsome document. I responded, thanking him and our two friends, Mojzer and Poprády who had made this all possible. The formal session was immediately followed by a very nice buffet. There was wine with which we were toasted by the ministry staff. Pictures were taken and a very good time was had by all. I must admit that it was a proud moment, not only because of the award, but even more importantly because of the recognition of Father's contributions to Hungary.

My parent's first child, Mária, was born on September fourteenth, 1914. Someone, probably her proud father, called the baby *Puppe* which is the word for "little doll" in German. The word was modified to Puppa in Hungarian and she was known to family and friends by that name for the rest of her life. In May of 1916 another baby girl was born – Johanna who was always known as Hanna and whom family and friends called Hancsi. George was next in the summer of 1918 and six years later I was born in 1924. The whole family was at Ireg that June day and three prominent physicians were also in residence; an obstetrician, a pediatrician and a family physician. I have been told that Mother's labor was prolonged and that when I finally made my appearance I was reluctant to join this vale of tears: I was unable to breath. With the application of slaps and spankings, at last I lost the dark blue color and breathed normally.

My parents' marriage initially was not a particularly happy one; their interests were different. Mother was much more socially active than Father who was quite reserved in some ways, preferring his books and his writing. Also, he tended not to be particularly demonstrative of his feelings. My mother told him repeatedly that she knew that he loved her but that she also wanted to hear him say so. Another problem was that her father, Manfréd Weiss, was not overly fond of my father which influenced my mother's feelings. She truly believed that her father was never wrong. The couple managed to get through the difficult years of the First World War at the end of which came first the Károlyi revolution and then the Hungarian Soviet Republic. Because of his education, social standing and financial resources, the Soviets would have considered Father "an enemy of the people" and would have imprisoned or even assassinated him. He therefore had to flee Budapest to avoid arrest. Mother and the three children managed to get to safety in Vienna.

During the years 1920-21 my mother was seriously considering leaving my father for good. However, by that time Manfréd had learned to like and appreciate my father and so advised my mother strongly to stay with him. This carried the day and while the marriage might not have been a particularly intimate and loving one, for many years it was peaceful. As a child I had no indication whatever of any tensions or problems between them. As the years went by the relationship continued to improve and, particularly after the separation enforced by the German invasion in 1944, it became a very happy and loving marriage and remained so until Father's death twenty-four years later.

Mother was almost pathologically devoted to her father. An example of these feelings is the fact that after he died she wore full mourning clothes complete with a heavy black veil every time she left the house for an entire year. She told me many years later that after her father had died she resented the fact that the sun was still shining.

During the nineteen-twenties and thirties Father led a very active life. He was a member of the Upper House of Parliament, having been appointed by the Regent in 1926 shortly after the Upper House was established. He was a member of the Board of Directors of the Hungarian National Bank, was actively involved in the management of Csepel and was very active in the agricultural and industrial activities at our estate in Ireg. He was actively supporting a number of young promising Hungarian writers, and artists. As early as 1919 he wrote a very courteous note to the greatest Hungarian poet of the twentieth century, Endre Ady, who at the time was destitute and very ill. Father asked him for permission to transmit a fairly significant sum of money to him in recognition for all of the pleasure his great poetry had given Father over many years. The offer was gratefully accepted and Ady died in peace and comfort several months later. Father was also very close to another great poet, Mihály Babits who became a good friend of my parents and even used the informal, second person singular, form of address with them. This would have been most unusual at the time. Not much after that Father was instrumental in supporting the important literary magazine *Nyugat* (West). He also personally helped one of the editors. Father subsidized a number of other young writers, many of them belonging to the rather radical "Village Explorer" group which was writing, for the first time in Hungary, about the miserable living conditions and the destitution that characterized much of the rural population. He was instrumental in establishing an English periodical, *The Hungarian Quarterly* and a French one, *Le Nouvelle Revue de Hongrie*. These two publications were to help in making Hungary better known to the leading nations in the west. He was also one of the major supporters of a daily newspaper, the *Magyar Nemzet* (Hungarian Nation) which became an important publication being the principal anti-German paper in Budapest.

Shortly after the publication of *Le Nouvelle Revue de Hongrie* Father wrote an article for it that was published in the December, 1933, issue under the title *Les deux routes*. In this he described the two political pathways that were potentially open to Hungary to follow. These were the German path and the Danubian path. The former path would have led to an increasing alliance with Germany, both politically and economically. Father described both the advantages and disadvantages of such an alliance. The advantages would be the likelihood of at least a partial reversal of the Trianon Treaty and economic support. The disadvantage would be the vassalage to a great power with the eventual loss of independence. The Danube plan would have led to an alliance with the nations of the Little Entente and some form of federation among the four or five countries inhabiting the Danube Basin. The advantage of this plan would be the maintenance of independence, the improvement of the position of the Hungarian minorities in the neighboring countries and the creation of a substantial block somewhat similar to the old Austro-Hungarian Monarchy. The disadvantage would be the historic antagonism between Hungary and its neighbors that would be extremely difficult to overcome.

Father drew no definitive conclusions but it is clear from the tone that he was very concerned about the German path. After all, Hitler had become the Chancellor of Germany just a few months earlier, in January, 1933. What is perhaps the most interesting issue in connection with this essay is that it triggered a response from no less a person than Franz von Papen who had been Chancellor of Germany in 1932 and was now Hitler's Vice Chancellor. In this article, also published by the *Nouvelle Revue*, in March, 1934, von Papen took issue with what he perceived as Father's conclusions and took a strong stance in favor of the German path. He believed for a variety of reasons that this was the only rational path for Hungary to follow. The fact that a response came from such an elevated source is a clear indication of Father's position and of the careful eye that was kept on him by important political personalities in Germany as early as 1933.

Mother was active in a number of benevolent organizations. She visited the Maria Alice Obstetrical Hospital, which her father had built in memory of her mother, every few months and made suggestions about repairs and maintenance which, of course, she then paid for. She was always busy with projects helping others.

My oldest sister, Puppa, received all of her secondary education at home with tutors. She also studied music, focusing on piano and voice. At the end of her schooling she took the *Matura*, the final exam, and was accepted in the doctoral program of the Department of History at the University of Budapest. It was typical at the time in Hungary for a student to continue their education in a doctoral program straight out of secondary school. At some point in her teens, Puppa became the mistress of a man twice her age: one János Zwack. Married to my mother's cousin, Vera de Wahl, he had one son. It was an odd combination – Puppa the intellectual with her love of music, art and books and Zwack who had none of these interests. Men always benefit from such arrangements. He had a comfortable home with a loving wife and his much adored son and – a young mistress. Although the future in the relationship for Puppa was bleak, it continued at Zwack's convenience until the war. I disliked him intensely.

Unfortunately, her academic career at the university ended early due to a falling out with her thesis advisor over the scope of her proposed investigation into the medieval development of the Hungarian cities. He wanted her to reduce the size to what he considered a more manageable plan but she refused. The life she had planned for herself in research and teaching and writing was over. My poor sister – these choices, early in her life, had major consequences later on. She remained financially dependent on our parents throughout much of her life and, except for a brief time in Portugal when she lived with a Spanish artist, she actually lived with them.

Hanna was home schooled for several years but then attended the Catholic gimnázium of the English Sisters and passed her comprehensive final exam, the *Matura*. She loved sports – skiing, swimming, tennis and skating and had an active social life. After high school she spent the next years working with Mother in her various charitable endeavors. Hanna met and fell deeply in love with Aladár Szegedy-Maszák, a brilliant and handsome young man in public service with the government. He was the descendent of a distinguished Hungarian noble family that included his maternal uncle the famous artist Miklós Barabás. Following postgraduate work in Paris, he joined the Hungarian Ministry of Foreign Affairs. His first diplomatic post was as secretary of the legation in Berlin where he stayed for about three years.

My brother György was a fine athlete but was not particularly intellectual. He graduated from the Piarist gimnázium, passed the *Matura* and served in the army as an officer candidate. After a six-month period he was commissioned a lieutenant. Mother and I attended the ceremony. He then served in the army for about a year and became a reserve officer.

Following his discharge he went to work in the Weiss Manfréd factory at Csepel which kept him from being inducted into a labor battalion at the outbreak of the Second World War. In 1943 he married Erzsébet Kawalsky who was known as Elza, a very pretty and lovely young woman. They had one son, Stefan, always called Stevie. I was very fond of Elza and was quite sorry when the marriage did not last. Some years later György married Maria Vessely. They had one son, George junior.

Chapter Four

Summertime

The village of Iregszemcse is about ninety miles from Budapest and twenty-five miles from Lake Balaton. It was there in 1913 that Grandfather Weiss bought an estate as a wedding gift for my parents and it was there that I, the youngest of four children, was born. We always called it Ireg. When I was growing up we spent the winters in Budapest working and going to school but most of the time in the summers we were in Ireg.

The village had a population of about thirty-five hundred people. Most of them were farmers with some officials and one or two professional people in addition to shopkeepers and artisans like shoemakers, tailors, carpenters, brick-layers, smiths and others. The houses in the village were all of one story and most of them, when I was a small child, did not have electricity or running water. It was only in the 1930s that electricity became available to all houses and at the same time plumbing was introduced generally. Many of the houses had thatched roofs which were gradually replaced by very ugly tiles. The only public buildings were the City Hall and the gendarmes' station. There were two churches, one Catholic and one Reformed Protestant and a small elementary school with grades from one to nine. Any child who wanted to have a secondary education had to leave the village and become a boarding student in our neighboring town of Tamási.

The people living in the village were almost all Hungarians with only a very small number of ethnic Germans. They were simple people, honest and hard-working. Some of the older ones and even some of the younger ones could not read or write. Many of the older men and women had never traveled away from Ireg. In 1938, at the time of the Eucharistic Congress in Budapest, my father made arrangements for fifty of the villagers to go there to see the man who would become Pope Pius XII, Cardinal Pacelli. The train station was about eight miles from the village but several of the older villagers who went on the trip never had seen a railroad train let alone travel on one. This would be the first time that they were ever so far from home. I stood at attention with my fellow Boy Scouts on Andrássy út looking toward Heroes' Square and watched the ceremonial parade including the papal delegate. The best thing about the Congress for me was that we had several days' vacation from school.

There was a doctor in the village, an older GP who was not very good but he was a nice man who delivered babies in the homes, attended to minor injuries and set fractures. There was also a public health nurse whom Father supported. She was the Green Cross nurse, who assisted the doctor and who also provided health care to the people on her own. In fact she probably did more for them than the old doctor. She and I became good friends.

The Catholic Church was served by the pastor and by a younger priest who assisted him. The old priest was the one who baptized me and when I grew up we became quite friendly. Oddly enough he could speak Latin fluently and when once a French Jesuit came to visit, he and the priest could converse in Latin. The Catholics represented about three quarters of the population with the rest being Protestant. There was little love between the two groups and while there was no open hostility there was surely no intermarriage. Catholic and Protestant children also kept strictly apart. We, of course, attended the Catholic Church with my father being a patron. That meant that any time something had to be done for the church he was called upon. Once the clock in the church tower stopped and the council, consisting of about five or six elderly peasants, met and decided to ask my father to have the clock repaired because its hourly chiming was very much missed. When it came time to talk to Father about the money one of the old peasants raised his hand, "I don't think we should have the clock fixed because if it is fixed the Protestants will also benefit by it." Needless to say the clock was repaired.

The estate was adjacent to the village with the chateau and at the western edge. The chateau was in a park of about twenty-five acres which included lawns and a three-acre garden for vegetables and flowers. The latter was cared for by the chief gardener who was my best friend and with whom I spent a good bit of time. He taught me about gardening and I enjoyed working with him planting, seeding, grafting and all the other gardening exercises. Eventually he married my nanny, Teta Liesl, which became very important to me in 1944.

The chateau was built about 1820 and had undergone practically no changes until Grandfather bought it. At that time the building needed relatively little repair on the outside but inside considerable work had to be done: bathrooms had to be added and the old tile stoves that heated the rooms needed repair. The building was rectangular with the first floor having a beautiful library-sitting room, a salon, a large dining room, sun porch, three bedrooms, kitchen, pantries, servants' dining room, etc. When you entered the building there was a sitting area with a wood burning fireplace and a lovely curved staircase leading to the upstairs where there were nine bedrooms and a small workshop where an old master cabinet maker worked when I was a little boy. He and I became friends and I was very sorry when he died in 1928 and the wood shop was turned into a small bedroom.

A large salon on that floor opened to a balcony. In the salon was a grand piano which was used occasionally when Mother played some classical music or accompanied Puppa who was studying voice.

The house had no central heating but each bedroom and each public room had a large tile stove which was heated with wood. The library-sitting room was large and one of the long walls was completely covered with books from floor to ceiling. There were comfortable chairs around a central table and there was room for a card table, liquor cabinet and one cabinet for the Britannica Encyclopedia.

The dining room was very large and had an oval table that accommodated twenty-eight people when completely extended. Along one wall there was a beautiful cabinet which I believe had come from a church. Above it was a very large and quite beautiful eighteenth-century Gobelin tapestry depicting a Greek mythological scene. We were told that in 1945 the Russian soldiers covered their trucks with it. My mother sat at the head of the table with my father on the right side. As the youngest, I of course, sat at the end of the table which was fine with me because there I was not under Mother's surveillance. Once, Hanna and I were together at the end of the table and were making fun of one of the guests. We started giggling and could not stop. Finally Mother told us to leave until we could behave ourselves. The table was set with Herend porcelain and crystal with sterling silver place settings. The food was served on silver platters and we helped ourselves from the dishes.

In general lunch and dinner both consisted of soup, a main course of meat or fish with vegetables and was followed by a dessert that was usually very fancy. This was followed by fruit. Breakfast was informal and while we could have eggs and bacon or ham or sausage we generally just had toast and butter and jam. We usually had tea in the morning and coffee in midmorning with some cookies or pastry. We also had afternoon tea consisting of sandwiches and pastries. Why we did not all weigh three hundred pounds is probably due to the fact that we were very active during the day.

Before the war, on weekends, the gentlemen wore black tie and the ladies had long gowns at dinner. This came to an end when the war broke out but we still had to wear ties and jackets. Lunch was more informal but no shorts were permitted. I remember how upset my father was the first time a lady guest, the wife of a cousin, wore slacks rather than a skirt. I think I remember that she was asked to wear a dress the next time she was invited. We usually had a house full of guests, particularly on the weekends when it was not unusual to have up to twenty-five people at the dinner table. We also had guests who stayed most of the summer. These included classmates and close friends who took their vacation with us. Ernő Jónás, Antal Géber, Cousin Stupszi Kornfeld and Puppa's dear friend, Éva H. Balázs, were among these. Elemér Terták was also a summer visitor. A friend and classmate of György's, he became a figure skating champion and represented Hungary at the Olympics. His family survived the Russian siege and Elemér became one of the leaders of Hungarian sports activities as a senior official in the Department of Education.

Distinguished guests, Baron von Krobatin and Baron Samu Hazai, were the first two people to sign the guest book. Aylmer Macartney, a British historian who specialized in the history of Central Europe, particularly Hungary, visited several times. The son and daughter-in-law of Nobel Prize winner Rabindranath Tagore stayed for a few days in the early thirties. Mrs. Tagore not only signed the guest book but also added a very nice pen-and-ink drawing of an Indian woman carrying a jug on her head. Other guests arrived for a weekend or for just a few days. They included friends and beaux of my sisters, my classmates Peter de Balogh and Johnny Graham and, of course, friends of my parents including Baron and Baroness Dobblehoff and their daughter Annemarie. Faithful attendees of Father's Thursday bachelor lunches, János Meltzer, Jenő Kőnig, Zsiga Thaly and Pál Bakonyi came occasionally.

Mother's cousin, Else Mauthner and her husband Stefan, the famous artist, painted many of his beautiful watercolors in Ireg and decorated the guest book with a number of delightful colored drawings. There was also the Szily family. Dr. Aurél Szily was a distinguished professor of ophthalmology at the University of Münster in Germany who lost his job under the Nazi regime and moved to Hungary with his wife, a descendant of a distinguished German aristocratic family, and their son and daughter.

Until about 1935 telephone service in Ireg left a good bit to be desired. We had an old-fashioned crank telephone which lived in the coat and gun room on the first floor off the hall leading to the kitchen. The operator, who was in the village, was the postmistress and the telephone switchboard was in her house. She responded to calls only for an hour in the morning, an hour at noon and an hour in the evening. I remember what a sensation it was when the first dial phone was installed and we were no longer dependent on the mercy of the postmistress.

In addition to the park and gardens mentioned above, there was also a fruit garden with peaches, pears, cherries, apples, and apricots. A large greenhouse supplied the fresh bouquets which were put in the rooms every other day. The park also had a tennis court and a swimming pool. The tennis court was not used much but the pool was pretty busy all day; sixty feet long by thirty feet wide the depth at one end was six feet. Once, a guest forgot to bring his bathing suit; the morning was hot, he removed his shorts and dove into the pool. At that moment Father came out of the house with his newspaper. He took a chair by the pool and proceeded to read. An hour later he was still there with the young guest still in the water in acute discomfort and embarrassment. There were also lawn areas and walks. There was some mix of pine trees, oaks, acacias, beach trees, aspens and many others; most of the trees where sixty to one hundred years old.

Adjacent to the main building was a guest house with twelve additional bedrooms. Directly in front of the house was a fountain in the middle of a rose garden. On the other side of the fountain area were the stables where the horses were kept and a building for the coaches. There was also a garage and, attached to it, a room where the chauffeur lived. On the back of this building was a laundry where women from the village came every day to do the washing for the house. Next to it was the icehouse where in the winter ice was laid down in considerable volume and covered with a thick layer of straw. This icehouse was used for the storage of food as well as a supply of ice. In those days we did not use ice in our water and only a little ice was used in some beverages. Iced coffee and iced tea was not known. The ice of course was also used in a large icebox in the pantry where food was stored. Two large pantries kept food supplies and, much to my pleasure, excellent hard sausages were kept hanging by a string ready for me to come and cut a piece to eat with a piece of bread. I did this fairly regularly most afternoons.

The front entrance to the park opened on the county highway but there were two other exits, one leading to the village and the church and the other toward one of the farms. I well remember walking to church every Sunday at a quarter to ten. We left through the small gate and walked down a village street, past the elementary school and the rectory. The church was only about a half mile away so it did not take us long to get there. I remember carrying my mother's missal. Entering the church through the sacristy we walked in front of the altar and sat in special "patron's pews" to the left of the altar.

In 1919 land reform legislation mandated that all large estates give up a certain amount of land to be distributed to the landless peasants. At Ireg the remaining four thousand acres were mostly arable land divided into forty-acre parcels with rows of walnut trees along the edges. There were also eight or ten fishponds which were separated from each other by dikes and linked by sluices. The ponds were stocked with carp and catfish and a special Hungarian fish called *fogas*. In the fall the ponds were partially drained and thousands of pounds of fish were collected and sold to a large wholesaler. On fishing day there was a festive outdoor luncheon when, naturally, fish was being served. There was an excellent Hungarian paprika fish stew, poached fish and fried fish with lots of wine and beer. There were usually also thirty or forty guests and we all had a wonderful time. Following the family party the workers had theirs.

The property was divided into four farms, each with a specific function, where some of the farmhands lived and where there was usually a forge, a carpenter shop and a home for the supervisor. In a poultry yard adjacent to the park chickens, ducks and geese were raised. We had Rhode Island Reds and Leghorn Whites. They produced the best and largest eggs most of which were sold to a wholesaler. Mother was very fond of this area and frequently took guests to show it to them. On the way there was an apiary with ten or twelve hives. Mother loved to help take care of the bees, but once she was stung and became very sick. After that she stayed away. The bees made excellent honey.

Immediately beyond the park wall was an acre of vegetables, mostly tomatoes and next to that, butting up against the poultry yard, were about three or four acres of hops. This area had poles about eight-feet long stuck vertically in the ground with wires strung across the tops. From the wires at two to three foot intervals wires came down to the ground where they were anchored by pegs. The hops were planted next to each peg and when they grew they climbed up the wires to the top. When the hops ripened they had clusters of "fruit' which looked like little green leafy pine cones. At harvest time the wires were unhooked at the top and the plants fell to the ground. Then women and children swarmed over them and picked the little cones by hand and put them in baskets. Eventually they were beaten with sticks to shake out the yellow powder which was then gathered up and sold to a brewery.

We did not make beer but we did have a seven-acre vineyard where both white and black grapes were grown. Grape harvest was a festive occasion. The grapes were picked by hand and then most of them were put in a press and crushed. The juice was laid down in barrels and eventually became wine. We had both white and red wine and while they were not equal to the really good Hungarian or other wines they were perfectly potable and, indeed, that is what we drank with our meals unless there were distinguished guests. The wine was made by a very nice elderly man who was in charge of the vineyard. The residue of the grapes, skins, stems, some leaves and whatever was sticking to them were placed into very large wooden tubs which were then covered with mud. Eventually this mess fermented and liquefied and was then taken and subjected to a distilling process. Since this was illegal in Hungary at the time very little was said about it. The end product was a rough, extremely potent brew which was called *pálinka* and was a kind of grappa or "red-eye". I happened to quite like it and it was very popular with some of our guests in Ireg who would have drunk kerosene out of the lamps if there had been nothing else available. Father did not approve.

The farm closest to the park was Bántava where pigs were raised. The others were Csehi, Okrád which was fairly central and where much of the farm machinery was located, Hékút, which was the farthest from the park and nearest the forest.

It was just about that time that mechanized farming equipment was first introduced. I well remember wheat being harvested by twenty or twenty-five men with scythes in slanting line working their way back and forth across the field. They were followed by women who gathered up the wheat, tied it in sheaves and stacked them in what were known as "crosses". Threshing was already being done by machines driven by a steam engine and fed by hand. There was one instance when the feeding hand was itself fed into the machine with disastrous result. I remember the first tractor which I believe was a John Deere. It was a sensation but was looked at with great concern by the farm workers who feared that such machines would make them unnecessary. This actually turned out to be true and many estates let people go when they switched to machines. Father was again the exception because he never allowed any good worker to be laid off. They were kept on and given some other tasks to do.

Near to the park on the other side of the highway there were the management buildings and a large storage building for wheat and corn that was grown on the estate. Adjacent to this was a mill where the wheat and the grains where ground into flour; this mill also served the people in the village. Next to the administration building there were small farm-oriented factories that my father planned and had installed. One of these made starch and one was a press for various oils and there was also one where soybean were made into a paste which I guess today would be called tofu. These little factories were an innovation unique to our estate.

About a quarter-mile away was the dairy farm where the cows were kept and there were also two or three prize bulls for breeding. Attached to the cow sheds was a milk-processing room where milk was pasteurized and bottled and where some of the milk was put in a centrifuge with the cream taken off and churned into butter. Across the yard from the cow barns were the workshops again including carpentry, foundry, smithy, and general metalworking shops that served all the farm equipment that needed repairs. Essentially the place was completely self-sufficient and we very rarely had to go outside for help of any kind. I loved these workshops and spent quite some time there with the workmen. While I was obviously a nuisance to them they were very nice and taught me the rudiments of carpentry and metal working.

At the end of the Hékút farm there was a three-hundred-acre forest which was well populated with the Hungarian roe deer, elk, pheasants and a variety of other animals. When the fall deer-hunting season started on September first I went hunting at dawn. Since my bedroom was next to my parents' I did not want to use an alarm clock. What I did was to tie a very long string on my ankle with a piece of firewood at the other end that I dropped out of the window to the ground below. The night watchman had instructions the pull on the string at three thirty in the morning upon which I got up, thanked him, got dressed and went out to the carriage waiting for me. It was five miles to the forest where the hunt master was waiting for me. We walked down a path to the edge of the woods where the deer liked to feed in a meadow. Many times there was nothing there but occasionally we did find a nice buck that I then managed to shoot. We lifted it into the carriage, took it back to the house where I helped to clean it and from there it went into the icehouse for use the next weekend.

One of the big events of the last few years at Ireg was my brother György's wedding in the summer of 1939. There were many guests and the parents of his fiancée came from Vienna. Her name was Elza and she was quite beautiful. I was very fond of her. The wedding at the church was spectacular and then a big reception was held at the house outside on the lawn with a nice buffet. Other nice events were the annual harvest festivals when people from the village who had participated in the harvest, came to the chateau with flowers and flags. There were speeches to which my father responded and everybody had a grand time.

During the summer my sister Hanna and I went riding most mornings at about seven o'clock and rode for about an hour coming back at eight o'clock for breakfast. I was not an enthusiastic rider but I did rather enjoy it and we had a good time. Of course we did not go out riding alone; the riding master was always with us. One summer the father of my friend and classmate, Peter de Balogh, leased a piece of land near Ireg for the deer hunting in the fall. Hanna and I with the riding master rode over to see the property as Peter was expecting us. On our way we met a group of peasants standing in the road talking. We asked directions and one of the women said, "Look at the tits on that lady hussar"! The riding master and I were hard put to stop laughing. Hanna was NOT amused.

During the day I frequently went out in the coach to do some shooting mostly for waterfowl around the fishponds. I shot a good many ducks which I then gave to the coachman to take home to his family. After having learned to use a 32-gauge shotgun in Derekegyháza I started out in Ireg with a 28-gauge single barrel shotgun but then graduated to a 20-gauge and eventually to a pair of 16-gauge Hungarian-made shotguns which I liked very much. Actually my hunting career started much earlier: I first had a 22-gauge single shot rifle that could fire small round bullets. The stock was shortened for me and I was given this gun when I was about five years old. The first thing I shot was a squirrel of which there were many in the park. My mother was very proud of me and had the squirrel stuffed and mounted. It was in my bedroom all through the years. When I was about six or seven years old my teacher, Prof. Balog (no relation to Peter's father), who spent the summers with us, and I went to Bántava, the pig farm, three or four afternoons a week where I shot sparrows with my little 22-gauge rifle. There were hundreds of sparrows there causing a lot of trouble by eating the food that was put out in the troughs. Bántava was only about a mile from the house but that was too much for Professor Balog to walk so we had the horses hooked up to the carriage and drove there. We raised two types of pigs, Yorkshires that were nice and pink and also a Hungarian breed that was dark gray in color, almost black, and very unfriendly. Both gave excellent meat and bacon and also provided the kitchen with fat that was rendered down to lard which was the principal source of cooking fat.

The estate was a model of its kind – way above in quality to most of the estates in Hungary. My father saw to it that all the houses of the farm workers had electricity installed and also had indoor plumbing which was practically unheard of in the rest of the country. He also had wood floors put down. In fact he was accused by other estate owners of spoiling the workers and making it very difficult to maintain the old customs.

Another memory of my childhood was the lessons I had almost every morning from Professor Balog. He was a very interesting man who had come to the family many years before as my grandfather Kornfeld's Hungarian language teacher. Balog at that time was an instructor at a prominent high school in Budapest. He was a most learned man who read Latin and Greek fluently and who was an excellent teacher. He started teaching me to read and write when I was less than five years old and by my fifth birthday I could do both quite well. It was thanks to the professor that when I started school a year later I could read and write. Professor Balog read Shakespeare and Homer to me in a slightly bowdlerized version more like a story then a play or an epic. Once in a while my mother sat in on my lessons and at the end asked me a lot of questions about what I heard and understood.

Professor Balog also had history discussions with the others in my family and occasionally even with some of the guests. We sat around in the living room or out on the lawn and the professor would ask one of us to pick a date, any date. If one of us said "fifteen ten", the next question would be: what happened in the world on that date? He might continue – who was the king of England, what dynasty, who was his father, who inherited the throne, what was going on in Spain and France, in Italy, in Hungary and Austria, in the Americas at that time? We usually spent about forty-five minutes to an hour in these discussions and learned an enormous amount of history, art, philosophy, etc. I still, many years later, maintain a very warm memory about the sessions.

Every summer my mother had a total of two hundred young women factory workers from Csepel come for two-week vacations in groups of fifty. They were put up very comfortably in a large building at the Hékút farm. Toward the end of their stay they usually put on a little performance for my mother: dances, songs, recitals, etc. and then there was a picnic supper by a pond with fires where we roasted bacon and all had a very enjoyable time.

My brother and sisters liked the life at Ireg, but they were not nearly so attached as I was. I loved the place dearly and felt deeply about it. Once, when I was about twelve, someone asked me why I was so involved in everything that went on in the running of the place. I said that I had been born there and that I believed that not only did I belong there but that it belonged to me. When I decided to become a doctor, I also decided that after I finished my training I wanted to live at Ireg and establish a free clinic for the village. Such was not to be.

Since there was no central heating we did not use the estate for ourselves in the winter. The house was closed and the servants, with their usual wages, had a long vacation which they spent with their family somewhere in the country.

When I was a late teenager, before I started at the medical school, I did go down occasionally in the winter and stay with my Teta Liesl and her husband, the head gardener, in a nice house which we had built for them when they got married. I enjoyed being there in the winter and we had parties and poker games with some of our friends in the village and had a very good time.

Until the war began we spent part of the summer abroad with the time being divided between Westend in Belgium on the North Sea and Sils Maria in Switzerland. Westend is a small community about ten miles from the larger, more commercial and more prestigious town of Ostend. My mother adored swimming in the sea; she felt it had therapeutic properties. She also thought that the clear air was especially healthful. I well remember these trips as far back as when I was about four years old. I almost invariably got sick on the way and on one occasion I had a high fever and was hallucinating about a lion coming into the train compartment. Frightened, Mother asked the conductor if there was a doctor among the passengers. A German doctor very kindly came to examine me. He told my mother that I was going to recover but also told her that if I should die she still had three other children. Mother angrily told him that it was always the sick one that mattered most.

By the time we got to Belgium the next day I had recovered and, after settling in at the hotel, my brother György and I went to a store where we purchased shrimp nets and a pocketful of small round brown stones – the local specialty. When dropped on the pavement, these stones made a loud explosive sound. We thought they were wonderful; the adults did not. Most of the day was spent on the beach catching shrimp, wading in the water and, occasionally, riding around on an old donkey that was saddled and could be hired for a few pennies for a fifteen-minute ride on the beach.

At the end of two weeks we took the train to Switzerland. Leaving in the evening, we would arrive in Basel at about five the next morning. Because there was a three-hour layover, my mother would decide that the time had to be used constructively. On at least two occasions she bundled us into a taxi and took us to the cathedral. She found out where the verger lived, roused him out and in exchange for a very handsome contribution asked him to get dressed and open the cathedral for us. I still remember the two statues on the façade of the building: St. George slaying the dragon on the left and St. Martin dividing his coat with a beggar on the right. When, many years later, I stood before the Basel cathedral, the two saints were still there like old friends.

In Sils we stayed at the beautiful Waldhaus Hotel. I was four on my first visit to Sils. My family was very amused to see that on the hotel bill only five and one half people were listed. I, being younger than ten, was the "half" person. My dignity was mightily offended while my sisters and brother were delighted. Just behind the hotel there was a large rock that I loved to climb. I also went for walks and later, when I was ten years old I started to do some gentle mountain climbing which consisted primarily of going up a very steep little path to the top of one of the smaller, non-glacial peaks called the Marmoree. When I was twelve, my cousin Pisti and I did go on a climb with a guide. We slept in a cabin and the next day climbed the Corvatch glacier. It was a truly exhilarating experience. A nice thing about Sils was that it was on the way from St. Moritz to Italy and on a couple of occasions we drove down through the Maloja pass with its hairpin turns to the beautiful Italian Lakes. Once we even drove to Milan where I was taken to see Leonardo da Vinci's painting of the Last Supper. Being a very religious nine-year-old at the time, seeing the painting was a major experience for me.

There were two years during my childhood when the summer trips did not include Belgium and Switzerland. During the first one we spent three or four weeks on the Semmering, a moderately high mountain close to Vienna. It was a resort area with several large hotels with allegedly very beneficial bathing facilities. On one occasion my father had some business to attend to in Budapest and left us for a few days. He was supposed to return early the following morning but finished his business earlier than expected and was able to catch the last train of the evening by just a couple of minutes. The next morning, about ten o'clock, Uncle Feri, who was also vacationing on the Semmering with his family, called my mother and in a very agitated voice asked if my father had returned. My mother, who did not quite understand Uncle Feri's concern, said that Father had arrived safely the night before and asked for the reason for the call. It turned out that the morning train my father was supposed to take was in a terrible accident when a crazy man, named Matuska, dynamited the viaduct at Biatorbágy and the entire train crashed into a river. All the people in the first-class wagon died.

Another memory of the summer on the Semmering was a visit to Trattenbach, the summer villa of Stefan and Else Mauthner. Stefan was the artist who painted and drew beautiful pictures, several of which decorated my parents' home in Chevy Chase and are at this writing in our present apartment. His wife Else was my mother's first cousin; her mother, Jenni and Manfréd being brother and sister. Stefan and Else lived in Hungary after the Anschluss but were captured by the Germans in 1944, transported to Auschwitz and killed. It is my understanding that the artist Stefan Mauthner is now very highly regarded in Austria and that his paintings are considered to be very valuable.

During the summer of 1936 we spent three weeks in Bad Gastein, in Austria, where Father and Uncle Feri wanted to take the baths. The Chorins stayed at a large hotel while we stayed at a small pension close by. The pension was owned and operated by a very nice Austrian family who "adopted" me and with whom I had dinner whenever my parents dined somewhere else.

The Chorin girls and I spent much time together. Twice daily we took a trip of about a mile to a small river in which was a group of little islands with streamlets of water between them. With small spades and shovels we redirected the flows, made new little islands and had a grand time doing it. We called it the Muki Island and we all became Muki residents. Erzsébet was the Hairy Muki, Daisy was the Heavy Muki and I was the Big Nose Muki. Rózsa, Aunt Daisy's maid who had to accompany us, was known as the Clip-Clop Muki because of the way she walked. The only other thing about Gastein that I remember vividly is the large number of squirrels along the walks. They were totally unafraid of people and came to take nuts from our hands. There was also a stand along the walk where white, freshly pressed grape juice was sold. When we walked together, my mother usually bought me a glass of the juice which was delicious. While I was having fun at Muki Island, György went to the 1936 Berlin Olympics with Monsieur Jacqier, our French teacher and friend.

For reasons which I do not remember we stopped going to Westend and Sils and spent three weeks of the summer in St. Moritz in Switzerland. It was there that I played golf most days. This was a gift of Uncle Jacques Kanitz who was Grandfather Weiss' nephew and who lived in Switzerland. Occasionally we played together but when he did not feel like playing I played with a caddy. This was a luxury that I thoroughly enjoyed and under the caddy's guidance my game improved considerably.

In 1938, the second year that we went to St. Moritz, Puppa and I traveled ahead of the family. We stopped in Vienna and visited Mother's cousins, the Eisslers who, after the Anschluss, were in considerable difficulties. The reason for our visit was not only to see them but also to take some of their valuables with us to Switzerland where they would be safe from confiscation. I remember that we left with Puppa wearing several large diamond rings and my pockets stuffed with pieces of jewelry. We arrived safely in St. Moritz and put the valuable things in a safe. The Eisslers shortly thereafter moved to Hungary where they lived for about two years when they emigrated to Argentina.

True to form I promptly got sick with a fever. Puppa took care of me and also called a doctor. He was an older man called Dr. von Planta – the offspring of a very ancient and distinguished Swiss family. I don't know how good a practitioner he was but I rapidly improved and in a couple of days I was quite well again. It was then that I started to play golf again with Uncle Jacques Kanitz.

This was the last time that we went away for a summer vacation because by July, 1939, the European political situation was grim and it was likely that there would be a war. In fact it began on September first when Germany invaded Poland. I clearly remember that day. It was the first day of the deer-hunting season in Ireg and I went to our small forest at four thirty in the morning. I didn't shoot anything and got home rather late expecting a scolding from my mother. Instead of a scolding, however, my mother was very relieved to see me. She told me that the war had broken out and she was terribly concerned about what would happen to György and to me.

Chapter Five

Derekegyháza

By 1914 it had become the custom of wealthy families to buy country estates from impoverished aristocratic families. The new owners sometimes settled on the properties or, more often, used them for vacations. Sometimes the estates were simply a financial investment and were visited by the owners only occasionally. The year after Grandfather Weiss bought the estate at Ireg as a wedding gift for my parents, he decided to make a purchase of this kind as an investment but also for the rest of his large family to use for vacations. It was not an easy decision – he had always lived modestly and the idea of becoming an estate owner and, in essence, a part of the gentry was difficult. In fact he made the decision without having seen the property known as Derekegyháza. The transaction was handled by his twenty-four year old son, Alfonz, who later made the comment that this was the first time his father consulted with him about a financial decision.

Derekegyháza consisted of close to ten thousand acres and was located in the area between the Danube and the Tisza rivers about one hundred miles south-southeast from Budapest. The road there led through Kecskemét, Kiskunfélegyháza and Szentes, the county seat, which was a nice little town of about twenty thousand people ten miles from the estate. Derek, as we called it was situated near the end of the major railway line. That area of Hungary was mostly flat with very gently rolling hills in certain areas. In most of the land between the two rivers the soil was black and fertile and the principal industry was agriculture. All standard crops were grown including sugar beets. The estate had belonged to Count József Károlyi and had been in his family for generations. He did not live there and visited only once a year for one day for a hunt.

When Uncle Alfonz negotiated the purchase the chateau, having been much neglected, was in poor condition and was in need of extensive repairs. In the entire building there was only one bathroom. The large park, consisting of almost one hundred and eighty acres of woods and meadows, was also badly neglected. Close to the chateau there were some enormous trees including a giant oak tree, known as the Matthias Oak, which allegedly had been planted in the time of the reign of King Matthias Corvinus at the end of the fifteenth century. Very large horse chestnut trees surrounded the chateau and the edges of the grassy areas were lined with lilac bushes.

The roads on the property were in abominable condition. Being knee-deep in mud after a heavy rain made them practically impassable. The people working on the estate lived in the most primitive conditions which was not unusual at the time. Three or four families had to share a common kitchen and the floors of the rooms were of beaten earth. The barns were old and decrepit but the cattle, including the Hungarian variety of the Brahma bull with enormous horns, were numerous and reasonably well cared for. There was a large flock of sheep including a sizable group of Merinos which produced excellent and very expensive wool. The arable land was divided into forty-acre parcels and at all four corners of the plots there was a small rectangular wooded area. On several hundred acres of the estate the soil was alkaline and of very poor quality for agriculture. Some of it was used for grazing but most of it was left fallow and was essentially useless.

The chateau, which was built sometime between 1765 and 1769 in the baroque style, was quite large and square.

It was a very nice, comfortable and well-furnished house although there was no central heating. The three-foot thick walls provided insulation both in winter and summer. A spacious foyer had numerous coat racks and several gun cabinets. It connected to a very large room that was used as the dining room. Thirty and more people were easily accommodated around the enormous oval table. In one corner of the dining room there was a huge armless settee on which six or seven adults could sit or several children could lie down and roll around. On each side of the dining room there was an additional fair-sized room that was used as a sitting room and for card games. A huge oak staircase led to the second floor where the bedrooms were located. The staircase continued to the third floor where there was a large attic that had been used for the storage of grain. Above it was yet another attic that was also used for grain. Needless to say, the lower attic was converted into bedrooms and the upper attic was used for the storage of household items.

One wing of the chateau was connected to a small chapel that seated about twenty-five people and where, with the local priest visiting, we attended Mass on Sundays and on holidays like Christmas and New Year's Eve and Easter. At the opposite end the chateau was connected to a kitchen with pantry and storage facilities. It was not uncommon for rural chateaux to have the kitchen separate from the main building, partly for fear of fire but also because of cooking odors. The food was carried from the kitchen to the dining room in large covered dishes and, as I recall, arrived there still being quite warm. The food at Derekegyháza was not nearly so good as in Ireg but, considering the enormous quantities in which it had to be prepared, it was really quite tasty.

A guest house was immediately adjacent to the chateau. Fairly simple, it was very comfortable. Unlike Ireg, which was used only in the summer, Derekegyháza was available for use all year long. Each bedroom had its own tile stove that was tended from the hallways. At six o'clock on winter mornings I remember the sound of the stove being cleaned of ashes and new wood being installed and lighted. As the room warmed I would turn over and go back to sleep.

Shortly after the purchase was complete major activities began to bring the place up to par. The first step was to provide decent housing for the people who worked the estate. When this was finished each family was provided with its own house with a kitchen and wooden floors. I don't know if running water and electricity were introduced at that time but I doubt it. I suspect that these improvements were made during the late twenties and early thirties.

The next step was the grading and improving of the roads and the installation of a narrow-gauge rail system to transport produce to the nearest freight rail depot in Szegvár which was ten miles away. This made it both possible and lucrative to increase the production of sugar beets. Manfréd considered the building of a sugar producing plant at one time but this did not come about. Instead an ingenious arrangement was made with the Szolnok sugar plant whereby beets from Derekegyháza were handled separately from other suppliers and the profits were returned to the estate. Shortly after the end of the First World War a hemp-processing plant was built in Szegvár and received large quantities of Derekegyháza hemp.

One of the major problems on the estate was the distribution of water. In some areas there were large puddles but in other, fairly extensive areas there was a shortage of ground water and the surface was arid. This problem was largely resolved by the ingenuity of Uncle Jenő, an engineer, who had artesian wells drilled in a number of areas and had an extensive system of canals dug which were filled from the wells. He also had a boat equipped with a powerful pump and spray system which watered the fields adjacent to the canals. So far as I know this was the first estate in Hungary with a system for watering. Irrigation made it possible to grow large quantities of legumes which, in turn, lead to the building of a vegetable drying plant that cooperated with the family cannery in Budapest which distributed huge quantities of dried vegetables nationally and internationally. A vegetable drying plant of Uncle Jenő's design was set up in Egypt under the direction of Cousin Georg Eissler.

Among the other additions at Derekegyháza made by the family was the building of a church for the community and a home for the priest. Aunt Elza also financed the building of a small hospital where the people working on the estate could get free medical care.

An interesting personality at Derekegyháza was Pál Tóth, known to his friends as Baligoma which translates "Friend Bali". He was known to all as "Bali". It was he who was in charge of forestry and hunting. He was a very good friend to us youngsters and it was he who started me off with a small 32-gauge single barrel shotgun with which I shot my first pheasant when I was eight. We used to go out in a carriage to shoot pigeons or doves, whatever happened to be around. He was fairly abrasive and most people didn't like him very much but he was clearly an expert in hunting and pheasant breeding and had fine general organizational ability. He and his wife kept an open house and some of my cousins and I regularly spent a couple of hours with them in the afternoon.

One of Tóth's major accomplishments was the forestation of the large dry and alkaline areas. He was a very forceful character who, contrary to expert opinion, insisted that done properly the alkaline areas could be planted with trees. With support from Aunt Elza, who liked Tóth very much, and my father, who did not like him at all but who appreciated his ability, the reforestation was begun and, after very heavy work on Tóth's part, proved to be a major success. The young trees prospered and grew surprisingly well eventually covering several hundred acres. One of the reasons why the trees did so well was that Tóth devised a system, unheard of at the time, of having a machine, very much like an ice augur, drill foot-wide holes into which the little trees were placed in good earth. This not only was excellent for the trees but also made the procedures much faster and much less expensive. An interesting side effect of the forestation program was the discovery of a number of Avar graves dating back to before the Hungarian conquest in the tenth century. The graves contained a number of artifacts which were deposited in the museum in Szentes. The museum staff actively participated in the dig and was very pleased to receive the items which had been uncovered.

On the property there were the usual administrative and farm buildings. There was no nearby village because in that part of Hungary the type of agriculture resembled the American farm system with the peasants living on their plots of land which ranged from ten to fifteen to hundred acres or more. Twenty to twenty-five miles apart there was usually a small town where the farmers went for their purchases. Actually most of the farm stands were completely self-sufficient and the shopping was mostly for items which might be needed and could not be made at home.

Hunting was a major activity at Derekegyháza. In the park adjacent to the chateau a very large number of pheasants were bred. Hundreds of pheasant eggs were collected in the spring, allowed to hatch under controlled conditions, and the chicks were raised the same way poultry would be raised. When old enough they were released in the park. The woods were divided into five or six-acre parcels with strips of lawn between the parcels. The park provided superb pheasant shooting. Every fall there was a major two-day hunt with about ten stands on each lawn between the wooded parcels.

On the other side of each parcel from the hunters stood a group of about twenty-five or thirty young men called the beaters. They lined up and started walking towards the hunters. This caused the pheasants to rise and fly away from the beaters towards the stands with the shooters. This was repeated on all of the lawns and by the end of the first day approximately four hundred to five hundred pheasants were shot. Shooting was limited to cock pheasants and a hunter who shot a hen was criticized fairly sharply. The hunters each stood behind a little palisade which had a number on it. When they went to the next strip of lawn each man went to the same numbered stand. Each hunter had a gun carrier whose job was to load the shotguns and hand them to the hunter. Each man had a pair of shotguns and always had a loaded one in his hand. One lot of pheasants was given to the beaters but most were sold to a meat packing house. On hunt days an elegant, festive picnic lunch was served outside, and at one of these Mother would smoke her annual cigarette.

My Uncle Feri and, possibly Father, usually invited several highly distinguished political and social figures to participate in the shoot. They included such eminent persons as former Prime Minister Count István Bethlen, future Prime Minister Kállay, Minister of the Interior Ferenc Keresztes-Fischer, Jenő Horthy, the regent's brother and several others. During the two days a total of close to a thousand pheasants were shot. These were almost all cocks. As youngsters we were not included among the shooters and I participated only once, in 1940, when I was sixteen. I was allowed to walk with the beaters and shoot those pheasants which flew towards the rear. Even in this lowly position I managed to shoot about thirty pheasants in the two days.

The estate belonged to Grandfather and after his death was inherited by his six children one of whom was my mother. Since we had our own property at Ireg we spent very little time at Derekegyháza. It was very well run by Aunt Elza who had been widowed and who spent much of the summer there. My family usually visited during the Christmas vacation. Arriving on December twenty-sixth, we stayed on till after the New Year. Between family and guests a group of about thirty people was not unusual.

During that time we had two or three spectacular hunts for hares. On a good day with about twelve hunters we shot fifty to one hundred hares. It was known as a circle shoot with the hunters separated from each other by two or three local youngsters. We walked in a very large circle. When the circle was closed a trumpet would be sounded by the hunt master. We all turned towards the center. The hares which were surrounded were trying to run out between the shooters but most of them were shot. Initially we could fire toward the center. But when the ring closed, the trumpet sounded which meant that we had to let the hares run out of the ring and then shot them once they were outside.

It is now an institution for mental patients. I have been there only once as an adult and looked in from the gate. The building seemed to be in good shape but I have no idea what happened to the park or to the swimming pool that was beyond it. Apparently it is a good hospital and takes good care of the patients.

Chapter Six

Growing up

My childhood in Budapest was happy and very comfortable. Many memories are from when I was about three and a half. My first ones are about going for walks every day with my nanny, Teta Liesl, or with Mother when Teta had the day off. We walked in the Városliget (City Park) but more often in the Zoo which was very close to the apartment. I got to know most of the animals and spent about an hour to an hour and a half in the Zoo wandering around and occasionally feeding the animals. I guess I was about four years old when I went to the Zoo once with my mother. We walked by a guard and Mother asked him the way to the bird house. As soon as we turned away from the guard I stopped, looked up at her very sternly and said, "Mother, when you are with me you don't ask a guard where things are in this Zoo. I know it as well or better than he does". With this I turned around and walked off in the direction of the bird house.

I must tell you about my nanny. A Viennese girl from a simple background she had had two years of training in child care. Her name was Liesl Böck and she was referred to as Teta Liesl. She came into the family when I was a baby and she looked after me as though I were her own son. She was kind and nice and I loved her dearly. Because of Teta, I spoke German earlier than I spoke Hungarian.

I don't remember when I started ice skating but I doubt if it was much later than age six. Once I started I went just about every afternoon and skated for about an hour with Teta

Liesl sitting in the warm waiting room until I was ready to go home. One episode with Teta stands out in my memory. We were traveling in the summer and found ourselves in Munich. I guess my parents and siblings went to the museum and I was left with Teta to go for a walk. I must have been about five. Somehow we wound up in the famous Marien Kirche, also known as the Onion Church because of the onion-shaped towers. Teta was very religious, so we went into the church and prayed. On the way out of the church there was the gift counter that is so common in the major European churches. Feeling that I had been awfully patient with all of that praying, I begged Teta to buy me something. She selected a small silver crucifix. This crucifix is very precious to me and has accompanied me on all my numerous travels. It was with me in the U.S. Army and has always seen me home safe and sound. Now, many years later, I still have it and still cherish it.

In our family small children did not eat with our parents in the dining room but had our lunch and dinner brought to us in our bedroom. I started eating at the table when I was about ten years old. Shortly after that Teta left to marry the head gardener in Ireg, Ferenc Oleár.

I started school at age six in a small private elementary school owned and operated by a lady named Louisa de Chatel. There were only about fifteen of us in first grade among whom were Cousin Alice, Johnny Graham and Peter de Balogh with whom I am still touch. Three or four of us knew how to read and write which put us in a very privileged position because when the others had their lectures and practice in reading and writing my literate classmates and I proudly marched to the front of the class where in a corner by the window there was a table with the books we had brought from home and that we were allowed to read while the other kids worked. I well remember my book, a fascinating story about a family of bears which dressed, talked and acted like human beings.

They had all sorts of adventures which I enjoyed very much. In addition to the regular class work we also had instruction in religion and manners. The school was located in the apartment of Mrs. de Chatel in a private building just behind the Academy of Science. It was much too far to walk so I was driven by the chauffeur in the morning and picked up again at noon. Elementary education in Hungary at that time was four years for those who went on to what was known as the *gimnázium* which corresponded to the American junior and senior high school – a full eight years.

Grade school ended the first week in June but my mother felt that at the end of the school year it would be more useful if we went to Ireg and I could have the final exam at the elementary school there. This was quite an event. The classroom was decorated with flowers by a girl who was not much older than I and who lived in a house just outside the park on the street which led first to the school and then to the church. The exam was a joke. The schoolteacher in Ireg received part of her salary from my parents and treated them with the greatest courtesy and consideration. At the exam I was asked my name and one or two questions about arithmetic, writing and reading. The whole thing took about fifteen minutes and I got my certificate, with a grade of A in all of the subjects that I had completed for the year.

Secondary education in Hungary at the time was good but also fairly complex. Most of the children of the urban middle and upper classes attended private schools many of which were operated by the Catholic religious orders. There was the Piarist school which George and I attended. There were Jesuit, Benedictine and Cistercian schools, as well as Lutheran and Calvinist ones. Identical in structure, they were under the general, albeit very lax, supervision of the Ministry of Religion and Education. There were also a few *gimnasia* which had no religious affiliation. Attendance at one of these schools was required for all who wished to continue their education at the university.

The other type of secondary school was the so-called Reál Gimnázium which did not emphasize the humanities but focused primarily on technical subjects both practical and theoretical. They varied in quality more than the other type but the good ones turned out very bright people who had no difficulty finding jobs in industry and business. Many of them were also accepted at the Technical University and became engineers and architects.

The universities were not religiously affiliated and they were to be found only in the larger cities. Most of them were in Budapest but there were also very good ones in cities like Debrecen, Pécs and Szeged. Education was free at all levels and the only expenses we had were books, notebooks, etc.

The gimnázium I went to was located in downtown Budapest near the Danube. It was a large building that housed both the school and a monastery for the priests. The school had sixteen classrooms to accommodate two classes of boys for each of the eight years of the program. The curriculum was completely fixed and the students had no opportunity to select courses. The only exception to this was that, prior to the beginning of the fifth year, we had to choose to take either Greek or French. Those of us who planned on a university education in the humanities, medicine or law actually had no choice – we had to take Greek which was an admission requirement.

There were sixty of us in the class and we stayed together for the whole eight years. We lost some students but we also acquired some transfers so that we finished up with fifty-nine at the end. The boys in my class came from all layers of society from middle class to aristocracy. Most of them were university oriented and, in fact, all of them made it. We sat in three rows of benches with two of us to a bench, arranged according to height. I sat in the second row from the back. There was some cliquishness but by and large we were all friends.

Classes began promptly at eight a.m. and each class lasted fifty minutes with a ten minute break in between. The third hour ended in forty-five minutes followed by a somewhat longer break. There was no cafeteria but there was a small stand where we could buy a snack and either white or chocolate milk. Soft drinks were unknown in Hungary at that time. Each day was composed of five classes with school ending at one p.m. On Saturdays there were only four classes so that we finished at noon.

In the first year, which was the equivalent of fifth grade in the United States, we studied Hungarian language, mathematics, history, religion, Latin and geography. The same subjects were taught every year and in the second year German was added and in the third, seventh, and eighth years we also had physics. The curriculum in the seventh and eighth years also included differential and integral calculus. As I mentioned above, during the last four years we also had Greek. In the third and fourth years we had a kind of biology class which covered, in a superficial manner, such subjects as botany and zoology. Not every subject was taught every day with the exception of Latin and Hungarian. The class work was very demanding with lots of homework mostly in essay form. In class we were called upon to report or to answer specific questions. When called upon we had to stand up, at attention, and answer as best we could. We were also given written exams at the whim of the instructors all of whom were Piarist priests.

We had physical education classes three times each week. This consisted of calisthenics, rope climbing and team sports such as basketball. Weather permitting we could also play soccer in the school yard which had goal posts at each end. The gym teacher and I got along very well and I could also play ice hockey. I got quite good at it and actually became the team captain for a couple of years.

There was a very lovely chapel in the school where we attended Mass daily as well as on Sundays and Holy Days of Obligation. From the fourth year on we also had to take two week stretches of serving as altar boys at six thirty in the morning. We usually served two and occasionally three masses. The masses were silent (i.e. no music) and some of the priests rushed through them in fifteen minutes. Some obviously took longer. The school year started on September eighth, the feast of the Nativity of the Blessed Virgin Mary in the Roman Catholic tradition, and ended about June tenth with a ten-day vacation at Christmas and a week at Easter. We also had all national days and church holy days off.

The quality of instruction varied somewhat from teacher to teacher but generally the level was high and we covered an enormous range of the humanities and sciences. The more advanced history classes included world history, although the focus was on classical Greco-Roman and European history. We learned relatively little about America and next to nothing about the Far East or Africa.

When I was thirteen, in the third year of the gimnázium, I became ill with what we first thought was just a bad cold with high fever. When it did not seem to get better, Mother called our old pediatrician, Dr. Preisich, who diagnosed pneumonia. There really was nothing to be done as this was several years before the discovery of penicillin. I was given aspirin for the fever and drank a lot of sparkling water, a very special treat which I could have only when I was very good. In this instance it was very much appreciated. Several things from this illness stand out in my mind. One morning, still fairly early in the illness, my father came into my room and sat down by the bed. We talked and I believe that this was the first time that he and I had such an intimate, one-on-one conversation. I was very happy because now I felt truly close to my father which I had never done before. I had always respected him and loved him, but always from a distance. I suddenly felt that the pneumonia was small price to pay for this monumental event in my life. Happily, our relationship continued to be excellent and remained so for the next forty years, until he died.

Another memory of that time was that Mother and I switched rooms. I was moved to her large room and large bed while she moved into my much smaller room next to it. I believe this was done so that the doctors could get at me from both sides and also so that my Teta Liesl, who came up from Ireg, could sleep in the same room on a cot near my bed. I was also attended by Dr. Ferenc Borbély, an outstanding internist who two or three years later married my cousin Maria, "Baby", Mauthner. There was not much Dr. Borbély could do for me but it was nice to have the attention of such a good physician and nice man. At one point in the illness I was given an injection of whole blood which had been donated by my brother. What this was supposed to do for me I can't even begin to guess. It was done, it hurt when it was done and I rather suppose that the only ones who benefited from it were the doctors. At any rate I weathered the traditional crisis of a severe pneumonia, turned the corner and then rapidly improved. In fact I felt increasingly well and since I had eaten nothing for about a week I had lost a number of pounds and suddenly became ravenously hungry. I must have eaten five or six times a day and could hardly wait for the next meal.

About two weeks after the illness started it was decided that for me to recover fully and as quickly as possible it would be best if I went away for two more weeks to recover in a nice mountain resort with good food and lots of fresh air. It was a resort hotel on the Kékes Mountain, the highest point in Hungary, about three thousand feet above sea level. Teta Liesl was going to go with me. I was taking a lot of school books and note books because somebody in the family, perhaps Puppa, went to the gimnázium and talked to my senior teacher. He agreed to my being away an additional two weeks and sent me a sizable amount of homework, reading and writing to do. He indicated that if I would do all of that work, I would have caught up with the class and everything would be all right.

That being so, Mother, Teta and I were driven up to the Kékes Rest and Recreation Hotel where I was settled in a nice room with a balcony and a splendid view. Teta and I had a very pleasant two weeks on the mountain. She taught me to do counted cross stitch and I loved sitting on the balcony with her, stitching a pillow cover and looking at the mountains. Frankly, I was not too anxious to go home. Obviously there was no choice so the chauffeur came, picked us up and off we went. Back at school I was pleased to note that with the homework I did and all the reading I had not fallen back too much and quickly caught up with the rest of the class. All in all it was an interesting experience. I was told later that one of the physicians, the older one, told Mother that I had a very good chance of not making it. I guess I was a lot sicker than I thought. I felt tired and sort of blah but I never felt really sick. A major positive aspect of the experience was that it brought me much closer to my father.

Less than a year later I started having pains in my lower abdomen. The diagnosis was appendicitis. The only way to proceed was to remove it. Thus, after having been examined by the surgeon, I was admitted to the Fasor Sanatorium, a very fine small hospital for the well-to-do patient. The surgery was scheduled for the afternoon and was going to be done under local anesthesia. The surgeon, Professor Lajos Ádám, had had much of his surgical training in the United States, mostly at the Mayo Clinic where much of the surgery in those days was done under local anesthesia. Ádám was a small man with small but powerful hands. He was very kind and considerate and he treated me courteously, almost like a friend. I was given some sedation and then I was taken to the operating room, accompanied by Mother who wore a gown, a cap and a mask. My belly was prepped (cleansed) and then Dr. Ádám said, "You will feel a small needle. We will then wait for about ten minutes. I will tell you when we start and you must tell me if you feel anything." I was quite sleepy and I really did not feel any pain at all. I felt a slight pulling on the lower right side of my belly but that was all. The next thing I knew was when Dr. Ádám said, "Well, that wasn't too bad, was it?" The operation was over and it had taken about twenty-five minutes from beginning to end. Mother was allowed to watch and told me that it was a "beautiful" operation with practically no blood loss. My appendix was moderately inflamed proving that the diagnosis was correct and the procedure was indicated.

I was in the sanatorium for five or six days. Having some discomfort in the evening after the operation I asked for some pain relief, was given a shot and slept the whole night. When I woke up the next morning I was feeling quite well and had only minimal discomfort when I was trying to sit up. I was allowed a liquid diet the first day but after that I was served regular food. I was surprised how good the food was and I certainly did ample justice to it.

Tonsillectomy was a routine procedure in those days and very few children grew to adulthood in the proud possession of their tonsils. My procedure came just a few months after the appendectomy and, while obviously a minor procedure, was much more unpleasant. I had had a number of sore throats and eventually had to go to an ear, nose and throat physician to have my tonsils looked at. A nice man and a competent surgeon, he scheduled the surgery during Easter vacation so I would not miss any school time. Insult was added to injury. The procedure was again done at the Fasor Sanatorium and again under local anesthesia. This was not at all a pleasant experience. It did not hurt except at the very end when the surgeon scraped off my adenoids. Fortunately the whole thing only lasted about twenty minutes, albeit at the time it seemed to be considerably more. When the anesthetic wore off I had an extremely sore throat so that I could neither talk above a whisper nor swallow. I was given a shot to help me sleep and by the next morning my throat, while still hurting, was much better. I was in the sanatorium for one more night. By the time I got home my throat was just a little painful but I could eat and talk. I had four days left of my Easter vacation and I'm sure I made the most of it. These stories show that, at least at some levels, medical care in Hungary in the middle 1930s was of a very high order.

When I got to the third year of the *gimnázium* I became eligible to apply for admission to the Boy Scouts. It was 1937 and the Boy Scout movement was very strong in Hungary. The national president was Count Pál Teleki who had been prime minister and would be again. Teleki was also a high official in the International Boy Scouts. The troops were always affiliated with a school and the Piarist Gimnázium had a long history of a strong and active group. My brother György was also a scout during his last five years in school.

I was accepted and that year about thirty of us in the two classes joined. We were assigned to patrols of about ten; my patrol was called the "Dove". We had two or three orientation sessions followed by a formal ceremony, with the parents present, during which we had to take an oath of allegiance to God, country and the Boy Scout movement. This was the first time that I wore the Boy Scout uniform that Mother and I had bought. Included were short pants, shirt, belt with special buckle and neckerchief. Best of all was a fancy hat with a broad flat brim like the hat worn by some state troopers in the U.S. I loved wearing that hat. We met once a week in the afternoon for about an hour and discussed the various Boy

Scout activities and the meaning of the Boy Scout rules. We also went on hikes on Sundays, usually in the Buda hills.

During the summer between my third and fourth year we went to a Boy Scout camp for two weeks at Lake Balaton in the Tihany area. Mother contributed a generous amount of canned meats and vegetables which made a considerable difference in the meals we were given. We swam in the lake, went for hikes, played games, sang folksongs and had a generally reasonable time. I did not really enjoy it very much but it was better than I had expected. As soon as it was over, Mother came in the car to pick me up and we headed around the lake toward Ireg. I was filthy, needed a haircut and a manicure in the worst way. We therefore stopped in Siófok and I was deposited in a barbershop to have my hair cut and my fingernails made socially acceptable. I was in my tattered and rather filthy Boy Scout uniform and I overheard a German lady say to her husband in a shocked voice, "A Boy Scout is having a manicure. What is the world coming to?" I thought it was funny. During the next school year we continued with weekly Boy Scout meetings and went on hikes in the Buda hills. I did not attend the summer camp that year because the family was going to Switzerland again. The following year we became Water Scouts. Instead of hiking we went to the lakes and rivers, first in eight-person row boats and later in two-person kayaks. I remember several very nice kayak trips up the Danube for a few miles and then drifting lazily down the river back to Pest. Ernő Jónás and I usually shared a kayak and had a good time.

The following summer, in 1939, we went to a part of Hungary that had recently been returned, having been awarded to the country from what had become the defunct Czechoslovakia. This was known as the First Vienna Award. A mountainous part of northeast Hungary, it was primitive but very beautiful. There were few inhabitants in small villages and many of them were Jewish of a particularly orthodox persuasion. They were hospitable and kind and once a family gave me and my patrol of eight boys a very good meal. It is sad to think that probably none of them survived the war with all but a very few of them winding up in Auschvitz. After we hiked around the mountains for a week we ended up along the upper reaches of the Tisza River where our large rowboats were waiting for us. The next week was spent on the river. It was enjoyable and very pleasant except for the innumerable mosquitoes and other bugs. There were of course no such things as insect repellants so that we just swatted them and tried to ignore them as best we could. It was just about six weeks later that Germany invaded Poland and the Second World War began. That autumn the Boy Scouts were organized into air-raid teams and messenger-service teams. I was part of the messenger-service group and when there was an air-raid practice, I raced around the empty streets on my bicycle in full Boy Scout uniform delivering messages from one point to another. It was an exercise in total futility but I must admit that at the time it was rather fun.

The first few weeks of the war were characterized by a flood of Polish refugees, men and women, crossing the border into Hungary. The two countries had cordial relations and the Hungarian government, contrary to the wishes of the Germans, opened the border to the Polish refugees. Many of them remained in Hungary but most of the young men, particularly the former soldiers, left, traveled through Yugoslavia and eventually got to Britain where a Polish military organization was established that eventually participated actively in the war against Germany. Many of the young Polish women found employment in Hungary and were initially supported by Hungarian families. My mother took in three of them. One was a peasant girl who was given a job in the household in Ireg as a maid but the other two were well educated and intelligent. They were able to find jobs in Budapest after a while but they spent a good bit of time with us in Ireg in the summers until 1943. One of them was a very nice and attractive girl named Nina with whom I had a brief flirtation. We remained good friends. She survived the German and Russian invasions and returned to Poland after the war. We learned later that some months after her return to her old home she died of typhoid fever. I do not remember how the information reached us in Portugal but I assume that it was via some friends in Hungary.

That was the last winter of my Boy Scout career and other than a long and very fatiguing bicycle excursion where we rode for about sixty miles there is not much to say. When we got back to the edge of Budapest I excused myself saying that I would fall behind and rest for a while. I told the patrol commander to go ahead and not to worry about me and that I would find my way home slowly and leisurely. In fact, as soon as they were out of sight I waved down a taxi and had him take me and the bike the rest of the way to Lendvay utca. In retrospect I am not very proud of this episode but at the time I felt very smart. The only other Boy Scout event worth mentioning was a rather fancy show that the troop put on at the gimnázium for our parents and friends. It was a performance of Hungarian folk songs and dances. I was on the dance team and I well remember the rather elaborate twenty-minute dance that we performed in full Hungarian peasant regalia. It was fun and the parents obviously thought that it was wonderful.

That brought my Boy Scout career to an end. I could have gone on for another year but chose not to for several reasons. One was simple laziness and the feeling that what I was doing with the Scouts was a total waste of time. More importantly, I left because the scouting movement became increasingly militarized. The German Nazis did not approve of scouting and, indeed, in Germany scouting was forbidden. There was pressure in Hungary also and the leaders of the

Hungarian Boy Scout Organization endeavored to counteract it by becoming more nationalistic, militant and anti-Semitic. I felt no hesitation in leaving the troop.

As we approached the end of the eighth year in school the final exam became increasingly threatening. Called the *Matura*, it was also known as a Baccalaureate exam and consisted of both a written and an oral part. The written part covered most of our fields of study in Latin, Greek, German, Hungarian history and Hungarian literature. The oral exam consisted of all of the above and also included mathematics and physics. This was a very important exam because admission to the university depended on getting a good set of grades. It was particularly important for admission to medical school or other professional schools like dentistry, pharmacy, engineering etc.

Much of the seventh and eighth years were spent in class talking about the exam and most of the teachers were coaching us about what to study, particularly how to answer the questions, what to say, and what not to say, etc. It was mostly in retrospect that we realized what they were doing. The last class in each subject was essentially a thank you and good-by session with the teachers and nothing of importance took place. The one exception was the last class in Greek when the teacher suddenly started asking some questions about words and tenses. This made no sense whatever until one of my ingenious classmates figured out that the words clearly came from the Odyssey. He also managed to find the section where they came from and it suddenly became obvious that it was the section that we would have to translate at the written exam to come. Needless to say all of us became thoroughly familiar with the twenty to twenty-five lines.

The written exams, each of which took up a whole morning, lasted a week. They were essay type in literature and history while in the languages we were given a text that we had to translate. Dictionaries were not allowed. By and large they were not too bad and I did very well in all of them. We now had to look forward to the oral exams which were two weeks away and which were going to be a major trial. In preparation for them four of us, Ernő Jónás, Peter de Balogh, Johnny Graham and I went to Ireg accompanied by a tutor. We worked for three hours every morning and every afternoon covering mathematics, physics, history, literature, Latin and Greek. We worked hard but still had a good time. Returning to Budapest on the Friday before the exam we spent the weekend with more study.

I don't remember exactly how we were scheduled but I do know that the exam took two full days with the seven subjects being divided with two in the morning and afternoon of the first day, two in the morning of the second day and the last one in the afternoon. It was a very formal event. I sat by myself at the middle of a long table facing the examiners. Across from me sat the representative of the Ministry of Religion and Education who happened to be a Cistercian priest in full black and white garb. Next to him sat the principal of the gimnázium and then the teachers on each side. It started out with Hungarian literature and then came history. In the afternoon I had mathematics and Latin. All four of them went well but by the end of the day I was totally exhausted. I went home, studied for another hour, had something to eat and went to bed. The next morning I had German which was a breeze and physics in which I did not do very well. In the afternoon we finished up with Greek. I was never very good at Greek and I had trouble with the text I was supposed to translate. I was also totally exhausted. Anyway it came to an end and, as it turned out, I got an A in every subject except physics in which I got a B. This was good enough to get me into medical school. However, the whole experience was so traumatic that I had nightmares about it for many years afterward.

On the Saturday following the *Matura* there was a party at the home of one of my classmates. Ten or twelve of my friends were gathered at the villa on one of the Buda hills and the evening consisted almost entirely of complaining about the exam and drinking brandy. I participated mostly in the second activity and, being at that time an inexperienced drinker, overindulged and relatively soon began to feel the effects of the brandy. To put it more bluntly, I became thoroughly drunk. I have only the vaguest memories about how I got home but I do remember that I had great difficulty in getting the key into the keyhole of the door of my house. By sheer chance the gentleman who lived in the apartment above ours came home and opened the door for me. Getting to my bedroom I promptly became sick and vomited partly into the sink but partly also on the floor. Somehow I got my clothes off and fell into my bed. When I woke up the next morning, with a substantial head ache, I found that the room had been cleaned up, my clothes were put away and that there was no sign of my dissipation. While I was not particularly hungry I did go to breakfast expecting to have a stern lecture. Much to my surprise and pleasure nothing was said other than a polite inquiry about whether the party had been a success. I found out later that Father had given strict instructions to my sisters and to the servants that no mention should be made to me about the unfortunate event. This was the first and last occasion in my life that I drank to such excess.

When the last year of the gimnázium came to an end there was no graduation ceremony as in the U.S. On the last Sunday of the school year we went to church as usual and then walked, with the lower class students lining the halls, through the school singing the old German student song: *Gaudeamus igitur, iuvenes dum sumus...* (Let us be happy while we are still young...).

Zsigmond Kornfeld
(Painting by Philip de Laszlo. Courtesy of the Historical Gallery of the Hungarian National Museum)

Móric Kornfeld in the garden of the home in Washington, D.C.
(Photo courtesy of Ágnes Széchenyi)

Manfréd Weiss (Photo courtesy of the author)

Manfréd Weiss and his wife Alice Wahl with four of their children
(Photo courtesy of the Hungarian National Museum)

Ferenc Chorin Senior and Junior
(Photo courtesy of the Hungarian National Museum)

Mrs. Móric Kornfeld, née Marianne Weiss and her four children
From the left: Tamás, Hanna, György and Mária (Photo courtesy of Ágnes Széchenyi)

Hanna, Mária and György Kornfeld

György Kornfeld and his younger brother, the author of this book
(Photo courtesy of the author)

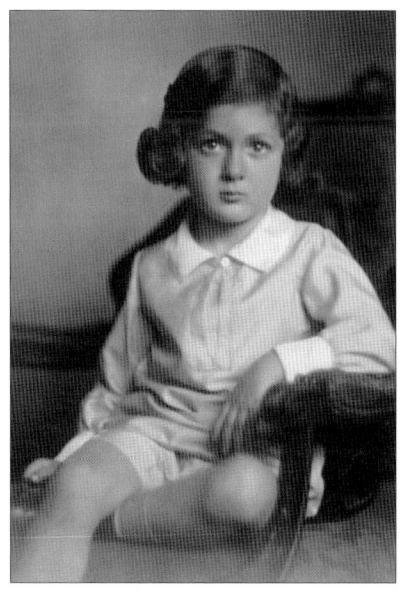

Thomas DeKornfeld
(Photo courtesy of the author)

The house in Lendvay Street where the Kornfeld family lived in a rental apartment. Presently the French Embassy (Photo by Zsolt Kováts)

The Chateau at Ireg, from the garden (Photo courtesy of the author)

Another picture of the Chateau from the garden (Photo courtesy of Ágnes Széchenyi)

Enclosed porch of the Chateau (Photo courtesy of Ágnes Széchenyi)

Dining room of the Chateau (Photo courtesy of Ágnes Széchenyi)

Ármin Balog, who translated Bacon and Spinoza into Hungarian and his young pupil Tamás in the garden of the Chateau in Ireg (Photo courtesy of the author)

The library in the Chateau at Ireg

The staircase in the Chateau at Ireg
(Photo courtesy of Ágnes Széchenyi)

Standing behind the family Packard automobile are members of the family and friends (Photo courtesy of the Hungarian National Office of Architecture and Cultural Heritage)

Móric Kornfeld and his wife with guests in the garden at Ireg
(Photo courtesy of Ágnes Széchenyi)

Hanna Kornfeld on horseback (Photo courtesy of Ágnes Széchenyi)

Hanna Kornfeld and her friend Éva Balázs in the garden at Ireg (Photo courtesy of Ágnes Széchenyi)

Mária Kornfeld (Puppa) at Ireg (Photo courtesy of Ágnes Széchenyi)

Near the swimming pool at Ireg. The guests include Marquis György Pallavicini, Jr., Tamás Perczel and Éva Balázs (Photo courtesy of Ágnes Széchenyi)

Passport photo of Marianne DeKornfeld at the age 75
(Photo courtesy of Ágnes Széchenyi)

Thomas DeKornfeld, Professor of Anesthesiology

Thomas DeKornfeld and Daisy Chorin. The cousins are chatting at the publication of the book by Móric Kornfeld by Corvina Publishers in 2006
(Photo taken by Tamás Szigeti, courtesy of Ágnes Széchenyi)

Thomas DeKornfeld in 2008 (The picture was taken by Helen DeKornfeld, courtesy of the author)

During the years I was at the gimnázium I lived most of the time, from the second week in September to the middle of June of the following year, in Budapest. Because the family stayed in Ireg beyond the time when the school started I was essentially the only one in Pest. The first two years I still had Teta Liesl so that I was well taken care of. The third year I was placed with the Mauthner family, my cousins, who had a summer place on the Budakeszi út in the Buda hills. I was put up in a small room in a guest house next to the main house. The only other person in that building was the Mauthner grandfather Ödön, a singularly unpleasant old man, who disliked me nearly as much as I disliked him. I also had to associate with my cousin István (Pisti) who always gave me a hard time and whom, consequently, I could have cheerfully killed and with a happy smile on my face. When my parents came back to town that year, and I could move back home I told my mother that if she made me go back to the Mauthners again the following year I would disappear and they would never find me.

So, for the next three years I spent the fall with my Chorin cousins on the Svábhegy. I had three cousins, Erzsébet who was two years older than I, Daisy who was one year younger and Ferenc who was four years younger. I very much liked my stay with them. I adored my Uncle Feri – we enjoyed each other very much. We played golf together and he arranged for me to take golf lessons. I had a very nice room on the second floor and had the companionship of Teta Marianne, the Chorin nanny, whom I liked very much and who was very fond of me and spoiled me.

My cousins went to school close to where my school was so that every morning, while I was staying with them, we were driven to school together. After class we were again picked up and taken back up the mountain to the villa. When I was about thirteen I occasionally stayed in town after school because of some sporting event or Boy Scout activity and when it was time to go back up the mountain I rode the bus to the cogwheel station, transferred to the little train and rode it up to the top of the Svábhegy. From there it was about a ten-minute walk to the villa, mostly downhill. It was in many ways an idyllic existence and when my parents came to town I was not all that anxious to go back to Lendvay utca.

The last two years of gimnázium I no longer spent the fall with the Chorins but stayed in our own apartment. This was a good time for me because Father was the only other person there and it gave me a unique opportunity to spend time with him. He occasionally took me out to dinner or to a Sunday lunch. Some of these meals were at the Gundel which in those days was considered to be one of the best restaurants in Budapest. Indeed, it was very good and the service was friendly and efficient. My father, of course, was known there which might have made a difference. During the Socialist era the Gundel deteriorated but in the early 1990s two Hungarian-Americans spent a great deal of money to modernize it and make it one of the showplaces of Budapest. The food is very good again but the place is terribly pretentious and the staff gives you the impression that they are doing you an enormous favor by letting you eat there. It is also very expensive so that we have found pleasant alternatives.

When my mother and my sisters returned to Budapest in the autumn life settled down in the usual way: school every morning after which I walked to my father's office which was about fifteen minutes away and then rode home with him in the car. Lunch was at two p.m. In the afternoon I did my homework, read and in the winter went ice-skating every afternoon. This was partly for exercise but mostly to see my girlfriend, a classmate of Daisy's, and skate with her arm in mine.

In the evening I frequently went to the opera. My parents being patrons, I could always get a free ticket. One winter

I had a huge crush on one of the sopranos and heard *La Traviata* about six times that season listening to her sing the role of Violetta. I also spent some time going to the movies. Until the outbreak of the war most of the films I saw were French, British or American. After 1940 most of the movies were German, Hungarian or Italian. I was very fond of the Italian movies because even then there was usually a scene where the heroine displayed her very impressive charms. Once every two weeks I also organized a bridge game with some classmates. I picked a day when my family was out so that we essentially had the place to ourselves and had dinner served to us.

Some of my classmates remained my friends through life and I am still in fairly close touch with two of them. Ernő Jónás was perhaps my closest friend; he spent most of the summers in Ireg with us. The other friends were Peter de Balogh who is currently living in Germany where we visited him and his wife a couple of years ago on one of our Europe trips. He was with me in elementary school so we have been friends now for eighty-two years. Another was Johnny Graham whose mother was a Hungarian aristocrat and whose father was a Scottish gentleman. Johnny was always a little odd but a good guy who is now living in Sarasota, Florida. Another very good friend was Tibor Fabinyi, one of the three non-Catholics in our class. He later became a Lutheran minister.

In many ways it was a wonderful life even though there was a war on and anti-Semitism, always present in Hungary, took on a very dangerous form. It became national policy and a series of anti-Semitic laws were passed which very seriously affected the considerable Jewish population in Budapest. The last of these laws, very similar to the Nürnberg racial laws, banned Jewish-Gentile marriages and for a Jew to have sex with a non-Jew was considered a punishable offense, criminal miscegenation. Personally it did not affect me. Our financial and social position seemed like a shield and, quite frankly, I paid very little attention to the whole very distasteful affair.

After the final *gimnázium* exam, in 1942, I applied to and was accepted at the medical school in Pécs. This came as a very pleasant surprise because at that time applicants, who were Jewish under the Anti-Semitic legislation, had great difficulty in gaining admission to university education, particularly in such fields as medicine or law. The reason I was accepted at Pécs was due partly to my very good scholastic record but mainly because my father had received an honorary doctorate from Pécs a few years earlier and was a major benefactor of the university and of the medical school.

That summer was spent in Ireg in the usual fashion with hunting, showing visitors around the estate, visiting the various manors, workshops and factories, sunbathing by the pool and playing bridge in the evening. We also followed the war as closely as we could by listening to the BBC on shortwave radio. This was illegal at the time, but nobody really cared. The war was at a critical stage with the Germans again advancing in Russia, getting close to Stalingrad and moving in the direction of the Caucasus. Leningrad was still under siege but Moscow was no longer threatened. In June, 1941, Hungary had declared war on the Soviet Union after the German invasion and Hungarian troops were fighting alongside the Germans and Romanians. This in turn led to a declaration of war by Great Britain. In December, 1941, after the Pearl Harbor attack, Hungary declared war on the United States so that now Hungary was formally allied with Germany and Italy. I was certain that the Allies would ultimately win the war and I looked at it with a certain idiotic equanimity considering my personal affairs to be of much greater importance.

I was getting ready to move to Pécs and found a nice room in an apartment owned by a widow whose son, Dódy Pilaszanovich, had finished medical school a year earlier and was now a resident in the Department of Surgery. Dódy and I became very good friends and spent a number of evenings together in a nightclub in search of entertainment. My room was fairly large with windows overlooking the street, a bed, a desk, a couple of chairs and a large armoire for my clothes. The bathroom was across the hall and there was another bedroom where Mrs. Pilaszanovich slept. There was also a living room and a separate dining room. Early in the mornings a maid arrived and made breakfast. Lunch was in the school cafeteria and dinner was either at home or in a restaurant downtown. Pécs was not a very large city and, not having a car, I walked everywhere. School was about ten minutes away and the center of town with the hotels and stores was the same distance in a different direction. Just outside of the town there was a small mountain called Mecsek. A small resort hotel with a spectacular view of the city was close to the top. The first autumn Puppa came to stay at there for a week while recovering from severe bronchitis. There was good bus service so that I could go up to the hotel and have dinner with her. We both enjoyed it.

The school year began around the first of September and the very first event was an interview with the dean of that year. In Hungary at that time the deanship rotated every three years among the department chairmen. He was the chairman of the Department of Physics, Dr. Császár, a notorious Germanophile, who after the war was one of the first at the university to be fired for his Nazism. At the initial interview he was very courteous to me and fortunately I never had any problems with him. He was not a very good teacher but since I had no interest whatever in physics I did not mind. I did well in the course and finished with an A. This was just an interim grade, there being a major comprehensive exam of all the courses of the first two years at the end of the second year.

The other courses during the first year were inorganic and organic chemistry and anatomy. Chemistry was well taught but, again, I had little interest in it and failed to see what it had to do with the study of medicine. The final exam had the reputation of being very difficult but I knew the professor's assistant, a very attractive young lady and I asked her if she would review the material with me. She agreed and we had two or three sessions with her quizzing me on the material to be covered by the exam. We became good friends and I found out that she was the girlfriend of my pal Dódy. I received an A on the exam.

The major course of the first year was gross anatomy. We had lectures and demonstrations every day and we also spent eight hours each week in the dissecting room. The Professor was quite elderly and his lectures, delivered in a rather monotonous manner, were difficult to follow. Fortunately he had some very good junior men in the department including several teaching assistants who were actually senior medical students having done very well in the course two or three years earlier. Medical education in Hungary at that time followed the Austrian-German pattern which consisted of a six-year-long curriculum followed by specialty training in a major field of one's choice. This was really a clinical apprenticeship rather than formal continuing education.

The teaching assistant in anatomy to whom I was assigned was a very pleasant and very bright young man named Dezső Merényi who spent considerable time with me and who helped me a great deal. It is indeed a most remarkable coincidence that almost sixty-three years later, in Towson, Maryland, we met again, he being the husband of the director of the retirement community where my wife and I decided to live. I must admit that I only had a somewhat hazy recollection of him, but he remembered me very well and cited several details of our work together in the Anatomy Department in Pécs all those many years ago. We then saw each other regularly and shared memories of time long past. At the end of the first year I had to take a practical exam in anatomy and dissect an arm. It went well and I received a good grade.

There were about hundred students in my class of whom there were only two or three women. Most of them came from the Pécs area although there were some who came from Budapest or from some other part of the country. I did not know any of them and during the less than two years that we were together I was friendly with a number of them but did not really form any deeper friendships and was generally on my own. There were two classmates who were Jewish, both of whom were the sons of prosperous merchants in Pécs. I had no real social life during that year other than going to a small nightclub at a hotel with Dódy a few nights of the week. We drank brandy and chatted with the girls who worked at the nightclub. Many nights were spent in my room studying, reading or listening to music on the radio. I was comfortable and reasonably happy looking forward to my progress in the medical school.

My small social circle included one other family in Pécs. Professor Géza Mansfeld was the chairman of the Department of Pharmacology and a noted scientist. He was an old friend of my father and he occasionally visited Ireg to collect the frogs he needed in his laboratory. I had known him for a number of years and liked him very much. I think my acceptance at the medical school was partly due to his patronage. The Mansfelds lived in a very nice house and had two daughters, older than I, with whom I became quite friendly. I had dinner with them about every two or three weeks.

Politically that year was a major turning point in the war with the battle of Stalingrad in the winter months, the surrender of the German Sixth Army and the beginning of the Soviet advance which eventually ended in Berlin. It was also the time when the German advance in North Africa was brought to a stop by General Bernard Montgomery at El Alamein. Mussolini was deposed and the Allies landed first in Sicily and then on the Italian mainland at Anzio. It became increasingly evident that the war was indeed going to end with Germany's defeat but none of us could foresee just what would happen to Hungary.

Dr. Ferenc Borbély, my Cousin Baby's husband, was very pleased when I started my medical education and he made arrangements for me to spend a month at the Csepel hospital during the summer between my first and second year in medical school. I worked mainly in the laboratory under the tutelage of the director of the laboratory, a delightful lady, Dr. Sára Rauschnig, who, tragically, became a victim of the holocaust. She taught me a lot of laboratory procedures on blood and urine samples and she also taught me how to draw blood. One day Dr. Borbély visited the laboratory and told me that he wanted to watch me draw blood from a patient. Needless to say I was pleased to show off, took the next patient, drew some blood from him on a second attempt and felt pretty good about it. When the patient was excused Dr. Borbély said he wanted to talk to me and took me to his office. There he read me the riot act and tore my performance to shreds. He said I did not approach the patient courteously enough, did not explain to him what I was going to do and why. He also said that I was not gentle enough with the patient and that my attitude left a good bit to be desired. He also said that unless I improved promptly he would ask me to leave.

This conversation was a novel experience. Nobody had ever talked to me like that and I must say that it was a real eye-opener. I was stunned. After I went home that evening I was thinking about it and realized that Dr. Borbély had done me the biggest favor I could ever have. It is not an exaggeration to say that in some respects it changed my life. I became a better person and eventually a better physician because of it. Later Dr. Borbély and I became friends and had lively discussions on many subjects. I saw him several times in Zürich where he and his family moved when we all left Hungary. I was very sorry to hear about his death in 1974.

The second year of my medical school training began in September, 1943, and the curriculum consisted of anatomy both gross and microscopic, physiology and a beginning of pathology. Anatomy continued to be agonizingly boring and was little more than an ongoing compounding of minute particles of information and a continuous stressing of the memory. Physiology, on the other hand, was fascinating. It was taught by a young professor who was extremely bright, fairly new at the job and an excellent teacher. He had had some of his training in the U.S. and told us many interesting stories about his work there. There was at that time no good up-to-date Hungarian textbook of physiology so we were expected to take extensive notes during the lectures and use them as the principal source when studying for exams. It so happened that there was an excellent German textbook available which I bought and which I used in my studies. Evenings were spent like those of the previous year with Dódy and me going to the night club two or three times a week and drinking more brandy than was necessarily good for either of us.

The war was increasingly tending toward the side of the Allies with the Americans and British in Italy and the Russians advancing toward the West. Hungary was politically committed to Germany although, secretly, there were anti-German groups beginning to make approaches toward the Allies. These were done with the knowledge of Prime Minister Kállay but most of the work was done by my future brother-in-law, Aladár Szegedy-Maszák and some of his colleagues at the Ministry of Foreign Affairs. The contacts were made in Sweden and in Ankara with British Foreign Office representatives. As it turned out later these attempts were totally unsuccessful for many reasons. At the time Hungary was completely surrounded by German forces and had no common border with any of the Allied countries. In addition, the British insisted that contacts had to be established with the Soviet Union and the Hungarians were not prepared to do that.

There were two incidents during my second year at Pécs that deserve mention. The first one involved my desire to purchase a small landscape painted by the noted Hungarian artist László Mednyánszky. I had become very interested in art some years earlier and was already the proud possessor of several small paintings. I really wanted the Mednyánszky but I did not have the five hundred pengő (about one hundred U.S. dollars) that I needed to buy it. I called my father and asked him if I could come up to Pest next day to see him. He asked me what it was all about but I said I would tell him when I saw him. I took the train the next day from Pécs to Budapest and went to his office. There I very hesitantly asked him if I might have five hundred pengő and told him why I wanted them. He smiled very kindly, reached into his pocket, took five one hundred pengő bills from his billfold and handed them to me saying, "I hope you will enjoy the painting for a long time". I took the train back to Pécs, got the picture and treasured it. It is still one of the things that I miss most from my life in Hungary.

The second incident was when I became involved with a group of young people, mostly university students, who were strongly anti-German and who met under the tutelage of a Catholic monsignor, an associate of the bishop of Pécs. I attended several of these meetings. We obviously accomplished nothing but had some interesting discussions and engaged in speculations about the future. We also had some guest speakers whom the Monsignor invited. In February or early March, 1944, at one the meetings the guest speaker was Árpád Szakasits who was the second in command of the Socialist Party, a deputy in Parliament and a well-known anti-German. He gave an interesting talk about the Hungarian labor movements and of the problems of the trade unions with the prevailing right-wing political system and the still prevailing strong capitalist trends. He happened to mention Ferenc Chorin as one of the prominent capitalists who was strongly anti-labor and who had been successful in suppressing labor unions in his mines and industries. He also said that, by contrast, Chorin's brother-in-law, a certain Móric Kornfeld, was just the opposite; that Kornfeld was a great friend of the labor movement and did everything to help the working people on his estate and wherever else he could. At the end of the meeting I went up to Szakasits, introduced myself and thanked him for his kind remarks about my father.

The next time I talked to my father I told him about this meeting. He was very upset and very concerned that I would get into trouble with the authorities and cause considerable embarrassment to him and to the family in addition to putting myself at great risk. He wrote me a very strong letter telling me to stay away from the group and never talk to anybody about it. He finished his letter by saying that he was disappointed by my thoughtless behavior. This letter was the last communication I had from my father prior to March nineteenth. When we met again in Purkersdorf in June he told me that he had felt very bad about his letter and about the fact that this letter could possibly be the very last communication between us in view of the fact that he was at that time already in the Mauthausen concentration camp and did not expect to survive.

My medical education in Hungary was rapidly coming to an end. On March nineteenth, 1944, early in the morning I received a phone call from a friend of our family telling me that the Germans had invaded Hungary and that my parents and siblings had gone into hiding with friends in Budapest. He advised me to pack a few things and to go to Ireg and hide out in the home of my old nanny Teta Liesl. By that time I noticed that German soldiers were riding on motorcycles back and forth in the street in front of our apartment building. I packed some things, including some books, walked to the station and took the train to the stop closest to Ireg. I rented a carriage and as we neared the edge of the village I asked the driver to stop, paid him, gave him a generous tip and walked to Teta's house.

Chapter Seven

March Nineteenth, 1944

It seems reasonable to provide a brief sketch of the situation in Central Europe which had led to the events of that dreadful day. To begin with, most historians have come to believe that the vengeful and injudicious peace treaties at the end of the First World War were directly responsible for the development of National Socialism in Germany, for Hitler coming to complete power and for the catastrophe of the Second World War. The major features of the 1919-1920 peace process were the dismemberment of the Austro-Hungarian Monarchy, the deprivation of Hungary of a huge part of its territory and a significant portion of its population, the establishment of Germany as a republic, with the loss of territory and people, the re-establishment of Poland and the imposition of crushing financial burdens on the losers of the First World War.

The destruction of the Monarchy led to the establishment of Austria as a republic, of Hungary as a fictional kingdom under a regent and of Czechoslovakia and Yugoslavia as separate states. Among these countries Austria did reasonably well after some initial difficulties and life there under the new republican system progressed quite well. Hungary was in very serious difficulties both politically and economically. The short-lived Hungarian Soviet Republic in 1919 led to Hungary being controlled by a strongly right-wing political system under the command of Regent Miklós Horthy. Additional political problems were created by the countries now surrounding Hungary, Czechoslovakia, Romania and Yugoslavia, forming the so-called Little Entente. Among these countries there was a profound dislike and resentment of Hungary. These animosities had been in existence for at least a couple of generations and were caused both by innate national antagonisms and also by the real or imagined oppression by the Hungarian authorities at the time of the Monarchy.

The political situation remained extremely tense for a couple of years until Count István Bethlen became the prime minister. His administration was very efficient, centrist in orientation and had as much of a democratic trend as was possible. Bethlen held his position for ten years during which time much healing took place. Hungary slowly and reluctantly began to realize that there was very little, if any, likelihood in the foreseeable future of regaining any of the lost territories and the country settled down to manage as best it could under the changed circumstances.

The situation in Germany was in many respects similar to that of Hungary but Weimar Germany had lost relatively little territory and had considerably greater social and economic strength which helped it to recover from the devastating inflation, the change to a republican system and the crushing war reparations. While economically Germany recovered quite successfully there remained serious societal stresses and a struggle between the growing presence of Communism and the fundamentally conservative, right-wing, unhappy, financially depressed and resentful lower classes prepared the ground for the eventual victory of National Socialism under the indomitable control of Adolf Hitler.

The Anschluss, in 1938, was welcomed by many in Vienna, but was viewed with alarm by most people in Hungary. Father was particularly concerned about the trends he saw occurring in Germany. The increasing military strength of the Third Reich was no secret and it seemed very likely that Hitler would use this strength for his frequently stated desire for increased *Lebensraum*. This, in fact, was precisely what happened. The cowardly surrender of France and Great Britain at Munich in September 1938 and the agreement to attach the Sudetenland to Germany led to the eventual destruction of Czechoslovakia and only delayed but did not prevent the outbreak of war on September first, 1939. Chamberlain's famous statement, "Peace in our time" which he made upon his return from Munich remains the most disastrous pronouncement of all time.

The outbreak of the war and the rapid destruction of Polish resistance placed Hungary in a very awkward position. She had refused to participate in the action and even denied the German request of troop transit through Hungary. As mentioned earlier my family was very active in helping the Polish émigrés and several young women were welcomed at our home in Budapest and stayed with us in Ireg the next summer. Father Béla Varga, the parish priest in Balatonboglár and the future Speaker of the House of Representatives, was establishing a school for Polish children where the language of instruction was Polish. My father was assisting him financially.

We were all very much concerned about the war particularly after the German invasion of Western Europe and the rapid destruction of France. We listened every evening to the BBC because we knew that the German newscasts were controlled by the Nazi Party. However, the news from Germany was regrettably accurate at the time and the battle in the West was over in a very short time.

A major change came in 1941 when Germany invaded Yugoslavia to assist in Mussolini's unfortunate fight against Greece. Following the suicide of Prime Minister Pál Teleki, Hungary could no longer resist German pressure and permitted troops to cross Hungary on their way to Belgrade and then into Athens. In June Germany invaded Russia. This time Hungary became allied with Germany and entered the war on the USSR after an alleged Soviet air raid on the city of Kassa which may well have been staged by German or Hungarian Forces.

By that time anti-Jewish legislation had been enacted but it did not seem to affect us in our daily activities. Of course my parents and sisters and brother were deeply concerned and we continued to listen to the BBC every evening. But we went on living our usual busy lives, understanding intellectually how dangerous the situation was growing, but emotionally rejecting the probability of it directly affecting us. I, in particular, buried myself in my studies in the last year at the *gimnázium* and largely ignored what was going on. In retrospect this seems incomprehensible. It had been evident for some time that a German occupation of Hungary was likely but the family made only few preparations for such an event. There had been some discussion a year or two earlier about leaving Hungary and going to Switzerland or to some other neutral country. This idea was abandoned for several reasons. Even if permission to leave could have been obtained we would not have been permitted to take any substantial amount of money or valuables with us. The senior members of the family were reluctant to leave Csepel and the other enterprises behind and there was also a strong, albeit in retrospect totally unreasonable, conviction that "this could not happen to us". As my cousin, Alice Cséry, said in her book about her family, "We were dancing on the edge of a volcano". It must be said, however, that there was some logic in our behavior: how could such a large and prominent family leave the country unnoticed? If some of us left, what of the others?

On December seventh, 1941, the Japanese bombed Pearl Harbor. Within days Germany declared war on the United States. Prime Minister László Bárdossy was strongly pro-Nazi and a dedicated anti-Semite. Although many in Parliament were against declaring war on the U.S., Bárdossy submitted to German pressure and war against the U.S. was declared on December thirteenth. Under the anti-Semitic laws those men who were considered Jews could no longer serve in the Army and therefore Jewish labor battalions were set up. György was exempt because he was employed at Csepel in a protected position; fortunately none of my cousins served in the battalions. Some of those outfits did go to Russia and many men perished there partly from Russian weapons, but more of them from mistreatment by the Hungarian commanders and/or the regular Hungarian units.

Bárdossy was dismissed by Regent Horthy in March, 1942, and replaced by the much more moderate Miklós Kállay, who did not like the Germans and was willing to find a way out of the war for Hungary.

On Sunday, March nineteenth, 1944, the German army entered Hungary and within a few hours took complete control of the country. There was no formal or informal resistance. Regent Horthy had been detained in Austria but was now permitted to return. He chose to remain in office and appointed Döme Sztójay, the former Hungarian ambassador in Berlin, as the new prime minister of Hungary to succeed Miklós Kállay. The German army was followed immediately by the German intelligence agencies and also by some of the notorious extermination groups. Many of the former Hungarian leaders went into hiding and this group included Father and Uncle Feri Chorin who were taken in by the abbot of the Cistercian Monastery of Premontre near Lake Balaton. Within a few days, however, they were arrested, taken to Budapest, interrogated by the SS, kept in prison for a short while and then taken with a number of other prominent people to the holding camp of Oberlanzendorf. From there Uncle Feri was taken back to Budapest while Father and the other Hungarian detainees were taken to the Mauthausen concentration camp in the Austrian Highlands.

During the time when Hanna's fiancé, Aladár Szegedy-Maszák, was secretary of the Legation in Berlin he met Hitler on several occasions and, even though he detested everything the Nazis stood for, he did recognize the remarkable charisma that Hitler had. Upon returning to Budapest he moved up rapidly in the ministry and eventually became the head of the Political Division. Along with some of his associates who were also strongly anti-Nazi he worked very hard to get Hungary out of the war. Their endeavors were not successful and, because the Germans knew about these strictly forbidden activities, he was arrested shortly after the German invasion and was taken to the concentration camp in Dachau. Fortunately, he survived and after his release returned to Hungary. He found his family surprisingly well, having endured the war and the Russian siege of Budapest.

While I went to Ireg and Teta Liesl, my mother, sisters and brother scattered – hiding out with various friends. They had to move frequently from one place to another because their extended presence would have generated a serious hazard for their hosts. György stayed for a couple of weeks with the Terták family. When I arrived at Teta's house I was welcomed most lovingly, fed and put to bed just as though I were still a four-year-old under her care. The next morning we talked about the situation and we agreed that my presence in her house should be kept a secret and that nobody beside her and her husband should know about it. Consequently for the next several days I lived a hermit-like existence, not setting foot outside the house, staying away from the windows and having the curtains closed whenever we had to put the lights on.

On the fourth or fifth day, late at night, I walked over to the chateau which was only a very short distance away, used Teta's key to get in and went up to my parents' room where I knew that there were some valuable things. I also knew that sooner or later the Germans or Hungarian authorities would come and search the house. Consequently, by the light of a flashlight, I looked through some drawers in the desk and found a small box with twenty-five gold coins in it. I took that and some other small valuable pieces of jewelry and returned to Teta's without anybody having seen me. It was a strange time. I spent several hours each day translating the leading German textbook on physiology into Hungarian with the thought that if I ever finished it I would send it to my former professor in Pécs for him to publish if he considered it satisfactory.

The principal contact among the members of my family was our chauffeur, János Schaffer, who had started his career in Ireg as a stable boy about twenty years earlier. He then became an accomplished chauffeur and automobile mechanic and was a valued member of our household servants. Now he was risking his life going about among the members of the family in their various hiding places. He once even went down to Ireg to see me and to tell me about the situation of the rest of the family. János survived the war and the Russian siege, later married and had several children, one of whom became an engineer. Puppa and Hanna visited him several times after the war.

We listened to the news but the only sources available to us were Hungarian and German news services which, of course, presented a much distorted picture of the war. The Hungarian sources dealt regularly with the ordinances against the Jews including the mandate that we had to wear a yellow Star of David on our coat any time we set foot outside the house. The Jewish owners of stores and businesses were deprived of their property, but the mass deportations did not begin until July and the slaughter of thousands of Jews in Budapest did not take place until after the Arrow Cross takeover in October of that year. In Ireg life seemed to go on exactly as before. The estate was managed by the old and trusted people. It did not take very long before it became known to at least a number of people that I was at Teta's house and one or two of our people came to see me.

One of my visitors was the young Catholic priest whom I had never met but who turned out to be an exceptionally nice and concerned clergyman who was sincerely trying to be of assistance to me. There was really nothing he could do, but I asked him if it would be all right if I went to Mass the next Sunday and to receive Communion. He said he would be pleased and right then and there heard my confession, preparatory to my going to church in a couple of days. When Sunday came I did go to the church, wearing my yellow star, and entered by the sacristy. I stayed there during the service but when the time came for the Communion, I went to the altar and received the Sacrament returning to the sacristy afterwards. When I turned away from the altar and looked at the people sitting in the pews I saw quite a few friendly smiles. I left just before the end of the Mass because I did not want to cause any embarrassment to any of the villagers.

It happened shortly thereafter that two gendarmes came to the house and told me that they had orders to take me to Budapest because there was somebody there who wished to talk to me. The two men who came to get me had been stationed in Ireg for some time and had met my mother and father whom they respected very much. My parents always supported the gendarmes and provided gifts for them at Christmas. The men were apologetic for having to take me to Budapest but said that they had no choice in the matter since the orders came from a high officer in the central office. We took a horse and carriage to the railway station that was about six miles away and when the train came they said very apologetically that they had to put handcuffs on me because technically I was their prisoner. I must admit that it was a strange feeling to have the cuffs snapped on my wrists but at least they had my hands in front of me and not behind my back.

When we got to Budapest I was taken to a major police station and was told to wait in a small room while the officer who wished to see me was called. I sat there for about an hour when my two Ireg gendarmes came into the room and said that the orders had changed and that they were told to take me back to Ireg. By this time it was late in the afternoon and the last train had left. Not quite knowing where to spend the night, it occurred to me that my sister-in-law Elza was living with her baby, the four-month-old Stevie, in their beautiful apartment and might be able to put us up for the night. I was allowed to call her and she said she would be very pleased to see us. She would feed us and we could spend the night there. This is what we did. As soon as we were off the street the handcuffs were removed and we actually had quite a pleasant evening with Elza. The gendarmes played a little bit with Stevie. She gave us sandwiches and beer and then we bedded down in the living room. I was lying on the davenport and the two gendarmes were reasonably comfortable in two large upholstered armchairs. I don't believe we heard the baby cry once during the night. The next morning, Elza gave us some breakfast and then we went to the railway station and traveled back to Ireg with me, of course, again wearing an elegant pair of handcuffs. I had no idea what all this was about and only later heard that it was a German officer who wished to see me but that negotiations between the Germans and my family were already being conducted and that therefore he no longer had to talk to me. In retrospect I believe that the whole matter rested on some misunderstanding. All in all it could have been very much worse. Elza, with whom I had a very good relationship ever since her marriage to György, could not have been nicer and I was very much obliged to her.

Back in Ireg things were quiet. I worked on the translation of the physiology textbook and led a very quiet existence until one morning, a week or ten days after my journey to Budapest. Teta came and woke me up saying that there were two German soldiers in the house who were going to take me to Budapest. I was seriously considering the possibility of escaping through the window and hiding out somewhere else but I very quickly came to my senses, got dressed and went into the parlor to meet the two Germans. They were SS non-commissioned officers who very politely informed me that they had orders to take me to Budapest. They also had a letter for me from Vilmos Billitz, a trusted high administrator at Csepel, who in a few lines told me that "everything was all right" and that I could safely join the two Germans.

I packed a few things in a small suitcase, said goodbye to Teta and her husband and joined the SS men in their car, a typical cream-colored German military vehicle. It was a teary leave-taking. What would become of Teta and her husband? What would happen to the village, to the estate, the chateau, the out-buildings... what would be the fate of our good people who were such a major part of our lives, whom we knew and loved so well? Who could possibly imagine the horror of the next years? My heart was very heavy.

The drive was entirely uneventful and we chatted amicably in German but when I asked where they were taking me all they said was that they had orders to take me to a place on the outskirts of Budapest. Imagine my surprise when "the place on the outskirts of Budapest" turned out to be the Mauthner villa on Budakeszi út. I knocked on the door which was opened by Aunt Annie who embraced me, gave me a kiss and then looking at my coat said that I should immediately remove the yellow star and throw it into the waste paper basket. I was happy to do so. I heard numerous voices coming from some of the inner rooms and when I went in I found to my complete surprise that the sounds originated from my extended family, including my mother and my siblings, the Mauthners, Weisses, Chorins, some other people I did not know and several high-ranking SS officers. Much of the conversation was incomprehensible to me since a number of people were all talking at the same time. Finally I managed to corner my brother György and asked him what in the world was going on. He told me that he was not entirely certain about the details but that it appeared that the family had reached an agreement with the SS that in exchange for Csepel they would take us out of Hungary and eventually take us to some neutral country. This seemed extremely unlikely to me but I kept my mouth shut and resigned myself to whatever might actually happen.

What did happen was in the nature of a major miracle. About nine o'clock, SS Colonel Kurt Becher, Himmler's Chief of Economic Affairs for Hungary, called for silence and asked the groups to separate by families. Then a German lawyer started to read the text of an agreement which was a very lengthy document, listing all the names of the family members and a large number of specific paragraphs describing the various components of Csepel and of the other Weiss Manfréd industrial organizations. The basic nature of the agreement was that the SS would lease the family's industrial holdings for a period of 25 years, free of charge, in exchange for which the SS would take the members of the family to a neutral country and also pay a substantial sum in U.S. dollars. One condition was that six members of the family would remain in Vienna as hostages in order to assure that the rest of us would not engage in anti-German activities. When Aunt Daisy learned that her brother Alfonz was to be one of the hostages she declared that she would not sign the agreement. Needless to say this caused considerable turmoil since it was obvious that if the agreement was not signed by all of us the alternative would almost certainly be confinement in a concentration camp. After some time and considerable pressure Aunt Daisy finally agreed to sign and the reading continued. The six hostages were Uncle Alfonz, György and his wife Elza and their son Stevie, my cousin János Mauthner and Vilmos Billitz, who negotiated most of the agreement and who was acceptable to the SS as a hostage. After the reading of the document was completed all the members of the family, a total of thirty-five people, appended their signatures as did the senior SS officers. As we learned later, the agreement was first approved by Himmler but he felt that it should also be submitted to Hitler for his approval in view of the fact that this was a unique event in the Germans' dealing with a Jewish family. Hitler allegedly discussed the matter with Himmler and then approved the agreement. We were told that the primary reason for Himmler to enter into this plan was to prevent Goering, whom he disliked, from gaining control of Csepel.

The signing was completed by about one a.m. at which time we were told to get our things together and prepare for a drive to Vienna. We did not have very much to prepare since most of us only had the clothes we wore and a couple of changes of underwear. Some of us had some jewelry, I still had the gold pieces I took from the chateau in Ireg, and some of the others had small suitcases of clothes and toiletries. We were then assigned to a number of small German military vehicles like the one that I rode in from Ireg to Budapest. The cars each held three or four people and consequently the convoy consisted of a total of about sixteen cars not counting the vehicles the SS officers and the guards rode in. I happened to be in a car with György, Elza and Stevie who was sleeping happily in a basket.

We crossed the Hungarian–German border without even slowing down and arrived in Vienna about six a.m. Several members of the family, who had relatives in Vienna, were allowed to stay with them. This group included György and his family who were to stay with Elza's parents, and the family of Krisztina Mauthner and her husband, Herbert Margaretha, who would stay with his parents. The rest of us were driven to Purkersdorf, a small town about fifteen miles from Vienna on the main railway line between Vienna and the rest of Germany. Here, on a siding were two Wagon Lits sleeping cars, a dining car, a salon car and two or three smaller carriages for the guards. I shared a compartment with my cousin Gábor Weiss. By the time we were settled it was morning but after a very stressful evening and a completely sleepless night most of us just went to bed and slept until noon when we were called for a meal. The cooking was done by SS men and the meals were also served by SS men wearing white jackets. Considering that this was the fifth year of the war the food was surprisingly good.

I believe it was on that same day, or perhaps the next day that Mother and Uncle Feri were driven to the Metropole Hotel in Vienna which was the local SS headquarters. My father arrived there about the same time, coming from the Mauthausen Concentration Camp. He was shaved from head to toe but otherwise seemed to be in reasonably good condition except for some minor swelling of the ankles. He was made to sign the agreement and then he, Mother and Uncle Feri were driven back to Purkersdorf where the rest of us welcomed my father whom we had expected to never see again. He was very tired but after a good night's sleep seemed to be his usual self. The swelling of his ankles was due to a very modest failure of his heart for which he was started on digitalis powder and recovered very rapidly. At Mother's insistence, later on when we were in Portugal, Father wrote a description of his experiences. He called it "The History of Ten Weeks", and the full text appears in *From Trianon to Trianon*, by Ágnes Széchenyi. I have excerpted parts of it here.

Uncle Feri and Father had discussed the possibility of hiding out in the Cistercian Monastery in Zirc and the Abbott, Vendel Endrédy, had agreed to take them. Thus on March nineteenth, after a very early phone call from Uncle Feri had alerted the family, Father and he proceeded to Zirc with Father Jusztin Baranyai while the rest of the family scattered and hid out with a variety of friends in Budapest.

The stay in Zirc did not last long. The second day two gendarmes came and asked for Uncle Feri. He decided to give himself up and was taken away. Father had the same experience two days later. "The two gendarmes detectives told me that they had orders to take me to Budapest. They begged me not to hold this against them... They also asked me to remember that they had performed this unpleasant task courteously... I could not take my suitcase with me. I did not mind this because the borrowed briefcase held only a few things but because the things in the suitcase represented the all-encompassing loving attention of my wife and was such an accurate representation of her entire being that saying good-by to the suitcase was like saying good-by to her one more time. Actually, during the following weeks, when I had to carry my things myself, having only a light briefcase was a distinct advantage."

In Budapest he was handed over to the Gestapo and was taken to the Astoria Hotel where in the basement the Hungarian political prisoners were kept. At the entrance, at a table two SS guards checked him in. "At this moment I ceased being somebody and became something." Here in the Astoria basement he again met Uncle Feri and a number of friends and acquaintances including General Sombor, the head of the Hungarian Political Police, General Andorka, Lajos Keresztes-Fischer, Count Sigray, Count Apponyi, Professor Laki and others.

That afternoon many of them, including Father, were taken to the Pest Area Court Jail in Fő utca on the Buda side.

The next day he was taken back to the Astoria for interrogation which continued all day and covered a multitude of subjects. Some of the interrogators were civil while others were rude and he was slapped in the face a couple of times. "Later on I tried to analyze what I felt in the depth of my soul at the time I was being slapped around. Even though the slaps made me reel to one side and then to the other, there was surprisingly little physical pain. ... Emotionally the slaps caused no pain either, perhaps because I considered them the forerunner of something much worse, but mainly because I considered them to be the manifestation of some elemental disaster which had nothing to do with my self-respect. In the final analysis only those can be humiliated who have neither enough pride, nor enough humility."

What saved him from some further slaps that day was a quotation that was found in a briefcase that had belonged to me. It said, "Every woman makes her man unhappy. If she is beautiful with her unfaithfulness and if she is ugly with her faithfulness." That is excellent, said the young SS man, and ten minutes later he made Father translate it again.

There were additional interrogations over several days but no hand was laid on him again. He describes the daily life in prison in some detail, the fun the guards had with them, the exercises they had to perform, the food or lack of it and whom he met and talked to in the several cells that he was assigned to.

After about a week he was summoned from the cell and lined up in the hall alongside Rassay, Sigray, Apponyi, Csekonics, Peyer and others. They stood in the hall facing the wall for a couple of hours and then they were packed into a truck and, after a trip of several hours, arrived "somewhere in Austria" but they did not know where. The next day they found out that they were in the camp of Oberlanzendorf, a few miles outside Vienna. This was not a concentration camp but a correction camp designed for short-time sentences to juvenile offenders.

Father stayed in Oberlanzendorf for six weeks and life in this camp was actually fairly good. He was interrogated repeatedly but in a reasonable and civil fashion very different from the Budapest experiences. A major event was when Uncle Feri was interviewed by two SS officers and then taken away from the camp. Father did not know at the time that this was the beginning of the negotiations with Becher that ultimately led to the family's leaving Hungary.

From Oberlanzendorf a large group, both Jews and Christians, were taken by bus and truck to Vienna to the railway station and then, by train, to the Mauthausen station where they arrived in the afternoon. From there they had to march for an hour uphill until they came to the gates of the Mauthausen concentration camp. This was not an extermination camp like Auschwitz or Bergen-Belsen but the prisoners were made to work very hard in an enormous quarry and hundreds of them died from accidents and illness or were killed by the guards. Father and his group were processed into the camp; they were given a shower, had their hair cut to a stubble and were shaved from head to toe. The only visible hair that remained was the eyebrows. Life in Mauthausen was fairly tolerable. Other than twice daily lining up for roll call the group of Hungarian inmates was not made to work and Christians and Jews were living in the same barracks. They were told that this was unprecedented and, according to Father, was viewed as a sign that the camp commander, suspecting that Germany would lose the war, was afraid of a war crimes trial.

"One of my fellow prisoners was György Parragi and it was through him that we learned that there was a Catholic priest in the camp.... There were many in our group for whom confession became a spiritual need, particularly because every moment could be our last one. Parragi became acquainted with the inmate priest who came to our yard and made it possible for us to have our confession heard. Naturally this could not be divulged to anybody outside our group. Therefore the confession was made while we were walking up and down in the yard and we could not even make the sign of the cross in order not to give the priest away. At absolution the priest made the sign of the cross in his palm as though he was showing us something."

Father had been at Mauthausen for two weeks when on May twentieth, "... a messenger came to fetch me. He said that I should gather my things and go with him. This meant departing from the camp. I seemed to be in a trance. The feeling of unreality which had never left me during the past weeks suddenly overwhelmed me. I could barely say good-by. I could not even shake Rassay's hand and when, an hour later I returned for a minute to pick up my glasses which I had left behind I was closer to somnambulism than to wakefulness. Ever since that minute my thoughts are almost constantly with my friends who remained behind. My heart aches for them and it pains me that having remained an object, I could do nothing for them."

Father was then formally discharged, having been made to sign a document in which he swore that he would never do anything against the German army or against German interests. After a few more insults he was turned over to a young SS man who was to accompany him to wherever he was going. As soon as they were out of the camp this young man took his parcel to carry it for him and also said that he had a letter for him. A few hundred steps further he gave him the letter. "A mistake had been made with this letter and the SS Chief apparently switched the letter addressed to me with one addressed to my son György which was also written by my wife. The letter contained a number of requests which, considering where I was just coming from struck me as funny. I did learn from this letter, however, that they were together in Austria and that we were headed for Portugal."

Little remained to be said. The SS man was very courteous and it became evident to Father that things had changed. When asked where they were going the man told him that the destination was Purkersdorf but that they had to stop in Vienna first. Father asked him whether Purkersdorf was another camp but the guard mumbled something about it being a "sleeping car". In Vienna Father was taken to the Metropole Hotel, the Vienna Headquarters of the Gestapo, where he was welcomed by my mother and Uncle Feri and where he had to sign the same document that we had signed in Budapest. They then came out to Purkersdorf where we greeted him and spent most of the rest of the night exchanging our stories. "We talked until morning about the sad and exciting events of the last few weeks and I became convinced that my life in captivity was more peaceful than theirs at home. Thus a new chapter of these unlikely events began."

Our life in Purkersdorf took on a regular routine which varied little from day to day or week to week. Every morning we woke to the loud calls by an SS non-com to his men, "Wasser pumpen!" meaning that water had to be pumped into the reservoirs of the sleeping cars in order for us to be able to wash ourselves and also have drinking water available. We had breakfast and then spent the morning in conversation, playing cards, chatting with the guards or walking around in a very limited area around the cars. Lunch was served at twelve thirty and the afternoon passed very much like the morning. We were given some books, mostly German classics, which also helped to pass the time. Dinner at seven thirty and by nine o'clock we were to be in our compartments and stay there for the night.

Twice each week we were driven in a couple of military buses to the Diana Bad, a celebrated Viennese bathing and swimming establishment where, segregated by gender, we luxuriated in the nude in a series of swimming pools filled with cold, lukewarm and warm water. Once Aunt Elza showed up in the women's section, fully dressed in her black dress and hat and carrying two black handbags. Everyone shouted with laughter saying, "there's the lady from the Gestapo". There were also steam rooms and on at least one of the visits each week we could have a professional massage if we chose, which, of course, I always did and most thoroughly enjoyed.

On one occasion we were taken to see a movie. This was a very peculiar event. We were put in the buses and taken to a theater which was closed to the public in order to accommodate us. While waiting for the projectionist to get ready the thirty of us were sitting in the foyer under a large bust of Hitler. We were then shown a rather good German movie, a comedy, which I enjoyed albeit the older generation was not amused and my Aunt Edith was convinced that this was a preliminary to all of us being shipped off to a concentration camp. I never understood how she arrived at this conclusion. We were provided with Vienna newspapers and could also listen to the German State Radio System. It was from this source that we learned on June sixth that the Americans and British had landed in Normandy but that the German forces were going to throw them back into the sea. Over the next few days the news became increasingly monosyllabic and it was evident to us that the landings had been successful and that another major step in the war had taken place.

I was quite chummy with some of the SS guards, all of whom had served on the Russian front, and thus were very happy with their present assignment. While they still stated that Germany was going to be victorious it was very obvious to me that this was bravado and that they had accepted the fact that with the German army retreating in both the east and the west the prospect of Germany winning the war became increasingly unlikely. Some of them said that they would like to fight the Americans and the British but most of them were very quiet and made it clear that they did not wish to have anything further to do with the war. They wanted to go home to their family and restart their life.

The days went by and on June nineteenth I celebrated my twentieth birthday. The surroundings were strange but the day was a festive one with presents from my parents and sisters. I even received some cigarettes from one of the guards. Only a few days later we had a visit from Becher's chief of staff, Major Karl Stapenhorst, who told us that our passports were in order, that we had been given Portuguese entry visa and that we would leave within the next two or three days. In fact, two days later, late in the afternoon, our two sleeping cars were attached to the end of the German express train going from Vienna to Berlin. It was a strange experience traveling at considerable speed through Austria, stopping in Salzburg and then in Munich. By this time it was dark but we could see that Munich had been heavily bombed on several occasions and that the damage was substantial. We then continued at a much slower rate, under strict black-out conditions from Munich to Stuttgart. I did not sleep at all but spent the night on the rear platform of the car looking at the countryside and seeing the damage caused by Allied bombers in just about every community that we passed through. We arrived in Stuttgart in the morning and were taken directly to the airport. There was a large Lufthansa commercial plane piloted by German Luftwaffe officers waiting for us. As we were walking toward the gate I saw some fresh orange peels lying on a windowsill. This was the first time that I had seen an orange peel in several years and it gave me a good feeling that we were heading in the right direction.

It was my first ever flight and I was fascinated. We landed in Lyons to refuel and just as the fueling was completed sirens started to wail indicating that an Allied air strike by fighters or bombers was expected. The doors on the plane were slammed and we took off right from the terminal without taxiing. We flew just a very few hundred feet over the ground in order to avoid the attention of Allied fliers. This again was an interesting experience but not having any flying experience I did not realize at the time the risks our pilots were taking to get us, and themselves, to safety. It was only after we crossed the French–Spanish border that the plane returned to normal altitude and we flew over the mountains to land in Barcelona for yet another refueling. Shortly after we had crossed the border, Major Stapenhorst, who was sitting facing me in the front of the plane, suddenly started to take his boots off and, much to my surprise, started taking out wads of U.S. one hundred dollar bills. He had obviously smuggled these past the German guards at the Stuttgart airport and this money constituted part of the settlement of the agreement. When we landed in Barcelona one of the Germans who were flying with us got off the plane and returned a few minutes later with a bunch of bananas which he distributed among us. This was another first after several years which we all very thoroughly enjoyed. I also now realized, for the first time that we had indeed "made it!"

The plane then headed toward Madrid where we landed about an hour later. Most of the family stayed on the plane and was continuing the trip to Lisbon, while for reasons completely obscure, my family and the Alfonz family were disembarked and taken to the Palace Hotel in downtown Madrid. We were told that we would stay in Madrid for two days and then continue to Lisbon. It was a delightful feeling to be free in a neutral country and we made the most of it. My cousin Gábor Weiss and I went to a nightclub and then enjoyed the favors of two very accommodating and attractive Spanish girls. The next day we visited the Prado Museum and the following day we were taken to the airport and flown to Lisbon.

Our escape from Hungary and from the war had ended. It was a stunning surprise that the Germans complied with the conditions stated in the agreement. Most of the family had serious doubts about their integrity. I think I might have been one of the only ones who, from the beginning in Budapest, was reasonably certain that all would end well.

It is important to understand that the reaction in Hungary, both at the time and later, after the war, was quite negative. The Sztójay government was enraged because they had assumed that they would take over the WM works. They were dismayed to learn that all had gone into the hands of the SS. Himmler had made the financial arrangements in his own self-interest to thwart the ambitions of his arch-enemy Goering. It was a power grab. Had he not done this the WM Works would have ended up in German hands anyway. In addition, many people, in deadly peril themselves, were understandably angry and envious. How could they not be? But had the agreement not come about the WM Works would still have been in German hands until the war ended and the family would have been in concentration camps or murdered which would have benefitted no one. The matter came up again, as might be expected, with some strongly critical voices about us "making a deal" with the SS. Curiously these articles appeared at the time when Hungary was already under rigid Communist control. All private property had already been nationalized and Csepel had become the Mátyás Rákosi Works, owned by the state and named for the head of the local Communist Party.

This brought to an end what was a most unexpected and significant series of events. Even if we had somehow survived the war, in a concentration camp, or in hiding in Hungary, our life would have been quite different and our future would almost certainly have taken a very different path. What happened was the result of a number of related actions and conditions: the SS wanting to acquire control of Csepel, the conflict between Himmler and Goering, the fact that the life or death of three dozen Jews meant little to the Nazi high command and the ability of the people conducting the negotiations on our behalf all combined to bring about a miracle, in the best sense of the word.

Chapter eight

Portugal

Our flight to Lisbon was uneventful but on arrival we were informed that our visa had been obtained illegally. It seems the Germans had bribed a Portuguese consular official in Brussels to stamp visa into all of our passports without the knowledge or permission of the authorities in Lisbon. Consequently we were to be classified as refugees and interned in a refugee camp. Fortunately, however, Aunt Edith knew the daughter of the Portuguese President, General Oscar Carmona, and was allowed to call her. That lady very kindly interceded on our behalf and thus we were classified as legitimate entrants and assigned, under police supervision, to a resort called Curia, located in the northern part of Portugal about thirty miles from the old university city of Coimbra. We stayed in Lisbon for two days in the Palace Hotel, did some sightseeing, exchanged money, including Hungarian pengős for escudos, bought some clothes and also Portuguese language books. Since we knew that we would be living in that country for some time it was essential to learn the language as rapidly as possible. However, communication with the Portuguese was easy since very many of them spoke French.

Two days after our arrival we went to the railway station that was adjacent to our hotel and, under the supervision of a police officer, started our journey to Curia. The train was very slow and the trip took almost eight hours. The station in Curia was tiny. Most of us got off while others started taking down the baggage when the train started moving again.

Fortunately someone in the family who was still on board had sense enough to pull the emergency line and the train stopped a couple of hundred yards down the line. There we managed to get all our belongings and family members off. By the station shed there were some hotel porters with hand carts onto which they packed all our belongings and started walking down a lovely tree-lined road toward the resort about half a mile away. Thirty of us following along must have made quite a spectacle. There were two hotels and a pension in Curia at that time and the family was split up. The Chorins, the Mauthners, the Jenő Weiss family and Aunt Edith stayed at the more elegant and expensive Palace Hotel while my family and the Alfonz Weiss family stayed at the older, less pretentious but very satisfactory Hotel Grande.

Our hotel was old but clean and comfortable. My parents had a nice large bedroom on the second floor and a private bath which was a real luxury. My sisters and I were on the fourth floor. They shared a nice corner room and I had a smaller single room next to them. Both rooms had a sink but the bathroom was down the hall. My room had a bed, a small desk, an armoire and two chairs. There was no telephone but there was a radio. Breakfast, consisting of a croissant or roll with butter and jam and coffee, was served in the bedrooms. Lunch and dinner were eaten in the dining room. The meals were simple but tasty and very generous. Fish was the usual first course, followed by meat and vegetables and at the end some sweet dessert or fruit. My cost for the room and three meals came to less than one U.S. dollar per day.

The resort was small, consisting of a very nice park with a small lake. A building called the Casino was used for lectures, motion picture shows and dances; no gambling was allowed. The tiny village adjacent to the hotel consisted of a couple of dozen homes and two or three little shops that sold groceries and household goods. Most of our shopping was done in one of the larger villages a couple of miles away and, if something more important was required the city of Coimbra, half an hour away by train, was the place to go. Our friendly policeman stayed with us and we were told that we could go on walks in the country but that we could not leave the immediate area without permission from him. This permission, incidentally, was a pure formality because so far as I can remember no request to go to a neighboring village or to Coimbra was ever denied. When we went to Coimbra, which happened regularly, we had to report at the local police station which was a very simple formality.

At the same time that the family was being rounded up in Budapest, our apartment was being entered by the SS. The servants were dismissed and the place secured. Somehow, and at considerable risk, the servants were able to return and rescue and hide some of our personal belongings which made their way to us over the years. Mother's wedding dress and some of her beautiful silk under-things, Father's full-dress uniform with his sword, many family pictures and other personal effects were saved. That those people would make such an effort under such risk to get the things and hide them for us is truly remarkable. At the chateau in Ireg it was still the winter season, so the place was empty. Teta Liesl, her husband and the estate manager's son, László Ribiánszky, went in and collected some personal things and family treasures. They buried the guns and other things, and burned others, one of which was the second guest book which contained the names of important people who were still alive. At this distance in time it is difficult to fully appreciate how the people who served us felt about us.

Our life in Curia was quiet and very pleasant. The Palace Hotel had two tennis courts where some of the younger members of the family played. There was also a mini golf course in the park that I enjoyed. Next to that there was a small counter where a very nice local man sold soft drinks and candy. He and I became friends and I practiced my Portuguese on him. He was very patient, corrected me and helped me to learn the language. We also organized learning sessions for the younger members of the family. My father and Uncle Feri talked about philosophy and politics. I gave a series of lectures on European history, from the middle ages to the present time. I also followed Dr. Balogh's example and used certain historical dates to discuss the various countries and ruling houses of a particular period.

In the afternoons we usually went for walks in the surrounding farm country and stopped to chat with the local people once we knew enough Portuguese. They were exceptionally nice simple people, courteous and kind, who frequently offered us a part of their lunch or dinner. At times, with permission, we walked to a neighboring village which had somewhat better amenities including a motion-picture theater. It was about three miles away but in those days a three-mile hike was no problem and usually took less than an hour.

In Curia we became acquainted with a most distinguished family, the Bourbon e Tavora, who were closely related to the former ruling family of Portugal. The elderly lady who was the head of the household was the niece of the last king of Portugal. I do not remember how we came to be introduced but I do remember the lady, the deep bow with which she was to be greeted, the kissing of her gloved hand and the completely formal brief conversation with which we were honored. Her granddaughter, Maria de Jesus, was a lovely young woman about my age with whom I went for a walk on their estate several times.

The highlights of the stay were the visits to Coimbra. We had to get permission to go and when we got to the city after a thirty-five-minute train ride we had to report to the local police station. After the second or third visit the policeman at the desk knew us, greeted us with a big smile and said that he hoped we would have a pleasant day. Coimbra is a beautiful and interesting city. It was built on the site of a former Roman city and there are still several Roman ruins. The city was the capital of Portugal for more than a century and also has the oldest University of Portugal founded in the early thirteenth century. It is the third most important city in Portugal after Lisbon and Porto having a population of over one hundred thousand people.

The university is spectacular and has a wonderful library. We became acquainted with the librarian and he and Father had lengthy discussions about a number of learned subjects. The librarian also allowed us to borrow books which we did in considerable numbers. I was reading mostly French, English and Portuguese literature, the latter being almost totally unfamiliar to me. I loved to go to Coimbra, enjoyed visiting the "Old" Cathedral which was built in 1180 to 1210 and the "New" Cathedral which was built in the early 1700s. I also enjoyed some of the restaurants which were a pleasant change from the routine meals at the hotel in Curia. So, with a tranquil and contemplative life in Curia, enjoyable visits to Coimbra and long walks in the countryside the weeks and months slipped by with amazing speed. Christmas came and we had a joyful and blessed festivity.

What we did not know at the time was that our arrival in Portugal had caused considerable concern and agitation among some of the Western diplomatic representatives. The British and American ambassadors reported our arrival to the Foreign Office and State Department respectively and asked for instructions. The ambassadors apparently wondered if we were German spies and could not believe that there had been an amicable agreement with the Germans. The British concerns were reported to Prime Minister Winston Churchill who ruled that we were probably harmless and should be left alone.

The Prime Minister's Personal Minute, Serial No. M.926/4 reads:

> Foreign Secretary. This seems to be a rather doubtful business. These unhappy families, mainly women and children, have purchased their lives with probably nine-tenth of their wealth. I should not like England to seem to be wanting to hunt them down. By all means tell the Russians anything that is necessary, but please do not let us prevent them from escaping.
>
> I cannot see how any suspicion of peace negotiations could be fixed on this miserable affair.

The minute is initialed by Churchill and dated 6.8.44.

The only major event in Curia was the arrival in early December of a large group of Germans, men, women and children, who had been expelled from Brazil and who were on their way home. Since Germany had already been invaded by the Western Allies on the Rhine and the Russians on the old Polish-German border, these people were stuck in Portugal and were living in Curia in the Palace Hotel. They kept very much to themselves and we did not get to know them other than saying hello and commenting on the weather.

At that time the war was continuing; in Europe the Germans started the Bastogne offensive and the Russians were besieging Budapest. We learned a lot about the battles in the West from the English papers and the BBC but very little about the siege of Budapest other than that it was going on. The horrors of the siege became known to us only after the war was over and we could get letters from Hungary and were able to talk to some of the Hungarian diplomats who came to Lisbon to represent the new Hungarian government.

One of my favorite activities in Curia was taking long walks. Inevitably, my thoughts turned to home and my friends and classmates. What was happening to them? How were they making out? Were they even still alive? Good memories of our times together were shadowed by fears for them. Where was Tibor Fabinyi? What was Aurél Dessewfy doing? They had both been actively involved in hiding Jewish people; had they been killed?

My stay in Curia came to an end early in January, 1945, when I was the first one to leave the resort and move to Lisbon where I found a room in the nice apartment of a very pleasant Portuguese family who had a son about three years younger than I. My room was very nice, adequately furnished and with two windows overlooking the street. As I recall it was on the third floor. I was served breakfast but had to go out for my other meals, which was no hardship because there were many small restaurants around serving simple but very good and very inexpensive food.

Shortly after getting settled in the apartment I went to the University Medical School office to ask whether there would be any opportunity for me to continue my medical education in Lisbon not knowing how long my stay would be. I was told that I would have to start from the beginning and even have to take some of the Portuguese high school exams before I could be admitted to the medical school as a freshman. I had no desire to do that and asked if there would be any research activity in which I could participate with or without salary. I was advised to contact the professor of physiology who had an active research program and was always looking for assistants. I did that and very soon started working in the laboratory of one of the senior members of the department of physiology. I spent about four hours every day in the laboratory and my job was to isolate the heart of small turtles which were kept in a large tank in the lab. I was shown how to do it and it took only a very few days before I became reasonably proficient in fishing out a turtle from the tank, securing it on a board on its back, amputating its head, sawing through the shell and then carefully dissecting out the heart and suspending it, still beating, in a nutrient solution. I also had to attach leads to the heart with which we could record the contractions on a smoked drum. We then perfused the heart with a variety of drugs, recording the effects of these drugs on the action of the heart. It was interesting work and I learned quite a bit both about the technical problems of setting up an experiment of this type, about the physiology of the heart muscle and about the effects of certain drugs on the heart. This work eventually led to a publication which, through the kindness of the professor, included my name among the authors. This was the first publication that had my name on it. Of course I was delighted but could not anticipate that this was just the first of some seventy publications, papers, essays and textbooks that would have my name on the title page.

During these weeks very major events took place in the world: the war in Europe came to an end in May with Hitler's suicide in the bunker in Berlin and with the unconditional surrender of Germany. I had applied for an American immigration visum early during the year and now that peace had come to Europe I hoped that the visum would be granted soon. The U.S. consulate general was very helpful and said that this was likely to happen within a few months. There were also local changes. My family left Curia and, after a very short stay in Lisbon, settled in Monte Estoril, a small resort town about forty minutes from Lisbon by a commuter train which went from Lisbon to Cascais about two miles beyond Monte Estoril. The commuter trains ran all day at frequent intervals and were a most convenient way of going either to Lisbon in one direction or to Cascais in the other.

Shortly after the family's settlement in Monte Estoril I became ill. I had a high fever and felt miserable. When things did not improve after a few days my mother came in from Monte Estoril to see me. She realized that I was much sicker than I thought and had a physician called. The doctor was a German refugee who had been living in Portugal for some years and had acquired a Portuguese license to practice medicine. He examined me very carefully and came to the conclusion that I probably had a moderately severe case of typhoid fever. He felt that I could stay in the apartment and that all things being equal I should recover in eight to ten days.

The Portuguese family in whose apartment my room was located was extraordinarily understanding and supportive. They agreed to my staying there and continued to provide me with breakfast. I was indeed fortunate and even now, many years later, I am still very grateful to them. Mother stayed in my room for the first twenty-four hours sleeping in a chair, but then got a room in a hotel nearby, spending most of the waking hours with me in my room. She also bought me a new mattress the one on my bed having the consistency of a slab of marble. It did make a substantial difference in my comfort and soon after I could rest and sleep so much better I started to recover. The doctor came to see me every day and was very pleased with my progress. I was most fortunate to have him as my physician and we became very friendly. When I was mostly recovered it was decided that I should not stay in Lisbon but should join the family at the hotel in Monte Estoril. This was obviously the right decision because I was not only quite weak but was also on a strict diet for at least another three to four weeks. I packed my things, bid a most grateful good-by to my Portuguese host family and was driven by a Hungarian friend of my family, the owner of a philately shop, to the Hotel Monte Estoril in Monte Estoril. This was sometime in late May and I lived in that hotel with the family until my departure for the United States at the end of the year.

I thoroughly enjoyed Monte Estoril. The hotel, on a hill above the main road and commuter rail line, was old fashioned but spotlessly clean and most accommodating; my room overlooked a eucalyptus grove. It was similar to the room I had at the Grande Hotel in Curia and the bathroom was again at the end of the hall. A large front terrace with chairs and tables overlooked the estuary of the Tagus. There some elderly guests at the hotel walked up and down for about an hour every day to get their exercise. Included with the group were an old English lady and an equally old English gentleman with whom we became very friendly. Another resident of the hotel was a Catalan painter who had had to leave Spain.

The hotel had a large and attractive dining room where we took all our meals. The food was very good although for the first three weeks of my stay I was still on a diet which consisted mostly of boiled fish for both lunch and dinner. It was good but after a few days, when I was feeling quite well again, I became heartily tired of it and swore that I would never eat boiled fish ever again.

Our life in Monte Estoril was very pleasant and peaceful. We walked over to Estoril frequently and spent some time with the Chorin and Weiss families. We also went to Cascais, a most attractive small town. It was a fishing port and a few times I went over there early in the morning to watch the boats come in after a night of fishing. The fish were unloaded in large boxes which were then auctioned off to a group of women who made their living by selling the fish in the streets of Cascais. Another reason to go to Cascais was to get some books from a beautiful library that was located in an old mansion. The librarian was a delightful elderly gentleman who became very friendly with Father and who allowed us to take books out without charge. The collection consisted of complete sets of French, English, German, Spanish and Portuguese literature, history, philosophy and art. Since I hoped to leave for the United States shortly, most of the books that I checked out were in English so I could learn the language better. It was there that I became acquainted with Dickens and fell in love with the *Pickwick Papers*. Even now, many years later, it is still a favorite which I re-read every so often. I also read *David Copperfield* and some of the other Dickens novels for the first time. Among the French works I stuck close to the eighteenth century, reading mostly Voltaire and Rousseau.

One of our Hungarian acquaintances, who also lived in Estoril, had a car and on several occasions invited us for rides in the general area. We drove along the coast to a magnificent beach some twenty miles away where we had a picnic lunch. On two or three occasions we drove up to Cintra which was about twenty-five miles away in the coastal mountains. It is a lovely and very old city with an old royal palace in town and a "new" royal palace, built in the nineteenth century on the top of a mountain. The old one is lovely with a spectacular huge kitchen with two enormous chimneys which are the hallmark of the building. The more recent castle on the mountain was built in the worst possible Victorian style and is furnished accordingly. We only walked through it once but that was quite enough. The only good thing one could say about it was that it had gorgeous views over the ocean to the west and toward the mountains in the east.

An interesting Hungarian acquaintance was the Gábor family – Mr. and Mrs. Gábor and their daughter Magda. They were Jewish but were able to leave Hungary because Magda was a good friend of the Portuguese minister in Budapest who had protected them while there and who successfully insisted that the Hungarian government permit them to accompany him to Portugal on a Portuguese diplomatic passport.

Mr. Gábor, who had a jewelry store in Budapest, returned to Hungary after the war, but Mrs. Gábor and Magda joined the other daughters who had been living in the U.S. for some time.

I celebrated my twenty-first birthday in Monte Estoril. My parents gave me a number of presents including some badly needed clothes and also some cash. Wearing the former I took the latter to the Casino in Estoril where I managed to add to it at the roulette table. The Casino had a movie theater that we visited from time to time, a large lecture hall and the gambling rooms which I also visited from time to time. By and large I did reasonably well and by the time I left in December I was ahead financially.

It was at this time that I had my first opportunity to play doctor. Uncle Feri developed a number of boils and his physician prescribed a series of six or seven penicillin shots. Penicillin had just come on the market in Portugal but was available only in injectable form. Uncle Feri was told that he had to go to the hospital in Lisbon for his shots unless he could make some arrangement in Estoril. He called me and asked if I would be willing and able to perform this task. I was delighted and happily agreed. Consequently over the next week I went over to Estoril every morning and, using a sterile needle and syringe, administered the penicillin that rested in a refrigerator in the Chorin's room at the Palace Hotel. When the course of treatment was finished, Uncle Feri gave me a very generous present that I soon took to the Casino and managed to make even more generous.

Politically the big news was the Potsdam Conference where President Truman negotiated with Stalin and with Churchill and, after the elections in the United Kingdom, with the new Prime Minister, Mr. Clement Attlee. It was there that the decision was made to drop the atom bomb on some city in Japan. The first bomb was dropped on Hiroshima on August sixth the second on Nagasaki on August ninth. The

Japanese surrender followed on August fifteenth and the instruments of surrender were signed on September second. After six years, the Second World War was officially over.

Once peace was declared I checked again with the American consulate general and was told that my immigration visum would be issued in the next few weeks. When I was notified that the papers were in order I went to the consulate to pick up my passport and immigration papers. One more formality had to be met: the application for and issuance of a permit by the British to cross the Atlantic Ocean which apparently they still regarded as their private pool. So, off to the British Consulate General I went. I had to pay about fifteen British pounds and waited for almost two months before the permit was finally issued.

The end of the war also meant that my sister, Hanna, would be able to return to Hungary and marry her fiancé, Aladár Szegedy-Maszák. Sometime in November or early December, 1945, Hanna received a message from Aladár telling her that he was back in Budapest and that he had been designated the first Hungarian minister plenipotentiary and envoy extraordinary to Washington. He asked her if she would consider coming to Budapest so that they could get married and then, after the first of the year, travel to Washington together.

Hanna was delighted and immediately responded, saying that she had to make the travel arrangements and would proceed to Budapest as soon as possible. Travel in Europe, just a few months after the end of the war, was still a complicated matter. There was little, if any, air travel and even rail travel was not up to the usual European standards. Nevertheless, Hanna made inquiries about getting home and was told that the only way this would be possible was to take the train in Lisbon, go via Spain to Paris and then from there to Budapest. The travel agency advised her that they could help her as far as Paris but that then she would be on her own.

She bought her ticket to Paris and about December fifteenth departed from Lisbon. Within twelve hours she was back because she apparently did not have all the required documents. A few days later she started again and this time the trip to Paris was relatively uneventful except that at Irun, on the Spanish-French border, all passengers had to leave the train and walk across the bridge to France where they then could board a French train to Paris. Arriving there she found out that it would be very difficult to go on. She did the smart thing, went to the American Embassy, told them the purpose of her trip and asked for help. The response was positive and arrangements were made for her to proceed to Vienna. This leg of the trip was smooth and from Vienna she had no trouble getting to Budapest.

She had notified Aladár about her arrival so that he and Èva Balázs were at the station in Budapest when she arrived. It was a most happy reunion. But Hanna was appalled by what she saw in Budapest. During the Russian siege a year earlier the city had been largely destroyed. All the bridges between Pest and Buda, across the Danube, were down and only a couple of pontoon bridges carried passenger traffic. Hanna told us that she did not expect that Budapest could ever be rebuilt to what it had been. The wedding, attended by Aladár's family and a number of mutual friends took place on the twenty-seventh or twenty-eighth of December and the new couple, accompanied by the legation staff left Budapest for Washington, by air, on January third, 1946.

Early in December I made inquiries about flying to New York and was told that it could take months before a seat would become available. Needless to say I was very disappointed. However, I learned that Magda Gábor was the very close friend of the manager of the Pan American office in Lisbon. I asked her if she would be good enough to talk to the manager and see whether it would be possible to get two seats on an earlier flight, one for me and one for my cousin Márta Weiss who had also received her American visum and British crossing permit. It appears that once again love conquered all and, with the help of Miss Gábor, we were given tickets to fly to New York on a Pan Am flight scheduled to depart on Christmas Eve, 1945.

All I had to do was to pack my few things. Mother bought me a warm coat because we knew that the winter in New York was going to be a little different from the winter in Estoril. We were taken to the Lisbon airport in the afternoon of December twenty-fourth, 1945, where a new Pan American DC 6 was sitting on the tarmac. I said goodbye to my family not knowing when I would see them again. Accompanied by their love, best wishes and some tears, Márta and I boarded the plane and a major chapter of our lives came to an end.

Chapter Nine

American Adventure

Our flight across the Atlantic was not without excitement. The plane developed some problems so we landed in Shannon, Ireland and were taken to the old Royal George Hotel in Limerick. An ancient hostelry, the rooms were small and the bathroom was at the end of a complex maze of hallways. Each passenger was given a small bottle of Jamieson Whisky as a Christmas present from the Irish government.

The next morning we were taken back to the airport and started our flight across the Atlantic. The plane again had some problems so that we landed at the U.S. Air Force Base in Gander, New Foundland, and spent Christmas night in the officers club sleeping on cots. There I made the acquaintance of slot machines which lined a wall in the club. They were nickel machines and I lost about twenty-five cents before I realized that this was not a very good idea. The following morning we departed for New York landing at La Guardia Airport about noon. While the night landings in Shannon and Gander were smooth and perfect and in a plane that had some problems, the landing in New York in bright sunlight and with a good plane almost put us in the bay. By the time the plane stopped rolling, we were about six feet from the fence with the water on the other side. We disembarked and cleared immigration and customs and were welcomed by Mr. and Mrs. Viktor Bátor who were friends of the family. Mr. Bátor was an attorney who handled some of the family affairs in New York. He had a nice apartment on East Seventy Second Street in Manhattan where we stayed as their guests.

The Bátors were scheduled to go on a skiing trip in Vermont a couple of days later and they invited us to go with them. Márta accepted but since I had not skied for many years I chose to stay in New York and try to become familiar with the city. It was a most interesting experience. I had never been in a city anywhere near that size and complexity and it was strange to walk the streets, look at shops on Fifth Avenue, see the Christmas tree in Rockefeller Plaza and gawk at the skyscrapers.

I contacted Mr. Tibor Eckhardt, a Hungarian politician who had been living in New York and who was the step-father of my good friend and former classmate Johnny Graham. He invited me for coffee and gave me some advice about America. He told me that things here were very good but quite different from Europe and if I expected to find the same things I would be disappointed. How right he was! The people I talked to were very friendly and helpful but kept asking me personal questions that I found strange. Where did I come from; where was I born; how old was I; what was I going to do; and so on. It was only later that I realized that this was not nosiness but a friendly and inoffensive concern.

There were two events of major importance. The first was finding out that under the immigration rules I was eligible for the military draft which was still in effect. When I made the appropriate inquiries I was told that I could apply for a six-months' delay but I decided that I would prefer to get into the army as soon as possible and then get out so that I could get back to school. Consequently I volunteered for immediate induction and was given a date about three weeks later to report for a pre-induction physical exam.

The second major event was the arrival of Aladár Szegedy-Maszák as the new minister of Hungary to the United States and Hanna, whom he had married in Budapest just two weeks earlier. I took the train down to Washington and went to the Carlton Hotel where they were staying. It was a lovely reunion and we were very happy to see each other looking so well and were very excited to be in a new country. I stayed with them and slept on their couch, hotel rooms being impossible to get at that time in Washington.

Returning to New York, I could no longer stay with the Bátors and was fortunate to find a room at a small hotel on Thirty-Fourth Street, directly across from Macy's original department store. The hotel was ancient, very simple, very inexpensive and, to be honest, not very good. It did suit my purpose, however, and I had no complaints. Immediately next door to it there was a Chinese restaurant on the second floor. Lunch was sixty-five cents and dinner was eighty cents. I had never had Chinese food before and really enjoyed becoming acquainted with a new cuisine. Not having much money I ate there twice every day, working my way down the menu from top to bottom. It was a peculiar culinary experience to say the very least.

I also spent a good bit of time in movie houses where the ticket was twenty-five cents and you could stay as long as you wished and watch the same movie twice. The winter was cold and one afternoon I went to a drug store which at that time had a food counter. I sat down on a stool and in my hesitant English asked the server behind the counter for a cocoa, hoping that the hot beverage would make me feel better. She misunderstood my order and served a large ice-filled Coke, which was about the last thing that I wanted. I have intensely disliked Coca Cola ever since.

While I was exploring New York, Aladár and Hanna were getting settled at the legation in Washington. The couple was welcomed with open arms by the diplomatic community. Aladár immediately set to work as the first Hungarian envoy extraordinary and minister plenipotentiary to the U.S. and Hanna became immersed in her new life as a diplomat's wife.

Fortunately, she was blessed with considerable social skills and, overcoming any anxiety she might have had, she rose to the challenges with grace, giving dinners and lunches and teas and meeting a host of new and important people. In later life one of her favorite memories was being invited by Mrs. Bess Truman for tea at the White House. This was probably the happiest time in her life.

The time for my pre-induction physical arrived and I went to the designated place, a large school gymnasium where about a hundred young men were getting ready for the physical. We were told by an officer to take our clothes off and we were assigned hangers to put them on. In those days in the middle of winter most of us had some head gear. There happened to be no place to put the caps and hats and thus all of us lined up for the physical, stripped naked but with a hat or cap on our head. The only thing I could think of was that this must be what a nudist synagogue would look like.

I passed the physical and was told to report in a few days for a pre-induction classification test that would decide to what branch of the army I would be assigned and where I would be sent for my basic training. The test was simple and I did well except, of course, some of the questions dealt with non-metric units about which I knew next to nothing. I had no idea, for instance, how many ounces there were in a pound, or how many inches made up a foot. Yet, combined with an oral interview, I did well enough that I was assigned to the Army Medical Service Corps and was told that I would go to Fort Sam Houston, Texas for my basic training. I had no idea where Fort Sam Houston was and I only had the haziest notion about where Texas was. In the New York Public Library on Fifth Avenue I looked up the area where I would spend the next few months.

At that time I still shaved with a straight razor. I had a pair of them in a nice case that I had for many years and which

I had managed to take with me when we left Hungary. Now, going into the service, I had some doubts about the wisdom of having only straight razors and so I thought that it would be nice to have one of the new electric razors about which I had read in the newspapers. I went across the street from the hotel to Macy's to get such a razor only to be told that they had a very few and that they were saving them for their regular customers. I looked sad and said that I was going into the army in a few days and that I hoped that I could have a new razor. The lady at Macy's smiled and said that if I was joining the Service she would be happy to give me an electric razor. In fact, she did give me one and I have been shaving with electric razors ever since.

> New York, January eleventh, 1946
>
> Dear Hancsi!
>
> I enclose a pair of nylon stockings for you. Since they are unavailable here these were given us by Aunt Franci. When nylons become available I will return a pair to her.
>
> Yesterday I was in Albany. I will probably need an affidavit from Aladár about my schooling at home. I will write to you about this later.
>
> Today I am moving. My new address is; The Herald Square Hotel.
>
> With many kisses for both of you, T.

My induction took place during the first week of March, 1946. I had to report in New York City and was then taken to Fort. Dix, New Jersey, which was the major U.S. Army induction center on the East Coast. It was a very large facility with numerous barracks and also permanent buildings. Everywhere you looked you saw groups of soldiers marching, admittedly somewhat irregularly, doing calisthenics or just wandering around. On my arrival I was assigned to a barrack and was then told to report to the supply room to be issued my uniform including boots and helmet liner. It was a very strange experience to put on the uniform and to suddenly become fully aware of the fact that I was now a soldier in the United States Army. It was a new start in life and one that I was looking forward to.

There must have been about sixty or seventy men in the barrack, forming a company. We were lined up in a formation and then marched around with a corporal yelling, "Left-right, left-right, left-right." Having had some training in marching in Hungary I was amazed at the inability of so many of my fellow inductees to walk a straight line and I suspected that some of them did not even know the difference between left and right. I was also amazed at the lack of any real form of discipline. I think I must have been the only one who stood at attention when I spoke to the corporal or to the sergeant who were in charge of our company. On the second day there was a written test and an interview with an officer who asked me a number of questions about my background and past history. At the end I was told that in two more days I would be shipped to San Antonio, Texas, to Fort Sam Houston and that I would receive my Basic Training in the Army Medical Service Corps affiliated with Brooks Army Medical Center. By this time I knew where San Antonio was and had also read about Texas without having any idea what it all really meant.

We did some more marching around the next day and the day after that we were told to pack our things and get ready to ship out. About midday we were taken to the Fort Dix railway station and put into a military transport wagon that had a sitting and eating area and that also had a large number of bunks. It was not particularly attractive but I didn't care and in fact found the whole experience most interesting. The wagon was pulled by an engine to the main Pennsylvania Railway track and eventually hooked up to the end of a regular train going from New York City to the West Coast via St. Louis, Missouri.

There were about thirty of us in that carriage. It was simple but surprisingly comfortable and we could lie down on triple cots. Since traveling through the United States was a new experience for me I spent most of my time by an open window looking at the scenery. I was enormously impressed with the extent of everything, with the numerous small towns, the stations where we stopped, the large farms and the enormous cultivated fields. Even though it was early March the weather was surprisingly pleasant and there was no snow on the ground. It must have been a very mild winter and spring came very early. It seemed to take forever to get to St. Louis and I think that it was early in the morning the day after we left Fort Dix. When we arrived our car was shunted to another track and hooked up to a train going to Texas. When we crossed the state line I thought that we must be getting close to San Antonio, having no idea about the size of Texas and not realizing that the distance from the state line to San Antonio was almost as far as from Fort Dix to St. Louis. In fact we spent another night on the train and arrived at Fort Sam Houston the following morning. I was enormously impressed with the whole trip and gained an entirely new and most favorable perspective of the United States. We disembarked and were taken to the basic training camp where we were put up in barracks.

I was assigned to Company A, Platoon One, given a bed and a footlocker and told that I was on my own until the next morning. I had dinner at the mess hall and was surprised at the quality of the food. Most of my meals were at the mess hall for the next two months. Breakfasts were excellent and I made the acquaintance of such local specialties as grits which I had never heard of before. Food was never inspired but always satisfactory although after a couple of weeks it became somewhat monotonous.

There were about twenty-five of us on each of two floors in the barrack. My bed was on the second floor and I was shown how to make it up each morning and get it ready for inspection. The daily inspection was performed by the Sergeant who was in charge of the barrack and by a Corporal, his assistant. The company commander, a Lieutenant who in civilian life was an elementary school teacher and whose IQ must have been somewhere between ninety and ninety-five, was actually quite a nice man and I never had any trouble with him. He inspected us once a week when we had to stand at attention at our bed. He always found fault with somebody but never with me. A number of the men in the platoon were from the lower orders of society and we had a couple who came from the slums of New York City and acted accordingly. I did meet a number of people and became quite friendly with some of them. My two closest friends were a lad named Charles Balderson who came from a very good family in Mobile, Alabama and who had a southern accent I found interesting and appealing. The other chap was Julian Kitay who several years later was a classmate of mine at Harvard Medical School and who had a very distinguished career as a neuroscientist.

Our daily activities were tightly scheduled, and consisted of marching in formation, calisthenics, running and lectures on numerous military and health-related topics. The war having ended, discipline was not very strict by my European standards and I had no difficulty in behaving according to what was expected. I was also about three years older than most of the others in the company and had much more education than any of them. This was recognized by the sergeant and I was always treated courteously. My knowledge of English was reasonable but I still had a fairly pronounced accent and worked very hard to learn to speak more understandably. I was apparently quite successful because I had no difficulty in making myself understood even by people who had never heard anybody speaking anything but American English with a Texas accent. Incidentally, I also learned a number of words that I had not been familiar with including one that apparently could be used as a verb, a noun and an adjective.

Life settled into a routine. We were doing a fair amount of marching. The longest one was about seventeen miles, with twenty-pound packs and our rifles. Several of the men dropped out and had to be picked up and taken back to camp in a truck. I was doing all right when a friend of mine said that he wasn't going to finish unless he could get rid of his gun. I took it and ended the march with my pack and two rifles. I did not think anyone noticed this or cared about it.

However, someone did: the sergeant saw me do it but said nothing at the time. A couple of days later he called me into the office and had me sit down in front of his desk. He said that he saw me carrying the two rifles and that he had looked up my record. He was impressed by my background and said that he thought that I would be eligible to get my American citizenship and that he would be pleased to be my sponsor. Needless to say I was delighted and made the appropriate inquiries. I found out that during the war any foreign national serving the U.S. Armed Forces was eligible for immediate citizenship. This was done so that if that soldier became a prisoner of war he could honestly claim American citizenship which would have provided him with considerable protection. Unfortunately, shortly after the end of the war in August, 1945, this rule was changed and I was no longer eligible. I thanked the sergeant very much and went about my business not knowing that the good man had done me another major favor by mentioning me favorably to the battalion commander.

We had target practice with the rifle. I missed the first day by being on KP duty and when I went to the rifle range the second day the master sergeant in charge started to give me basic instruction about aiming and firing a rifle. I told him that I had handled a rifle many times before and that I did not need elementary instruction. He said, "Okay, Wise Guy, here are five cartridges, show me what you can do." So I lay down, aimed at the target hundred yards away and fired. The target was lowered and then raised again and a red flag, known as "Maggie's drawers", was waved in front of it indicating that I had missed the whole large target. The sergeant made a rather derogatory remark about my skills upon which I insisted that it was not possible for me to miss the target and asked that it be examined again. Somewhat reluctantly the sergeant agreed, the target was lowered and then raised again with a white disc indicating that my shot had hit the target about an inch to the right from dead center. I said to the sergeant, "See? I told you and I am also telling you that this rifle is sighted a trifle to the left." He gave me a strange look and told me to fire the other four bullets. I did and all four shots were clustered in the black. The next thing I knew I was made an instructor and helped the other guys in the platoon who have never fired a rifle.

Fort Sam Houston, June twenty-fourth, 1946

Dear Hancsi!

Thank you very much for your birthday letter that I can regretfully only now respond to because until yesterday we were on bivouac. The bivouac lasted for one week and would have been awful if I had not hit the jackpot. When I saw on Monday that the whole affair was not to my liking because it was dirty and fatiguing I went to the Commander and asked him to entrust me with the health-safety affairs because that was my specialty. Much to my surprise he fell for this nonsense and I was really given the job. I immediately moved into the Command tent and, when the troops moved out, I moved into the ambulance. I even slept there which was very nice because every night I had a clean, protected and dry bed. The others, in pouring rain, muddy to their ears, shaking and with their teeth chattering crouched under a tree. During the day the others were occupied with military matters and walked for miles sweating and cursing while I was sitting on my increasingly spreading behind and smoked cigarettes. The most notoriously difficult week of the basic training thus became the easiest week for me that I have so far spent in the army.

Many, many kisses and love to both of you.
T.

The end of basic training arrived and we were waiting for our assignments. I had no idea where I would be sent or what I was going to do. The day that the assignments were to be announced I was summoned to report to the battalion commander. Entering his office I stood at attention, saluted and said, "Private DeKornfeld reporting as ordered, Sir!" The battalion commander, a very nice lieutenant colonel, had me sit down and told me that I did well during the basic training and that on reviewing my record he wondered if I would like to stay attached to Brooks Army Medical Center and become an instructor in the Medical Field Service School. It would be my job to teach anatomy and physiology to men who would eventually be assigned to units as "medics". The school had been in operation for some years and had a good reputation. It now needed some new instructors of which I could be one if I wanted the job. It sounded ideal to me. I liked the base and I enjoyed my visits to San Antonio so the idea of staying there in what seemed like a pleasant job appealed strongly and I told the colonel that I would be very grateful for the assignment. He smiled and said that it was a done deal, that

I could move to my new quarters the next day and that I would be asked to start teaching the following week.

In retrospect it is fair to say that basic training was a surprisingly non-traumatic experience which I actually rather enjoyed. I did not find it physically overly demanding and I even enjoyed getting into a better shape than I had ever been. The treatment was good, the food was adequate, the people around me were generally very pleasant and I became quite friendly with several of them. The occasional visits to San Antonio were also pleasant and two or three of us went together once a week to eat at a nice restaurant where a good dinner could be obtained with all the trimmings for less than five dollars. At a special steak restaurant for six dollars you were served what appeared to be half a cow. San Antonio in those days was still a small town which had one decent hotel, the Gunther, and one "skyscraper" of about twelve stories. Much of the population was Spanish speaking and there were obviously also a number of African-Americans, referred to as "negroes" in those days who were still strictly segregated.

Fort Sam Houston, July tenth, 1946

Dear Hancsi!

Please forgive me for not having written for such a long time and for not having thanked you for the most generous birthday present. It was a lifesaver pulling me back from the jaws of starvation. May it serve as my excuse that lately I have been very busy. After the basic training was completed I was transferred here to the Army Medical and Surgical Technician School and I teach anatomy and physiology. Can you imagine me standing in a white coat on the rostrum teaching physiology to forty men? The first few days were very strange. But now, after two weeks, I am "into it" like a puppy into barking. Everybody says that I am a good teacher. Every day I have two to three hours which is not bad at all. The food is excellent and generally the whole atmosphere is incomparably better than in basic training. I am very pleased and apart from the terrible heat I feel very well. My new address is Pvt. Thomas DeKornfeld 42278369 Co. A. MDETS. Fort Sam Houston, Texas.

I embrace Aladár with much love, and many loving kisses to you.
T.

Brooke Army Medical Center was one of the major hospitals in the army, serving a large area in the southern part of Texas with a number of military bases all around it. Associated with it was the Medical Field Service School which was under the command of a colonel in the Medical Field Service Corps and which also had a number of army nurses assigned to it as instructors. There were four or five enlisted instructors of whom I now became one. We had a building with classrooms and with one or two large rooms set up as wards with beds and all the usual facilities.

There was also a building for us to live in and much to my pleasure I was assigned a room by myself. After sleeping with more than twenty people in one room for the past two months this was a most pleasant change. I still had access to the mess hall and now that I had more time to myself I was looking for something to do. The camp library was surprisingly good and had a very large collection of both classic and contemporary American literature with most of which I was not yet familiar. I became a regular reader and soon became friends with the librarian, a pleasant and knowledgeable elderly lady. She once asked me if I would like to work in the library on a regular basis. I said that my schedule was such that I could work for a couple of hours every afternoon and also for several hours on Saturdays and Sundays. She promptly hired me for the munificent salary of one dollar per hour which, considering that my monthly net income was seventeen dollars and fifty cents, seemed like a fortune. I started working the next day and continued to do so as long as I was in the Service.

My teaching chores were relatively light and I enjoyed lecturing on anatomy and physiology to groups of fifteen or twenty men. Starting with anatomy in a general way, not going into minute details, I explained the body and its components as best I could. The physiology lectures were also quite basic and the purpose of the entire exercise was to introduce a group of totally ignorant people to the structure and function of the human body. The school had a decent collection of books and charts that I could use and I soon assembled a reasonable collection of material that I could hand out to the students. I also had to prepare quizzes and exams, including a final exam which, when passed, allowed the students to move on to other courses.

By and large it was an ideal existence and I have never had before or since such a carefree time. I became friendly with some of the other instructors and we used to go to San Antonio together for meals and some other forms of entertainment. Life in those days was very inexpensive. Cigarettes at the PX were twenty-five cents a pack and a movie ticket was ten cents. There were shuttle buses between the hospital and the city, which were free but even the commercial buses charged only twenty cents for a ticket.

Life was easy and the only unexpected event was a bout of virus pneumonia which forced me to go to the hospital. I was there for about a week and received absolutely first-class care from the physicians, the nurses and the ancillary personnel. I could not have had better care in the most expensive and prestigious private hospital anywhere. When I was recovering

I was granted a two-week recovery furlough which I decided to spend in Washington with Hanna and Aladár.

The trip home was an experience. I was told at the hospital that I could hitch a ride on an Air Force plane from the nearby base to Washington at no cost. This sounded good to me so I got myself to Lackland Air Force base and was told that in about an hour I could get a ride to Atlanta from where I could get a flight to Washington. This sounded wonderful. I boarded the plane and, still being somewhat tired from the illness, promptly fell asleep. When I woke up we were banking for a landing and when I looked out the window I saw nothing but blue water. Knowing that Atlanta was not exactly on the ocean I asked the sergeant in charge of the passengers where we were and he told me that our orders had been changed while we were in the air and that we were now landing at the Air Force base in Pensacola, Florida. When we got off the plane I was told that there was no way I could get a flight north and that I would do better to go by train or bus. There was another guy on the plane who also was headed toward Washington so the two of us decided we would hitchhike to Mobile and then catch a bus to Washington. This is in fact what we did and we were quite lucky in getting to Mobile with surprising ease. We were given a ride by a very nice lady from Pensacola to the half-way point and then we picked up another ride with a farmer headed to Mobile who actually took us to the bus station. We got on the bus to Atlanta where we had to change to another bus and eventually, some twenty-four hours later, arrived in Washington. I took a cab to Hanna's house where I just about collapsed and slept for the next eight hours.

My furlough in Washington was very nice. Recovering rapidly, I enjoyed my stay with my dear sister, Madame Ambassadress. Her house was lovely and she had several Hungarian servants including an excellent cook. When my furlough was coming to an end I decided to take the train back to San Antonio which I did with no particular problems other than the length of the trip.

Back on the base things went on as usual. Christmas came and it was odd to be all by myself at that time in a new country, in uniform and on an army base in Texas. Yet it was pleasant and after the New Year my work continued until March when we were informed that the draft law had been revoked and that we could be discharged from the army early in April. By that time I had been promoted to corporal and my official designation was T5, meaning technical NCO grade five. I was told that if I signed up for another three years I would be made a sergeant. I thanked them politely but said that I would rather get my discharge papers because I wished to go back to school and eventually get my degree. Thus late in March I received my honorable discharge and about one hundred dollars severance pay.

My friend of many years, Ernő Jónás, had come to the U.S. and was in Michigan at the University. I took the bus to Chicago – a twenty-four hour ride – and arrived there late in the afternoon. Feeling adventuresome I went into a bar, sat the counter and ordered a rye whiskey. A mistake: I didn't like it at all but drank it and then adjourned to the YMCA dormitory for the night. The next day I took a bus to Ann Arbor where Ernő had settled in with his uncle, a professor at the University of Michigan. Arriving there I swore a great oath under the sacred oak tree that I would never ride on a commercial bus again as long as I lived.

My visit with Ernő was pleasant but after a couple of days I felt an urge to move on and took the train to New York. After two or three days there I went down to Washington where I stayed with Hanna and Aladár. There was not much for me to do so I tried to help Hanna, running errands and, after I got my driver's license, acting as a tour guide for important visitors from Hungary. There were two tours: the long one that included Mt. Vernon for important people, the short one, just around town, for everyone else.

I also started to make inquiries about continuing my education and contacted the admissions office at The George Washington University in Washington. I was told that with my educational background in Hungary the university would grant me credits for three years and that I could matriculate as a senior in biology in September. I also learned that if I did all right I could get a Bachelor's Degree the next June and then apply to medical school. Both GW and Georgetown University said that I would get no medical school credit for my semesters at Pécs and that I would have to take the full four years of medical training. It was a disappointment but there was nothing I could do about it and I decided to make the best of it. Visiting the Biology Department at GW I met the chairman, Dr. Paul Bowman, who turned out to be an extraordinarily nice man and who welcomed me into the program. This made a considerable difference and I was looking forward very much to resuming my studies under a totally different system than the one I had been familiar with in Hungary.

It was now April, 1947. Much was happening politically. In Hungary a Communist regime took control of the government early in April and Aladár resigned from the ministership. He and Hanna were granted asylum in the United States, becoming citizens five years later. There was much to do: numerous documents had to be duplicated, messages had to be sent or delivered and I tried to help in all of these activities. Several of Aladár's colleagues also resigned although my friend Iván Nagy decided to stay at the legation which meant the end of our relationship. We also had to make new living arrangements because the house that we were living in either belonged to the legation or was rented by it. This meant a search for a suitable house and we were fortunate to find a smaller but pleasant one just off Western Avenue in Chevy Chase. We rented it and moved around May first, 1947. It was convenient because there was a bus that went on Western Avenue to Chevy Chase Circle from where another bus took us downtown. We, of course, also had the car, a Chrysler, and it was my job to act as the family chauffeur since Aladár did not drive at all and Hanna drove but not with any great enthusiasm. Actually, driving in Washington in 1947 was not too much of a problem. Traffic was still quite moderate and there was no congestion. It was quite different from what it became over the next ten years when driving in the District of Columbia became a chore.

Hanna was pregnant and during that summer a little boy, Aladár Jr., was born. He was a very attractive and nice little boy. He seemed to thrive but when he was about three months old he became ill one day and had some bloody stools. The pediatrician diagnosed a minor problem and prescribed some medicine. The child became much worse and was now diagnosed as having an intestinal intussusception, which is an obstruction of the bowel. He was rushed to the Washington Children's Hospital and was subjected to emergency surgery. The pediatric surgeon told us that there was very little hope and, in fact, little Aladár died that night with Hanna and me standing at the side of the crib. The tragedy devastated all of us. I think that Hanna and Aladár never really recovered. The other members of the family, still in Portugal, were deeply saddened at the news especially as they were so far away. Father, in particular, had looked forward with great enthusiasm to getting to know little Aladár. And Puppa was miserable at not being able to comfort her sister. The baby's death was the result of an obvious case of major malpractice but we were ignorant of its implication at the time and did nothing about it.

His little body had been taken from the hospital to the funeral parlor and it was my job to inform the priest at Blessed

Sacrament Church which the family attended on Chevy Chase Circle. I went to the rectory and rang the bell. When nobody answered I tried the handle and found that the door was open. As I entered the hall a priest came out of one of the rooms and started berating me for entering the rectory without permission. I very quietly told him that I had rung the bell and knocked before entering and that I had come to advise him that the infant child of one of his parishioners, a baby whom he had baptized, had died. He became a little more civil and said that he would come to the house to make the arrangements for the funeral. This took place a couple of days later and the baby was buried in a children's cemetery somewhere in South East Washington, miles away from where we lived. It was indeed a very bad time for all of us. Over the years I sometimes asked Hanna if I could help her bring little Aladár back to the family cemetery which was nearer to home. She always refused the offer: I don't think she could bear the thought.

During that same summer I was approached by an agent of the FBI and asked if I would be willing to work with the Bureau as a translator and consultant. I agreed and was then introduced to some agents at the FBI headquarters and was given a number of Hungarian letters and documents to translate. The work was easy and some of the material, particularly the letters from Budapest, was very interesting but terribly sad. There were reports about the events of the siege of Budapest, the activities of some of the Russian troops, the rapes, robberies, arrests, deportations, and so on. The news was ghastly. I worked with several agents and some of them became good friends. In fact, two of them sponsored me for my citizenship the following year. Fortunately the law had changed again and I became eligible for citizenship after having been in the military and having been in the United States for three years instead of the standard five years.

At the beginning of September I started my college education at GW in the Department of Biology. I took mostly science courses including two biology courses and a course in botany. During the second semester I took a course in parasitology and one in advanced botany. I also took some non-science courses including one on American literature and several others. Carrying seventeen credit hours in both the fall and winter semesters made me eligible for a Bachelor's degree which I received at the end of the academic year. I very much enjoyed my time at GW. The level of instruction was excellent. Some of the professors were leading scientists working for the federal government and teaching at GW in the evening. The classes were small and with very few exceptions the students were bright, interested and very pleasant. Many of them were working and attended school on a part-time basis. There was practically no "Rah-Rah" spirit and football and basketball were not a matter for discussion.

During the year I applied to medical school at both GW and Georgetown but at the same time returning veterans were applying to the medical schools in very large numbers and I was not accepted even though I was encouraged to apply again the next year. This being the situation I discussed my options with Dr. Bowman who suggested that I stay at GW and work toward a Master's degree which I could get in three semesters. It seemed like a very good idea and I immediately applied, was accepted, and started my Master's studies during the summer term of 1948.

One of the courses I took during that summer was organic chemistry. Although I remembered some of the material that I had studied at Pécs five years earlier, I still had to work pretty hard to get at least a B as required for the Master's degree. The chemistry lab was on the top floor of one of the large brick GW buildings. It was not air-conditioned and became so hot one day that the temperature approached the boiling point of ether and we were all sent home. I also took another course in American literature during the summer and became very friendly with the instructor, an extremely bright young assistant professor. The classes were three days a week at eleven a.m. so that he and I usually had lunch together after the lecture. I received an A in both chemistry and literature.

The Master's degree program required a research project resulting in a thesis. So during the summer I started to work on a project in biology under Dr. Bowman's guidance. It consisted of growing onions in a variety of aqueous media and then sectioning the rootlets, staining them and examining the effects of the media on cellular growth and structure. It was an interesting project and I had a lot of fun with it even though making literally hundreds of microscope slides of the rootlets became a major chore after a while.

During the fall term I continued my research project and also was asked to work as a teaching assistant in freshman botany. It was not much of a job and paid next to nothing but I really enjoyed working with the freshmen. I also took a biochemistry course which was the medical school course but which could be taken by graduate students in other fields like biology. It was given at the medical school in a different part of town which meant a daily commute between the main campus and the medical school. The only other course I took that semester was biostatistics, which I detested and had a very difficult time with. In all my years in school I have never had a course that I disliked so much or had so much trouble with. I knew I had to get a grade of at least B for my Master's and fortunately I had two classmates who had a lot of statistics background and who helped me particularly in getting ready for the exams. Thanks to their assistance and to the benevolence of the instructor I did get a B and swore that I would never, ever, take another course in statistics.

A major event of the late autumn was being granted my American citizenship. As I indicated earlier, the law had been changed and I was sponsored by the two FBI agents with whom I had become friends. The formal swearing-in ceremony was held on December seventh, 1948, the anniversary of the Japanese attack on Pearl Harbor. I took the oath quite literally with tears in my eyes. It was a very proud moment. I loved this country, was immensely grateful to it and was determined to do the very best I could to show my appreciation. An important side benefit of my citizenship was that it gave my parents a major advantage in getting their immigration visa since they were now the parents of an American citizen. Living in Switzerland at the time, they immediately applied and were granted their visa within a couple of months. In March, 1949, they arrived in Washington.

My studies at GW continued. The Master's degree required a reading knowledge of either French or German and we had to pass a written exam in which we had to translate into English a couple of paragraphs from a scientific article. This presented no problems for me but I had two classmates who were also working for a Master's in biology and who knew very little of either French or German. They asked me if I would coach them in French and I agreed. The arrangement was that I would work with them and if, as the result of my teaching, they passed the exam they would owe me fifty dollars. If they flunked they would not owe me anything. We worked for about three hours each week for a couple of months and I was very pleased when both of the guys passed the exam.

Sometime during that autumn the family bought a house. The one we had been living in was quite small and also was associated with the very sad memories of little Aladár's illness and death. The new house was on the Maryland side of Western Avenue on Summerfield Road just a few blocks from the Chevy Chase Circle. A pleasant house with four bedrooms, it had a nice but not very large yard. On the first floor there was a bedroom and bathroom which became my parents' home when they arrived in the U.S. The neighborhood was quiet and we had very friendly neighbors with whom we established excellent relationships. At the time we had considerable household help from the Hungarian couple who had worked for Hanna and Aladár during his ministership and who resigned from the Legation when he did. The man was an excellent cook and the wife was an efficient maid. When my parents arrived it was a pleasure to see them after a separation of more than four years. They were well and were very happy to be here and settled in a home with two of their four children.

I finished my thesis and having completed all other requirements I was awarded the Master's degree in biology. I even attended the graduation exercises because my mother was very anxious to see them. It was also about this time that I was informed that my application to Georgetown Medical School had been approved and that I could restart my medical education in September. As I found out later my acceptance was due partly to my background and very good performance at GW but also, and to a very large extent, to the sponsorship of Dr. Francis Horvath, a professor of medicine at Georgetown who knew my family in Hungary and who actually became my parents' physician in Washington. He was a fine internist and an exceptionally nice man. I was grateful for his help then and I am still grateful to him all these many years later. Had it not been for him I doubt it if I would have been accepted at that time.

Part of the summer was taken up with a most interesting drive to Calgary, Canada. Father had been a good friend of Bishop Count Mikes (Mikesh) who some time after the First World War had purchased property there – a ranch run by two brothers, the Barons Csávossy. Needing money, the bishop asked Father if he would like to purchase a one-third portion of the property. To help his old friend out, Father agreed. Now that they were in the U.S. my parents wanted to see the place. Since I was free and we had a car we decided to drive and invited my cousin Pic to come along and help with the driving. We started out fairly early one day in late June or early July.

The first day we were on the Pennsylvania turnpike from Breezewood to its end at Irvine a little east of Pittsburgh. We had not driven on a four-lane highway before and we both enjoyed the experience. After driving through Pittsburgh we eventually stopped in Akron, Ohio for the night, staying at the Hotel Akron and eating in the hotel restaurant. On one wall was the old poem, "I've never seen a purple cow, I never hope to see one, but I can tell you anyhow, I'd rather see than be one". My father was vastly amused. We got as far as Chicago and drove along the Lakeshore drive and the following day, crossing all of Wisconsin, we went as far as Duluth, Minnesota. Gasoline was twenty-five cents a gallon and there were no interstate highways west of Pittsburgh; travel was slow on the two-lane roads through all the small towns where the speed limit was twenty-five miles an hour. But my parents fell in love with the country; Father was particularly impressed by the huge farmsteads.

From Duluth we continued our trek west and finished the day at the Hotel Meier in Devil's Lake, North Dakota. The following day the temperature was in the high nineties and the car, not having air conditioning, was really uncomfortable. This was the first time that I ever saw my farther take off his tie and open the top button on his shirt. The car was running hot and we stopped several times when we found some shade to let it cool off. Eventually we arrived in Glasgow, Montana, where we found rooms in a small hotel. Being below street level the rooms were reasonably comfortable although the hotel was not air conditioned. We slept well but not for very long because a group of truck drivers who had rooms next to ours left at four o'clock in the morning making a considerable amount of noise. The day was still warm but not as bad as the day before. We made good progress and arrived at Glacier National Park in mid-afternoon, staying at the very good hotel in the park. It was quite cool and we enjoyed a lovely evening.

Finally, after six days and two thousand miles, we arrived in Calgary on a Saturday afternoon and could not find a hotel room for love or money. It seems that on Saturdays the ranchers from the area around Calgary came into town and occupied every available room. At one of the hotels we were told that if we drove another twenty miles we would come to a small village called Cochrane on the way toward Banff where there was a hotel that might have rooms available.

After spending the night in Cochrane we wanted to visit the ranch but were not entirely certain how to get there. The people at the hotel in Cochrane knew the Csávossy brothers and gave us directions. Pic and I started out. The road was only a dirt track which occasionally disappeared being replaced by ruts and gullies produced by the last rain storm. Once we thought that we had broken an axle and drove on at about five miles an hour. Finally we saw the ranch and also found that there was a far better road leading to it. Returning to Cochrane we decided that since the Csávossys had no telephone it would be best to go back to Calgary to get settled in a hotel before we attempted to contact them. Rooms were available at the Royal York Hotel, a very nice, more modest and less expensive hotel than the fancy Canadian Pacific Hotel called the Palliser.

Eventually we reached the Csávossys and they gave us perfect directions; that afternoon we arrived at the ranch, met the brothers and were shown around the property. There was a quite nice house, a stable for horses and several barns for the cows that were the principal feature of the ranch. Of the approximately six hundred acres many were used for grazing, some were worked and both corn and forage crops were grown. Everything seemed to be in good order and we were told that the ranch actually produced a reasonable income. The older brother was in charge of the agriculture while the younger brother was in charge of the animals. We stayed in Calgary for three or four days during which time we met the older brother's lady friend, Princess Tanya Obolensky, and her mother, the widow of a high official in the tsar's court until the fall of the tsar in 1917. As soon as the war was over they had left Russia and eventually settled in Calgary where Princess Tanya owned and operated a very upscale ladies' dress shop.

Continuing our trip we drove to Banff. The village is in the Banff National Park, about seventy-five miles from Calgary and the famous Banff Springs Hotel, one of the ornaments of the Canadian Pacific Railway Company, is just outside and above the village. It is a spectacular place: very large, beautifully maintained, and with a phenomenal view of the Bow River Valley and the Canadian Rockies. My mother fell in love with it and decided that we would stay there for a few days. When we checked in Father told the concierge that he did not bring formal clothes and asked if we could eat in the dining room in street clothes. The concierge, an elderly man of the old school, smiled and said, "Alas, those days are over. For the last three or four years you can eat in the dining room provided you wear a jacket and a tie." We were there for three days and thoroughly enjoyed it. Our excursions were fun as we visited the Valley of the Seven Peaks and drove along the road leading to the glaciers and skirting Mt. Eisenhower. The whole area was reminiscent of Switzerland and brought back some memories of years gone by.

We stopped in Calgary again for a couple of days, said good-bye to the Csávossys and started for home. Deciding that as long as we were that far west we might as well see some more of the United States, we drove south eventually reaching Salt Lake City where we stayed for a couple of days visiting the Mormon facilities that were open to tourists. Slowly we made our way back east and eventually got back to Washington having been gone a total of almost five weeks. My little Plymouth behaved very well and it was only once, in Salt Lake City, that I could not get it started because of a rain storm. Pic and I alternated driving and progressed steadily albeit fairly slowly, all roads being single lane. Fortunately traffic, particularly in the West, was minimal and there were not too many semi-trailers on the road.

During the brief time remaining prior to the start of medical school I continued to do some work for the FBI and reviewed some of my notes from my course in biochemistry at GW knowing that I would have to take it again at Georgetown unless they allowed me to test out of it.

The dean of Georgetown Medical School at that time was one Paul McNally, S.J., an astronomer who knew nothing about medicine but who had been appointed to the job based on his reputation as a disciplinarian. His demeanor was the exact opposite of the cordial men at GW and his opening remarks on the first day of classes were appalling. After telling us that we must obey all of the rules and regulations or risk dismissal, he predicted that out of the one hundred fifty of us thirty or forty would fail. It struck me that there must be something terribly wrong with the selection process. He added that failing any course or getting two D's in one semester would automatically lead to dismissal. He then introduced the professor of anatomy, Dr. Othmar Solnitzky and left the room without even saying good-by. I must admit that coming from the liberal and friendly atmosphere of GW I was flabbergasted and wondered whether I had made a terrible mistake in coming to Georgetown.

Dr. Solnitzky welcomed the class and explained to us that Georgetown had initiated a trimester system which meant that all of gross anatomy would be taught in one trimester and that consequently we would have several lectures each of four days and laboratory on the same days. We had a ten-minute break and he started his first lecture. Solnitzky was Canadian and an excellent anatomist. His lectures were precise, well delivered and accompanied by excellent drawings on the blackboard with colored chalks. He was the only person I ever knew who could draw simultaneously with both hands. That morning he lectured for two hours and then we were told to report to the dissecting laboratory after lunch for a two-hour session. Four of us were assigned to each cadaver that we would dissect completely before the end of the term. Having done dissections in Pécs all those many years ago I was not particularly concerned but some of my classmates were less than enthusiastic about the whole idea. One classmate took a look at the cadaver, turned around and walked out never to return. His entire medical education lasted exactly three hours. The anatomy lectures and the laboratory work progressed smoothly with a large number of short quizzes and several larger exams. I was fortunate to have no particular problems and did well on the exams. The dean's predictions turned out correctly and some thirty of my classmates failed anatomy and were dismissed.

The only other major course during the first year was biochemistry. I went to speak to the professor, Dr. Walter Hess, and explained that the previous year I had attended the medical school biochemistry course at GW and received an A and asked if I might be excused from the course or perhaps allowed to test out of it. Hess was a very nice man, a strict disciplinarian but fair and a very good teacher. He said that unfortunately Georgetown did not allow any student to be excused from or test out of a course and hence there was nothing he could do for me. I did not mind too much because obviously the course was easy. I enjoyed Hess's lectures and became very friendly with one of his assistants, Dr. Paul Hilmer, who remained a friend for many years. One thing that made the biochemistry course interesting was that while at GW the emphasis was on carbohydrates and fats, at Georgetown the principal subject for discussions was the proteins.

The house in Chevy Chase had become crowded and was a long way from Georgetown. My parents and I decided that it would be best if I were to rent a room somewhere near the school. Fortunately I found a nice place in a house owned by an elderly lady who rented rooms to medical and dental students. An additional piece of very good fortune was that two of the other tenants were classmates. Jack Adams and Bill Kitsko and I became very close friends. We went to school together, usually ate together and, before exams, studied together and quizzed each other. This was most helpful and all three of us did well in all of our courses.

The year continued and during the third trimester we started the course in physiology. The professor, Dr. Charles Morgan, was a very nice man but a poor lecturer and the course was second rate, except for one associate professor, Dr. Abraham Shane, who was an outstanding physiologist and an excellent teacher. He and I became quite well acquainted and at the end of the trimester he asked me if I would like to work in his laboratory at the Woods Hole Marine Biological Laboratories for a month during the summer. I would get no pay but room and board and could attend all the teaching sessions at the MBL without charge. Since I had nothing planned for the summer this seemed like a great idea and I accepted the invitation gratefully.

The school year came to end in mid-June. There was an early heat wave in Washington and the school was not air conditioned. The classrooms were sweltering and during the final biochemistry exam my friend Dr. Hilmer, who was proctoring the exam, told us that we could take our jackets off and loosen our ties. About ten minutes later the door opened and somebody looked in. He waved to Hilmer to join him in the hall. Three minutes later Hilmer came back in, beet red in the face, and told us that the dean ordered us to pull up our ties and put on our coats.

During the year we had one or two weekly lectures on a variety of medical subjects, including neurology, psychiatry, medicine, surgery, pediatrics and public health. It was not a particularly difficult year and I had a good time with my friends but I was very glad that it was over and was looking forward to my summer in Woods Hole.

At the southern tip of Cape Cod off the Massachusetts coast, Woods Hole is a small village with extensive waterfront properties and a smaller area of moderately priced homes. Its claim to fame rests on the fact that it is not only the ferry terminal to Martha's Vineyard and Nantucket but also houses two major and important research facilities. One of these is the Marine Biological Laboratory and the other one is the Oceanographic Institute. The latter was at that time federally sponsored and engaged in research and exploration along the North Atlantic Coast. It was the sister institution of the Oceanographic Institute on the Pacific Coast in California.

The Marine Biological Laboratory, usually referred to as the MBL, was a unique institution. It was a large three story building housing about twenty or thirty laboratories of different sizes. These were made available to research scientists from academic institutions who wished to spend their summers doing research under ideal circumstances and surrounded by other scientists of generally similar interests. In addition to these there was also a teaching program and a very high level physiology course was offered to carefully selected undergraduate and graduate students from a large number of universities. The course was not cheap. It was an outstanding educational program and as a worker in one of the MBL laboratories I was allowed to attend the course without having to pay for it. With Dr. Shane's permission I attended many of the lectures and during the four weeks of the course the eight or ten lecturers included three Nobel Prize winners.

My work in the laboratory consisted primarily of maintaining and cleaning the equipment, obtaining the animal specimens that Dr. Shane was working on and dissecting out the nerves that he needed for his studies. The two species we used were a type of crab and squids. It was my job to get the long leg nerves from the crabs and suspend them in a liquid medium for Shane to work on. The work on the crabs was relatively simple but the work on the squids was far from it. It was my job to dissect the giant axon of the squid, a large nerve running along the fins, covered by a sheet and surrounded within the sheet by a liquid. The dissection was not easy and the smallest nick in the membrane ruined the specimen. It took me a while to learn it but Shane was very patient; when he got the dissected giant axon he suspended it between electrodes and then recorded the impulses traveling along the axon in a variety of pharmacologic environments. I found it fascinating work and learned quite a bit both from Shane and even more so from the lectures that I was allowed to attend. Another very nice feature of the MBL was that all the laboratories were open to other investigators and to their assistants. This meant that I could visit any laboratory, introduce myself and ask what they were working on. In all instances I was always received cordially and was told about the work. It was a unique experience to meet all those nationally and internationally famous scientists and chat with them as though I were an equal.

The living conditions that year were rather primitive. I had a room in a small house and the owners were not particularly friendly. They never asked me to a meal or to sit with them for a chat. We were courteous to each other but had essentially nothing whatever in common. I ate most of my meals at the MBL dining room since this was included in the arrangement I had with Shane. The food was simple but good and I had no complaints. It was there, incidentally, that I became acquainted with cranberry juice that I never had before.

My work in the laboratory came to an end at about three o'clock in the afternoon and then I was free until the next morning. I found a small golf course nearby where as an MBL person I was allowed to play for a nominal fee. I had no clubs so that I drove down to Providence one Saturday and bought a basic set consisting of six clubs and a small bag. One of the nicest features of being on Cape Cod in the summer was that there were numerous summer theater performances within easy reach of Woods Hole. The performances were excellent and I saw a number of musical comedies and plays for next to nothing. Student tickets were fifty cents or one dollar. Another nice feature of the first summer at Woods Hole was that I met a very attractive young lady, Anne Powers, who was a student in the MBL physiology course. She came from Chicago but told me that her family was moving to Northern Virginia in the autumn and that she would transfer from Northwestern to the University of Virginia. I was quite smitten with Anne and we became good friends, going for walks in the evening and attending a number of plays together. All in all it was a splendid summer and I was sorry when August came around and it was time to get back to school.

The second year at Georgetown was a mix of the excellent and the abominable. The main courses were pharmacology, pathology, microbiology and preventive medicine–public health. In the second half of the year we started our clinical visits and had lectures in most of the major medical disciplines. Pharmacology was a very good course. The department was headed by Dr. Theodore Koppányi, a Hungarian scientist of major standing, who knew my family and had been a regular guest at our house. He also had a very good staff with whom I became very friendly and for one of whom, Dr. Alexander Karczmar, I did some library research. Pathology was also an excellent course. Dr. Charles Geschickter was not only an excellent teacher but also a renowned scientist and the author of a classic textbook of pathology.

Very far, at the other end of the scale of quality, stood microbiology, which was probably the worst course of my entire medical education. The chairman, Dr. Mollari, might have been a good microbiologist at one time but he was a terrible lecturer who spent most of the time on trivia and whose accent was so heavy that he was difficult to understand. It was during one of his lectures that I decided that I could not possibly stay at Georgetown, a school which tolerated that level of instruction. Preventive medicine and public health were taught by Dr. Mollari's son-in-law, a far better teacher than Mollari, but who also spent an inordinate amount of time on trivia. I planned to apply to Harvard for a transfer into the third year when I found out that Dean McNally had instituted a policy according to which any student who applied for a transfer to another school and was not accepted was automatically dismissed from Georgetown. I still wrote to Harvard and asked to be sent the necessary application forms for a transfer. When they came I found that they required a recommendation from the dean or from the registrar. I happened to know the registrar and understood that he was not a great fan of McNally's, so I told him that I was considering an application to transfer to Harvard but that I needed a letter of recommendation from him. I further asked him to make sure that this information would not reach the dean; I could not afford to be dismissed from Georgetown if I was not accepted at Harvard. He assured me that he would be pleased to do this. I trusted him and went ahead with my application.

That was sometime in the late autumn and shortly before Christmas I received a letter from Harvard telling me that I had to have an interview with a member of the Harvard Medical School Admission Committee who was in practice in Washington. I made an appointment and had a very satisfactory interview with a distinguished surgeon who asked me many questions about my background and education and who could not have been nicer or more courteous. In April I received a telegram from HMS informing me that they were pleased to approve my application and that if I finished the current academic year successfully I would be admitted to the third year at HMS in September. I still remember the joy I felt when I read this telegram and immediately sat down, as instructed, to respond to the telegram and indicate my intention to become a student at the HMS. I obviously told my family but I did not tell anybody else because I did not want this to become public knowledge at Georgetown. Eventually I did tell Dr. Koppányi and he later told me that when the dean found out that I was leaving he raised a substantial fuss at a faculty meeting.

The introduction to the clinical teaching facilities in the Washington area where Georgetown medical students received their clinical instruction was both interesting and enjoyable. In small groups we visited these clinical facilities where we were shown around, had teaching sessions with the clinicians and made rounds on the wards. In this way I became acquainted with the Naval Medical Center, with Walter Reed Army General Hospital, with the NIH hospital, with the VA hospital, the enormous District of Columbia Gallinger Municipal Hospital and several private hospitals.

These visits were the highlight of my stay at Georgetown and were an excellent introduction to clinical medicine. The physicians we met on these visits were all not only outstanding practitioners but also experienced and thoughtful teachers who enjoyed meeting with us and introducing us to what the practice of medicine really was all about.

We spent some time at Gallinger and were offered the opportunity of spending a night in the emergency room as an observer. Some of us took advantage of this offer and I spent two nights in the emergency room from about seven p.m. on Saturday evening until seven a.m. Sunday. These were fascinating experiences and I saw certain aspects of urban life that I had not known existed. The ER was very busy and I was put to work transporting patients and was also given my first opportunity to insert some sutures in people who were so drunk that they could not have cared less what happened to them or who was doing anything to or for them. I also talked for some time with the police sergeant in charge of the Gallinger detail. He told me a number of fascinating stories about some of the problems he and his staff became embroiled in.

The only other major educational event was taking Part One of the National Boards Examination which was a requirement at Georgetown. The exam lasted three whole days and covered all the basic sciences, anatomy, physiology, pharmacology, pathology, microbiology and biochemistry. The exams were three hours each and all, except pharmacology, were essays. This was the first year in the history of the boards that any exam was offered in a multiple choice, short answer format. Within two or three years all of the board exams were of this type which made a considerable difference to those taking them. I did well on the exams and was told that I had the second-best total grades in my class.

Dr. Shane again invited me to come to Woods Hole and work with him during the summer. I accepted but told him that I could stay only for a month because there was something else I had to do during the summer prior to going to Boston. This was agreeable to him and so I planned to drive to Woods Hole about the middle of June. I could not stay longer in Woods Hole because my parents wanted to go to Calgary again and I was only too happy to accommodate them.

There had been some major changes in the family over the past months. My brother György had arrived with his second wife, Mária, her parents and her daughter Angelica. Puppa also had arrived some weeks before and Aladár's job with the Voice of America had moved to New York City so part of the family – my parents and Puppa – were moving to Scarsdale, New York. My brother and his family continued to live in the house in Chevy Chase. György had decided to go into the hotel business and was taking a brief introductory course prior to his apprenticeship at the Mayflower Hotel in Washington. In due time he made a fine career in hotel management. Possessed of an easy charm, he had a personal elegance in both appearance and demeanor. Superb with guests he became an outstanding manager of people. He was president of hotels in Washington, New York and London and the Plaza in New York. Puppa took a two-year course in laboratory technology and worked in New York City for a doctor. When Aladár retired from the Voice of America, the family returned to Washington to live. At that time Puppa began working at the Suburban Hospital in Bethesda and later for a group of doctors where she stayed until her retirement.

About the middle of July I met my parents in Providence, Rhode Island and we drove north from there into Canada. We headed west and then took an overnight ferry the length of Lake Superior. It was a beautiful day and we enjoyed it very much. About thirty miles from Lake Superior I lost control of the car on a sharp bend and we ended up in the ditch. We were all okay but I could not get the car out of the ditch and so hitch-hiked with a nice Canadian couple to the next town some twenty miles away to get a tow truck to get the car out. Fortunately a couple of hours later we were back on the road again. We stopped in Winnipeg and Regina and then reached Alberta, stopping at Medicine Hat. Father had not been feeling well for a day and became quite sick with an elevated temperature. We did not know anybody in Medicine Hat so, with Calgary being only about four hours away, we decided to proceed and got to our friendly Royal York Hotel by mid afternoon. We called Princess Obolensky who recommended a physician. The doctor was a very nice and very competent general practitioner who came to the hotel, examined Father and made the diagnosis of an influenza-like viral infection. He thought that it would take three or four days of rest for Father to recover and that it would be good to stay at the hotel. After a few days when he was feeling quite well we went up to Banff for a few days. Although he was better, he was still tired and weakened so we decided that he should not ride back to New York but that he and Mother would stay in Banff for another two or three days, then spend a few days in Calgary and fly home from there. Mother decided that I should not drive home alone and called Puppa to come to Calgary and drive home with me. We got to Scarsdale in about five or six days. I was impressed with the house the family had found. Large, with a nice garden and some trees, it was convenient to the Scarsdale train station that Aladár used every day on his trip to New York City and the VOA. Since all my things was still in Chevy Chase I drove down there, spent a couple of days with György and Mária, packed up my belongings and departed to start my third year of medical school at HMS.

In Boston I found my way, with some difficulty, to the Medical School complex which included Vanderbilt Hall, the Medical School dormitory, where my room was. Small but adequate it had a bed, a desk, a couple of chairs and a dresser. The window overlooked the small circle where the main entrance was located. I also had a view of the medical school buildings and of the Lying-in Hospital. The bathroom was down the hall and reminded me of my days in basic training in San Antonio. We had our meals in the dining hall and the food was quite good albeit you could tell the day of the week by what was on the menu for dinner. My next door neighbor at Vanderbilt Hall was Philip Bromberg one of the brightest men in the class who became a good friend. He was a champion chess player and of the many games we played I won only one and tied two or three. Phil eventually made a very fine career in pulmonary medicine as a professor at Ohio State University. I had a number of other friends at Vanderbilt Hall and it did not take me very long to realize that while at Georgetown I was probably among the smartest in the class, here at HMS I was at best average with a number of classmates both smarter and more knowledgeable than I.

The next day the class met with the dean of HMS. There were about thirty transfer students, many of them from North Carolina, South Carolina and Georgia because at that time those states only had two-year medical schools. The Dean welcomed us warmly, stated that HMS was pleased to have us and would do everything in its power to make our stay both pleasant and successful. He assured us that we would all graduate, that nobody would flunk out and that if we had any problem, educational or financial, to be sure to come to the deanery for advice and assistance. I was stunned by the difference between this welcome and the one at Georgetown and realized that coming up here was probably the smartest thing I had ever done and even now, sixty years later, I still believe that to be true.

The class was divided into groups which were assigned in rotation to the HMS teaching hospitals for the various major disciplines. I was assigned to the Massachusetts General

Hospital for surgery and to the Boston City Hospital for medicine. OB-Gyn was taught at the Lying-in Hospital and pediatrics at the Children's Hospital. The last two facilities were across the street from Vanderbilt Hall which made it most convenient. Teaching in all of these hospitals was excellent and there were plenty of patients for us to work with. We also had a series of excellent lectures which were given first thing in the morning at one of the medical school buildings. It was after these lectures that we went to our various clinical assignments.

Life in Vanderbilt Hall continued to be pleasant. There were a number of clubs and groups and I joined one that was known as Argo. We had some social activities but most of the time we just played cards. Bridge and poker prevailed but I also had a couple of cribbage partners. Needless to say the card playing was for money although the stakes were low and nobody got hurt. Boston also offered numerous other opportunities for entertainment and instruction and I attended Boston Symphony concerts, visited the museums and spent considerable time and money in the numerous used book stores.

✻

I was having lunch with two classmates in the cafeteria of the Boston Lying-in Hospital one day in October, 1951, when a young nurse walked by. I asked my classmates if they knew her. When they said that they did not, I told them to take a good look at her because I was going to marry that girl. I know this sounds unlikely but actually it happens to be true.

I was working in the afternoons in the blood bank of the Lying-in for a very low salary but enjoyed it and learned a lot about typing blood, drawing blood and handling the required paperwork. Two or three days after I had seen her for the first time in the cafeteria, the young nurse came to the blood bank to get a pint of blood for a patient. I introduced myself and found out that her name was Helen Pickert, that she was from Wisconsin and that she was there for a post-graduate course in obstetrical nursing prior to becoming one of the head-nurses at a hospital in Milwaukee where she had trained. She asked me if I would type her blood for her sometime later that afternoon when she came off service. Needless to say I was very pleased. When she came back I typed her blood and we chatted for some time. She came to the blood bank several times over the next couple of weeks. About the middle of November I asked her if she would consider having dinner with me on Thanksgiving Day and going to a play. Much to my surprise and delight she agreed.

The evening was a huge success. I took her a bouquet of six red carnations and waited in the lobby of the nursing residence for Helen to appear. She was about ten minutes late but apologized profusely and we went out to have a very pleasant dinner at an Italian restaurant and then to a play that had its pre-Broadway try-outs in Boston. The play was not very good and, in fact, never made it to New York, but the evening was a huge success. When we got back to the hospital I asked her very hesitantly whether I might kiss her and when she nodded I kissed her very gently and with my heart in my boots. To make a long story short, this evening was the beginning of a relationship that, after some ups and downs did not come to an end until her death in 1996. We were together most evenings and in February, 1952, when she was recovering from a severe cold, I went to see her and, literally going down on one knee, asked her to marry me. Much to my delight she said yes and I put my signet ring on her finger to serve as our pledge until I could buy a more traditional engagement ring.

Helen's father, John Pickert, had died several years earlier and so she called her mother to inform her about this great event. Mrs. Pickert was very pleased and said that she would fly to Boston in a few days to meet me. I called my parents in

Scarsdale and told them about my engagement. They were pleased for me and came to Boston a week later to meet Helen. She was very nervous about meeting them but the evening was a great success and my parents became very fond of her, a relationship that lasted until their death.

A couple of weeks later Helen's mother, Lena, came to Boston to meet me. We met her at the airport and she and I established a good relationship. She was a registered nurse and was still doing some private duty nursing in Berlin, Wisconsin where she lived and where Helen was born. Her parents and her brother had migrated from Iceland to the United States when Lena was a baby. They settled on Washington Island, on the Wisconsin side of Lake Michigan, the home of the largest Icelandic settlement in the United States. A very simple person of average intelligence, little education and very little interest in any cultural activities, she was very conservative politically and she and I stood at the opposite poles of the political spectrum. She was a thoroughly honest and decent person and in spite of the differences betweens us, she and I were good friends and liked and respected each other.

Helen's brother Jack was a different matter. He had a difficult adolescence and joined the Marine Corps on the day after his seventeenth birthday, after having graduated from the Berlin high school. Shortly after his basic training his unit was sent to Korea and became involved both in the advance into North Korea and also in the winter retreat under continuous battle conditions with the advancing Chinese army. In one of the skirmishes Jack suffered a wound in his hand and was sent first to Japan for corrective surgery and recovery and then back to the United States. He was discharged in the autumn of 1951 and lived at home at the time when Helen and I became engaged. I think that he disapproved of me partly because of my foreign background and also because of my level of education. When we eventually met he slowly warmed up toward me but while we were very cordial to each other we never developed a truly close relationship. Jack was not very bright, was very opinionated and politically stood just a little to the right of Genghis Khan.

While his mother wanted him to get a college education, Jack wanted to become a forest ranger; Lena wanted him to have a more "intellectual" career. She heard about an outfit in Chicago that performed extensive testing on young people to determine the career for which they were the most suitable. Accordingly, Jack went to Chicago, underwent extensive testing and was informed that his best career choice was chemical engineering. He matriculated at the University of Wisconsin in Madison to work for a degree in chemical engineering. Needless to say, this was a total fiasco and, in fact, he had to drop out of the program toward the end of the second year.

Helen and I were living in Madison at the time and I was starting my residency in anesthesiology at the University of Wisconsin Medical School. We saw Jack fairly often and when he had to drop out of school he came to us for advice. We suggested that he should do what he wanted to do in the first place and get a bachelor's degree in forest and wildlife management. His mother was not very happy but eventually agreed and Jack went to the University of Wisconsin branch in Stephen's Point where they had a suitable program. He did well and after he obtained his degree he worked for the Wisconsin Department of Natural Resources as a ranger for many years.

Helen also had a much older sister, Doris, the daughter of John Pickert's first wife who died very shortly after Doris was born. Doris and Lena thoroughly disliked each other and the relationship between Doris and Helen was a friendly one but without any major emotional involvement on either side. I liked Doris. She was very bright and had an interesting job at the Institute of Paper Chemistry in Appleton, Wisconsin. After some years she moved to Palo Alto, California, got married and eventually died there. She and her husband came to see us on several occasions and the relationship between the two sisters ultimately became a very affectionate one.

After Helen and I became engaged we were fortunate to have the strong support of both Helen's mother and my parents. We spent all free moments together until her training program came to an end at the end of March and she had to go back to Milwaukee to the Hospital that sponsored her postgraduate training. She explained to the people in Milwaukee that she had become engaged and would not be able to continue to work for them. They were very understanding and allowed her to resign after about a month. She then returned to Boston where, in the mean time, I had rented a small furnished apartment, very close to the Medical School and to three of the major teaching hospitals. She stayed there for two weeks and we had a grand time anticipating the pleasures of married life.

Helen went home to Berlin to prepare for the wedding. I had to work through June and then planned to drive to Berlin with the wedding scheduled for the latter part of July. Everything went according to schedule. I drove out there and we had a very nice time including a delightful trip to Washington Island where Lena had grown up and where she still had many friends. In fact, she still owned her father's farm and we stayed there with the people who were renting the farm and were quite successfully operating it.

The wedding was a very nice affair. Lena organized it beautifully and generously. In the presence of all of both families we were married in the Congregational Church in Berlin by the Reverend Mr. Sneezby, an elderly and very nice Britisher who had lived in Berlin for many years. My best man was my brother György and Helen was given away by her brother Jack. The wedding luncheon, attended by about thirty-two people was held in a lovely restaurant on Green Lake and shortly after the end of the luncheon we departed for our honeymoon at Lake Louise in the Canadian Rockies. After a three-day drive we arrived at the Chateau Lake Louise and had a wonderful time exploring the mountains, taking long walks and enjoying each other's company. The hotel was excellent and our room looked out over Lake Louise to the peaks across the lake. In the mean time my parents and Puppa had arrived at the Banff Springs Hotel in Banff so when we started our drive back to Wisconsin we stopped for a day there and had a very pleasant visit with the folks. The drive to Wisconsin was uneventful albeit long and tedious. Fortunately traffic was relatively light and we made reasonably good time.

We stayed in Berlin only for a couple of days and then departed for Boston where my last year at Harvard was about to begin. Arriving there we settled into our apartment on the Riverway. Helen contacted a very nice obstetrician, Dr. Kirkwood, whom she had met when she was working at the Lying-in Hospital. Fortunately this man and his partner were actually looking for an office nurse and, having been impressed by Helen, immediately offered her the job. She was pleased to accept and started working the next Monday.

I started my fourth year a few days later with a rotation on surgery at the Beth Israel Hospital which was only a block away from our apartment. It was not considered, at that time, to be one of the best surgical rotations at HMS but I was not interested in becoming a surgeon and was pleased to have a somewhat less demanding rotation so close to home. My next rotation was also at the BI, this time in Medicine. Contrary to surgery, this was an excellent rotation and I spent the next two months working hard and learning a great deal. The practice of medicine was changing rapidly and I was among the first ones to attend a patient who was given steroids. This important and exciting substance had just been introduced at the Mayo Clinic and was instrumental in changing the prognosis for very many patients with a variety of illnesses. I well remember being asked to sit up with a patient all night while an infusion of a steroid solution was dripping slowly into his vein. It was my job to make sure that the IV remained open and that the infusion proceeded smoothly. I must have done reasonably well because when I told one my instructors that I was going into anesthesiology he was appalled and told me to change my mind and go into internal medicine. He said he could guarantee me a good internship and residency and that I should not, "throw away my life".

My next rotation was on Pediatrics at the Children's Hospital which was only a short walk from where we lived. I did not particularly enjoy that rotation. The Children's Hospital was clearly an excellent facility but most of the patients I had to deal with had some severe congenital disorder, cardiac or neurological, about which nothing could be done at that time. The weekly clinical conferences were also of little practical interest because the cases discussed were extremely complex and usually only a handful had ever been reported in the literature.

Christmas came and we went to Scarsdale to spend it with my family and also celebrate my father's birthday on December thirtieth. As we had discovered a couple of months earlier Helen was pregnant but was still working at the obstetrical office enjoying her work very much. Our life was very pleasant. Her cooking skills, which were vestigial first, rapidly improved and we had a lot of fun working together in the tiny kitchen of our apartment. We also had a number of friends, classmates from the Medical School and young Francis Nagy and his charming American wife. Francis, a student at MIT, was the son of the last Hungarian Prime Minister prior to the Communist takeover who had received asylum in the United States with his family. We decided to celebrate Thanksgiving at our apartment. Neither Helen nor I had ever fixed a turkey before and this first Thanksgiving became an interesting experience. On the day before the event I went to the local supermarket to buy the turkey. I stood before a giant cooler bin that must have held a hundred turkeys. I had no idea what to look for and therefore approached a very nice looking middle aged lady and asked her if she would recommend a bird for me. She said that she would be happy to help me and only asked how many of us would share the meal. When I told her that there would be just four of us she looked at some birds and then pointed to one saying: "That is the one". I thanked her profusely, took the bird, bought stuffing mix and cranberry preserves and returned to the apartment. That evening I unwrapped the turkey and found much to my dismay that it was not cleaned properly at all and that there were still numerous little quills sticking out from the skin. I spent the next hour laboriously removing all these bits with eyebrow tweezers, thinking unkind thoughts about the lady who picked it out for me.

The stove in our tiny kitchen did not have a temperature gauge, only a dial without any markings. We did have a meat thermometer, however, and thus we put the bird in the oven at about ten o'clock setting the temperature gauge at about half. Much to our dismay the meat thermometer indicated that the bird was done about one o'clock with the Nagys scheduled to come at five. They did not have a telephone so that I got into my car and drove over to Cambridge to ask them to come right away which they did and actually we had a good meal and a very pleasant afternoon.

My clinical responsibilities came to an end in December. In January, 1953, I started on a four-month elective rotation in the Department of Pharmacology. The department was under the chairmanship of Dr. Otto Krayer. He had been a professor at a German university but left when Hitler came to power and was the professor at HMS for several years. An outstanding pharmacologist, he had an international reputation. He was also a typical German *Herr Professor*, courteous but very formal. You could not just go and talk to him, you had to talk to his secretary who then entered his office and asked him if he would see you. He almost always said yes and was always very helpful in answering questions. I started on a research problem that he suggested and I was working a number of hours every day making reasonable, albeit slow progress. I well remember that once I thought that I had a brilliant idea and asked to see him. He listened very carefully to my presentation and when I came to the end he said that this was a very nice idea but if I were to consult the July, 1913, issue of the German Journal of Pharmacology I would find that somebody had already had the same idea and had done all the research on it. I left the office very quietly.

One of the young faculty members in the department was Peter Dews, a British pharmacologist who was assigned to be my mentor. He was an extraordinarily bright, knowledgeable and nice chap who was not much older than I. We became good friends and he not only helped me with my work but also let me work with him. He later had a distinguished career at the National Institutes of Health. By the time the fourth month of my rotation came to an end my project was not complete but Dr. Krayer was very satisfied with my work and said that one of his teaching assistants would continue the work after I had left.

The personal events confronting us at this time were the announcement of the results of the intern matching program, my final exam and Helen's forthcoming delivery. Her pregnancy had progressed smoothly and she had worked for the first seven months. Her due date was April thirtieth.

The results of the intern matching program were announced to us in the Dean's Office sometime around the tenth of April. This was the first year that the internships for all senior medical students were handled by a national matching organization instead of the previous practice where individual students did their own negotiations with the program of their choice. When we applied we were asked to rank order our choices. I listed the University of Wisconsin Medical School as my first choice because it was not only a very good program but also because Madison was only about eighty miles from Berlin and Helen's mother. The day the results were announced all of us seniors gathered rather nervously in the Dean's Office where we were given the envelope containing the match. I was fortunate in getting my first choice as did most of my classmates. There were only three of us who did not get matched with any of their choices and who now could make their own arrangements. As it turned out all three of them were able to get very good internships.

The final exam was scheduled for April twenty-sixth. It was an all-day written exam with a single, large question in the morning and four questions in the afternoon of which we had to pick three. I do not remember the afternoon questions but I well remember the morning one. It said very simply: "Discuss tuberculosis". We had three hours to respond and I used all but a few minutes of it. It was a typical example of the excellent sense and fairness of HMS. They were testing us not only on our knowledge but also on our ability to think clearly and logically and to present our thoughts in an organized and orderly fashion. It was one the very few exams that I actually enjoyed taking.

Just thirty-six hours later Helen went into labor early on April twenty-eighth and we quickly went to the Lying-in Hospital where she was immediately admitted to the labor room. Dr. Kirkwood came a few minutes later, examined her and told me that it would be a little while and that I could go and have some breakfast in the cafeteria. When I got back to the labor area I was told that Helen had been taken to the delivery suite ten minutes earlier and it was only about another fifteen or twenty minutes before Dr. Kirkwood came out and told me that I was the father of a nice healthy little boy. The next day we moved back to the apartment. Tom was a good baby and gave us very little trouble. Helen tried to breast feed but did not have enough milk and thus we started Tom on bottle feeding with me getting up in the middle of the night. My parents and Helen's mother came out to visit and inspect the new grandchild, but only stayed for a couple of days.

Graduation from medical school was a relatively informal event held on the lawn behind the dean's office. No diplomas were issued because these were handed out only at the formal Harvard graduation in the middle of June when most of us graduating from the medical school were already making our living arrangements wherever we were going to have our internship. Helen and I attended the medical school ceremony which consisted only of a few short speeches and lasted only about fifty minutes.

On June fifth I took Helen and the baby to the airport in Boston. From there they flew to Milwaukee where some friends picked them up and drove them to the Pickert home in Berlin. I packed the car and drove to Scarsdale to spend a couple of days with my parents and Hanna's family. Helen's brother Jack came to help me drive to Wisconsin. Leaving the next day we drove to Berlin in two days. I found Helen and Tom well and then I drove down to Madison to find us an apartment. Fortunately there was a nice one in an older house about four blocks from the University Hospital and only one block from the football stadium. The house was owned by an elderly German couple who rented out the first floor and also a smaller apartment on the second floor. We took the first floor apartment consisting of two small bedrooms, a living-dining room, bathroom and kitchen. It was reasonably well furnished and, while fairly small, suited us well. The other apartment was rented to a young couple with a small baby. He was a doctoral candidate in the English Department of the University and we became good friends.

My internship began on the first of July with a meeting of all of the interns, the dean of the medical school, the director of the hospital, several professors and the chief resident. There were only eleven of us interns in contrast to the usual twenty-two. The discrepancy was apparently due to the new matching program which Wisconsin did not handle correctly. Actually this worked out well for us interns because not every department could get one each month and thus we became more valuable and more highly appreciated.

The program was known as a rotational internship which meant that during the year we spent some time in each of the major departments and also had some elective rotations. We spent three months on medicine, two months on surgery, one month each on pediatrics, obstetrics and gynecology and psychiatry and we also had three months elective time.

My first rotation was pediatrics and on the second night I was put on call which meant that I was in charge of the department. Needless to say I was terrified but fortunately did not have a single call all night. There was an elderly British nurse, Miss Wilson, who took me under her wing. Whenever I had no idea what to do I went and asked her. She never told me directly what to do but said that under similar circumstances she had seen Dr. McDonough, the professor, do such and such. I will always be grateful to her for keeping me out of trouble.

My second month was an elective one and I chose anesthesiology in order learn more about the field, become acquainted with the department and decide whether I wanted to get my specialty training in Madison. By the end of the month I decided that this was indeed the specialty for me, that I liked the department and both liked and respected the chairman, Dr. Sidney Orth.

I then had two months of surgery, followed by three months of internal medicine. The medicine rotation was particularly good and I was fortunate to have the Dean, Dr. William Middleton, as my chief for two of the three months. He was a truly remarkable person. Not only an excellent diagnostician, he was also a fine teacher. His distinguished career in the military was capped by being appointed general in charge of the medical services in the European Theater of Operations during the Second World War. Referred to at Wisconsin as "the general" he was indeed a strict disciplinarian. He called me "sergeant" and we got along extremely well.

The medicine rotation was followed by two months of electives during which I was doing research in endocrinology with the head of that division, Dr. Edward Gordon. We were working on a problem involving the thyroid gland and it was my job to get a considerable number of such glands from the local slaughterhouse. I had never been in such an establishment and found it a most interesting experience. Literally hundreds of cattle were killed and processed every day and I was allowed to observe and then to collect a sizable number of beef thyroids for our research program. When I saw that federal food inspectors, standing along each slaughtered animal, condemned an occasional one because of some pathology, often a minor one, I asked the man who was in charge of me if the condemned animals would be used for dog food. He laughed and said, "No Way! Dog food has to meet the same requirements as people food only it comes from different parts of the animal. You may not know it but much of the dog food is consumed by people who can not afford regular meat." I was stunned.

After my two very pleasant months with Dr. Gordon I had one good and instructive month on obstetrics and gynecology followed by the last month of my internship on psychiatry. I had little interest in this area but the professor and the staff were pleasant and I actually had a good time. It was also about June first that I took the second part of the national boards. This entailed three full days but by this time all exams were of the multiple choice type which made them considerably easier.

During this year there were some changes in my family life as well. Tom was developing well and was a good baby. Helen had made arrangements with the people who lived upstairs to look after him while she went back to work on a part-time basis in the office of one of the senior obstetricians, Dr. Campbell. In the autumn she realized that she was pregnant again but continued to work for another couple of months. The second baby was due to be born sometime at the end of June but on June eighth, very early in the morning, she went into premature labor. I rushed her to the hospital where the senior obstetrical resident examined her, found her to be ready for immediate delivery, called her obstetrician and placed her on the delivery table. I was standing at the head of the table and administered some very light anesthesia while the resident delivered our second boy. It was at this time that both the obstetrician and the anesthesiologist arrived so that I could go and sit down and try to recover my equanimity.

As it turned out the baby, to be called Jim, was about four weeks premature and developed respiratory distress syndrome. The professor of pediatrics who looked after Jim told us that there was little chance for the baby's survival. Consequently we decided to have the baby baptized by the minister of the Congregational church that Helen and I attended most Sundays. The reverend came quickly and baptized the baby who was in a neonatal incubator struggling with every breath. Much to everybody's amazement within a few hours after the baptism the baby seemed to improve and thereafter continued to improve so that after about ten days we could take him home. Whether this was a case of *post hoc propter hoc* or not is not for me to say.

Jim was still a problem and required a great deal of care. With Tom being only fourteen months old Helen had her hands full. I was still finishing the last month of my internship, but psychiatry was not very demanding and I could be home in the evening, at night and during the week end. Fortunately Jim continued to improve slowly and Tom was a good kid who caused few problems other than his refusal to take naps.

Two events that had taken place somewhat earlier deserve mention. The first one was that earlier during the spring I had applied for a residency position in anesthesiology and was accepted to start in July, at the termination of my internship. The second event is mentioned to show what kind of a person Dean Middleton was. There was a requirement in teaching hospitals that interns were to get as many permissions for autopsies as possible. Wisconsin considered this an important matter because autopsies and the precise determination of the cause of death they provided were important from both an educational perspective and also because nationally one of the measures of the quality of a teaching hospital was the percentage of autopsies performed. This requirement presented the intern with a delicate problem – how to persuade the family of a deceased patient to permit the procedure. To encourage our efforts three prizes were awarded in the amount fifty, twenty-five and ten dollars. Toward the middle of June Dr. Middleton called me to his office and told me that I had come in second in the autopsy competition and handed me a check. He also asked how my son was progressing and expressed his hopes for Jim's continued improvement. I thanked him for his concern and for the check and left his office. When I looked at the folded check I found that there were two checks folded together. One for twenty-five dollars from the school for my autopsy win and another one, a personal check from Dr. Middleton for thirty dollars. I immediately went back to his office to thank him. He looked at me and said,

"I have no idea what you are talking about." I said, "Thank you very much anyway Sir," and walked out, quite literally with tears in my eyes.

My residency in anesthesiology started on the first of July, 1954, and I found it challenging. There were only four first-year residents so that there was plenty of clinical material for us to benefit from. We were assigned in rotation to different surgical areas, starting with simple and short cases and eventually progressing to the more complex and difficult surgical procedures. In those days anesthesiology was still a rather uncomplicated matter. We had only three general anesthesia agents, ether, cyclopropane and nitrous oxide. The first two were highly flammable and explosive so that elaborate safety procedures had to be rigidly enforced. Even so during the second year of my residency we had two explosions in the operating room. The first one caused little damage other than a ruptured ear drum of one of my fellow residents who was administering the anesthetic. The second one caused the death of the patient who was the wife of one of the representatives in the Wisconsin legislature. This caused considerable turmoil, with formal investigations and the calling in of nationally famous consultants. It took quite a while for normal activities to resume. Fortunately I was not involved in either case with both of them happening in the operating room next to the one I was working in.

In the department there were four second-year residents and five faculty members each of whom was an experienced, board-certified anesthesiologist. The faculty enjoyed teaching and was very skilled in introducing us beginners into the mysteries of our chosen specialty. The load was surprisingly light. We worked from seven thirty until about three with breaks for coffee and lunch. We then had to see the patients scheduled for surgery the following day and we usually got home by five o'clock. Night call came about once a week but was not a problem. The charter of the University Hospital stated that all patients admitted to the hospital had to be referred by a licensed Wisconsin physician. This meant that we had practically no emergency work all ambulance cases going to one of the other two hospitals in town. The only emergencies we had were the in-house ones which fortunately occurred only rarely. I think that during my two years as a resident I had to do only three or four cases at night when I was on call. My salary during the first year was fifty dollars per month which was raised by the department to one hundred. During the second year my salary rose to seventy-five dollars and this was again doubled by the department.

During the second year of my residency I spent three months at the U.S. Veterans Administration Hospital which at that time was restricted to patients with tuberculosis. Consequently most of the surgical cases involved pulmonary surgery which, in 1955-56, was still the primary therapeutic modality for this disease. I thoroughly enjoyed my time at the VA and giving anesthesia for thoracic surgery remained my principal area of expertise for the next forty years. The only curious thing about working at the VA was that I had to serve as the officer of the day every four or five days. This meant that I was the only physician in the hospital over night. Luck was with me and I never had any serious trouble. In fact I spent most of my evenings playing cribbage with the head guard.

It was in the autumn of my first year as a resident when I had to apply for a license to practice medicine in Wisconsin. I took the exam in November and passed it expecting to get my license within a few weeks. At that time the secretary general of the Wisconsin Board of Medicine was an elderly woman whose principal aim in life seemed to be to keep as many people from practicing medicine in Wisconsin as possible. When I had not received my license within a reasonable period of time I called the board office and was told that my application was not complete because I did not have a certificate of having completed high school in Hungary. I immediately went to the board office and spoke to the woman, telling her that I had completed eight years of middle and high school in Hungary but that I had graduated from college and medical school in the United States and could not understand what it was that was wanted. She informed me rather curtly that unless I could document my high school attendance in Hungary she would refuse to issue a license for me to practice in Wisconsin. Fortunately I did have a document that certified my eight years of attendance at the Piarist Gimnázium in Budapest. It was in Hungarian and I had to have it translated and then I had to have the translation certified and notarized. I took this document to the board office and eventually did get my license.

The two years of the residency passed surprisingly quickly and in the spring of the second year Dr. Orth asked me if I would like to continue in the department with a faculty appointment as an instructor. Helen and I enjoyed our life in Madison and therefore I thanked Dr. Orth for the offer and gratefully accepted the appointment to start on the first of July, 1956. My university salary was three hundred fifty dollars a month but this was also doubled from departmental funds. With seven hundred dollars a month we could get by modestly but quite well and we no longer needed as much additional support from my parents.

One of the major events in our family life during these two years was that we bought a house. An older house, it was in good condition and it had an attached garage and a small, fenced back yard. There were three bedrooms and one bath. The house was only a little over one mile from the University Hospital and even closer to the VA. My wife drove me to work on many mornings and I walked home in the afternoon. Tom and Jim continued to progress well. Tom was still a sleeping problem and Jim was a very fussy eater which caused Helen considerable concern. She became pregnant again and delivered, early in March 1956, a full-term, healthy little girl whom we named Anne.

July, 1956, was the beginning of my professional academic career which came to an end forty years later. There were only four other faculty members in the department at that time with my being the most junior. With true collegial spirit we were able to work together and meet our teaching and research responsibilities without any friction. I started my research at Wisconsin with a major review paper of the pulmonary surgery procedures performed at the hospital which had begun there about ten years earlier. In the review of several hundred cases I used an IBM machine to sort the cases on a wide variety of statistical bases. It was a laborious process involving a good many hours of standing by that voracious machine that occasionally shredded and ate my cards. When the paper was finished it was immediately accepted for publication being by far the largest review of pulmonary surgery cases in the United States. I also began to do some research with analgesic drugs. This work later became a major activity for me.

Dean Middleton retired and the new dean had his own agenda. His strong ideas about making changes in the medical school and hospital first made the relationship between him and the clinical chairmen difficult and then frankly hostile. Dr. Orth was furious and advised me to make a move because he did not think that the dean would allow him to pay half of my salary. Just by chance within a week Dr. Orth received an inquiry from Dr. Peter Safar, the chairman of the department of anesthesiology at the Baltimore City Hospital (BCH), asking if he knew of any young, well-trained anesthesiologist who would be interested in becoming an assistant chairman in his department. I went to Baltimore to be interviewed by Dr. Safar and he offered me the job that I was pleased to accept. It did mean a move with the family which by the then had grown to three children and one on the way but the job was very appealing in that it made me a junior faculty member both at the Johns Hopkins University and the University of Maryland. An additional feature was that because Baltimore was so near to Washington we would be much closer to my family that I had seen only a few times during the past three years. Our fourth child, another little girl, Christine, was born in July, 1957, just five weeks prior to our departure for Baltimore.

We took the three older children to the airport in Madison and arranged for them to be flown directly to Washington where my parents picked them up at the airport. In those days the airlines were most helpful in such cases and a flight attendant took excellent care of the children who were five, four and two years old at the time. A few days later Helen, baby Christine and I left Madison by car and with a stop over night somewhere in Indiana drove to Washington the next day. The house on Patterson Street was large enough to accommodate all of us for a short while.

Helen and I drove to Baltimore where a real-estate agent showed us an adequate albeit not very attractive house that was for rent by its owner. A senior faculty member at the University of Maryland, he was on sabbatical leave in Europe. We took the lease and moved within a few days. Soon after we moved I started to work at BCH.

※

Work at the City Hospital was pleasant. The anesthesiology department consisted of three faculty members, one fellow and six residents. We had to cover obstetrics and four operating rooms. Obstetrics was a busy service but the load in the operating rooms was moderate and we usually finished by three o'clock. The staff took call in rotation but we could take call from home and went in only for the fortunately relatively infrequent emergencies.

During the first few days of my attendance I met with Dr. Don Benson, the chairman of the department of anesthesiology at the Johns Hopkins Medical School, and with Dr. Martin Helrich, the chairman of the department at the University of Maryland School of Medicine. I was granted a faculty appointment by both schools as an instructor. I spent Mondays at the University of Maryland Hospital. It was an excellent rotation. The Hopkins rotation was not quite so pleasant and I spent very little time there. The department was staffed almost entirely by nurse anesthetists some of whom found it difficult to accept a physician anesthesiologist. However, Dr. Benson, and I became good friends. His tenure was not an easy one. Having been trained at Chicago, he was happy to return there sometime later.

Shortly after I started working at BCH I was put in charge of obstetrical anesthesia where I was struck by the difference in the patient population between Baltimore and what I was used to in Wisconsin. In Madison we could have two or three women in labor simultaneously but, other than a few moans, you heard nothing. It was very different in Baltimore – with only one patient in the delivery room there could be a lot of noise.

I soon became involved in research and was very fortunate indeed to be under the guidance of Dr. Louis Lasagna, the head of the clinical pharmacology research group at Hopkins. He was not only a nationally respected scientist and scholar but also an extraordinarily nice person. Together we devised a program of clinical research with analgesics and he helped me obtain very generous grants from the National Analgesics Research Foundation and also from a number of pharmaceutical companies in exchange for providing them with the results of our clinical investigations. The numerous papers that were published on the results of these investigations added a lot of weight to my résumé.

One of the studies raised considerable interest. We compared the effectiveness of four widely advertised aspirins available without prescription in any drugstore. They varied in price and at least two of them claimed that they were more effective in pain control than any of the others. We bought the aspirins in bottles of one hundred pills from several drugstores. We then repackaged them, coded them and had two technicians administer them to patients who complained of headaches or other painful discomforts. Much as we expected there was no difference between any of the compounds we compared: the least expensive being just as effective as the most expensive. The one unexpected finding was that the least expensive brand did not have one hundred pills in any of the hundred-pill bottles. The number varied from ninety-two to ninety-five.

It was because of this work that I was invited to Vienna in the spring of 1962 to chair a session at an international congress on pain and pain relief. I was happy to accept and with Helen flew to Vienna. It was her first visit to Europe and my first one since 1945. We had a wonderful time in Vienna with a ball at the royal castle, a reception at the famous Vienna City Hall, a visit to the Opera and a number of very interesting scientific discussions. We then rented a car and drove to Venice, crossed Northern Italy to the French Riviera and eventually arrived in Paris. We stayed there several days and then flew back to Baltimore. While we were away my mother and my sister, Puppa, took care of our children much to their pleasure. We were also very fortunate in having met a wonderful African-American lady, Isabel Nottage, a licensed practical nurse, who now worked as a family helper to take care of children when the parents needed to be away or simply wanted a very nice person to help with the children and with the household. She was very helpful while Helen and I were in Europe.

In addition to the small but very competent staff and residents at Baltimore City Hospital we also had students both from Hopkins and the University of Maryland. In this regard our department was unique because all of the other departments were serving only one of the two medical schools. My sole difficulty was my chairman, Peter Safar. He was an Austrian who had come to the U.S. after the war and had his anesthesia training at the University of Pennsylvania. Very bright and very creative, he was a good researcher who made significant contributions to both respiratory and cardiac resuscitation. In fact, mouth-to-mouth resuscitation was largely his idea. Unfortunately he was not a good department head. A micro-manager by nature, he wanted to be involved in every detail. I remember that when he asked me to be in charge of obstetrical anesthesia and I told him that I would be pleased to take on that responsibility. I had no sooner left his office when he called me back to tell me precisely how I was to do my job. It was a great relief when a year later he became the chairman of the Department of Anesthesiology at the University of Pittsburgh. Within a couple of weeks after his departure I was appointed chairman at a salary of twenty-five thousand dollars per year. Things went along well and I had a very pleasant life both professionally at the hospital and socially at home. I enjoyed my new responsibility and the authority that went with it. The chairmanship also meant that my relationship with the University of Maryland underwent certain changes. I was promoted to assistant professor and I no longer had to spend one day each week working at the University Hospital.

One outstanding memory of the first winter in Baltimore is of a heavy snowstorm that occurred one weekend. On Monday morning, I cleaned off the car and headed for the University of Maryland Hospital. Several times I had to drive with two wheels on the sidewalk to get around cars abandoned in the street. When I arrived at the hospital I was looked at as if I had just come from Mars, "What are you doing here", they asked. "Don't you know that we are closed for anything but emergencies and that the city has told people to stay off the streets?" Okay, I thought, got back in the car, drove home and had a three-day vacation. With the help of troops from nearby Fort Meade the streets were finally cleaned and the abandoned cars removed. It seems that it was common practice for the good citizens of Baltimore to panic in the face of a storm, leave their cars right smack in the middle of the street and walk home.

In the spring of 1958 we started to look for a house to buy and were very fortunate in finding a very nice, relatively new house in a residential area called Glendale off Loch Raven Boulevard. It had three large bedrooms, a den and a playroom. There was also an attached garage and a small, terraced back yard. It was a nice neighborhood and we soon became good friends with our neighbors on both sides. They had children of the same age as ours and the kids quickly became friends and played together.

Our social activities consisted of dinners with friends and neighbors, of visits to the symphony concerts and of a monthly music evening. The latter was attended by the Safars, the Bensons and two or three other couples. Some members of the group were excellent pianists, some were singers, Helen played her flute and one member was a cellist. Later, after Helen started taking flute lessons with Britten Johnson, the first flute of the Baltimore Symphony, Mr. Johnson and his wife also attended our music evenings whenever he could.

Helen worked as a volunteer for the Women's Association of the Baltimore Symphony and it was there that she met and became friendly with Helen Hiltabidle who was also one of the volunteers. The Hiltabidles and we became good friends. They had three children a little younger than ours and we spent a fair amount of time together. One of my memories is of a Fourth of July fireworks display that we watched together sitting on blankets in a park. Both Hiltabidles were extremely bright people who were working as research analysts and computer experts; Helen was also a remarkably pretty girl whom I both liked very much and admired greatly.

My son Tom started kindergarten in the autumn of 1958 and entered first grade the next year. Jim was one year behind him. The Baltimore county schools in our area were excellent and the kids got a fine start. Anne finished kindergarten before we moved away from Baltimore.

The decision to leave Baltimore was largely due to two facts. The first one was that BCH was not really an academic institution and it was increasingly difficult to find qualified residents. The second fact was that in the autumn of 1962 Parke-Davis, the pharmaceutical company, made me an offer to become their director of clinical investigation for the U.S. and Canada. Of course I was very interested and discussed the offer with both Dr. Lasagna and Dr. Orth both of whom thought that it was a good opportunity. I accepted the position and agreed to start working for Parke-Davis in Ann Arbor, Michigan in March, 1963.

Helen and I went to Ann Arbor and bought a house only a few minutes away from the Parke-Davis offices. We had decided that we would not move the children until school ended and therefore I would be in Ann Arbor by myself until June when the whole family would move. So, at the end of February, Helen and I drove to Ann Arbor again, pulling a trailer with minimal furniture sufficient for my needs. Helen flew back to Baltimore and I started my new job on March first.

I was assigned a nice office and an excellent secretary. My duties included monitoring ongoing research programs within the United States and Canada, setting up new projects in the same two countries and working with the basic scientists and other colleagues at Parke-Davis. The main offices of the company and much of its manufacturing facilities were located in Detroit. Once a week I had to go there for a meeting with the vice presidents for research and marketing. These were informal meetings and the tone was generally very friendly. The work was interesting and I spent much time setting up research programs in various parts of the country and in Canada. Once these were underway I checked on the progress periodically either by phone or with a visit. I met a number of interesting people and visited a number of universities and research hospitals.

I also made contact with Dr. Robert Sweet, the chairman of the Department of Anesthesiology at the University of Michigan. He received me most cordially and offered me an appointment at the associate professor level. I accepted with pleasure and attended the weekly departmental teaching sessions whenever I could. This appointment was a clinical one, had no salary attached to it and was not a tenure position.

A couple of months went by and Helen and I were planning the family move to Ann Arbor when one day, while I was in the office, Helen called me and said that Christine had to have heart surgery. What happened was that Christine had had a severe cold and before she could go back to nursery school she had to be seen by our wonderful pediatrician, Dr. Melchijah Spragins. Helen told me that when the doctor was examining Christine he suddenly became very grave and said that the child had a significant heart murmur that had not been present earlier and that had to be investigated promptly. Helen called me and I made arrangements to fly to Baltimore the next day.

Christine was seen that morning by a cardiac surgeon at Hopkins and the diagnosis of a *patent ductus arteriosus* (PDA) was made. This was a congenital defect affecting the vessels outside the heart and was not considered to be a life threatening condition as it is usually repaired within the first few months of life. According to the Hopkins cardiologists Christine's was only the third or fourth case in their huge experience where the defect had become clinically apparent at her age. The surgery was scheduled for a few days later and fortunately everything went very well. I stayed for a couple of days and then returned to Ann Arbor. Isabel Nottage came to the house and took care of the other three children so that Helen could spend much of her time with Christine. About three weeks later the time came for the family to move to Michigan. I again flew to Baltimore and helped pack our personal belongings while the general move was being done by a moving company paid for by Parke-Davis. On moving day Isabel Nottage and the three older children went with me by car while Helen and Christine flew to Detroit the following day.

The work continued to be interesting but it did not take very long for me to find out that I had made a mistake and so had Parke-Davis. I was disappointed because I had believed, naively perhaps, that the drug companies were different from other companies and that their primary interest was to do the best possible for the people who needed their drugs. It turned out that drug companies were no different from shoe companies and that their only concern was to make a profit. In fact they would have cheerfully put garbage into capsules if they had thought that somebody would buy them. They were also disappointed because they thought that I would be a good company yes-man when, in fact, I was nothing of the sort. When I was asked about my opinion about an issue

I told them precisely what I thought and not necessarily what they wanted to hear. This went on for just about a year. In April, 1964, I found out that one of the research studies being set up by my colleague somewhere in South America could seriously endanger the participants. Although the person responsible for the study was away I stopped it immediately. A few days later I was called to the office of the director of clinical investigation and was told that my services were no longer required. To put it more bluntly, I was fired. I could, however, continue to work for them for another sixty days before I had to vacate the premises! It was an interesting experience. As I found out later my colleague complained to the vice president in charge of research and threatened to resign if I was not dismissed.

My parents were visiting us at the time so they were there with my wife to hear what had happened. They were all obviously very supportive and asked what I was proposing to do. I said that I wanted to go back into academic anesthesiology and hoped that I could get a full-time appointment at the University of Michigan. The next morning I called Dr. Sweet, told him what had happened and asked him if he would take me on as a full-time faculty member. He said that he would like that very much but that the budget for the next year had already been settled and therefore he had to talk to the Dean to find out what could be done. He called back the following day saying that the Dean had been supportive and that I could start working at the University on July first as a tenured associate professor at a salary somewhat less than what I had made in Baltimore or at Parke-Davis. My family and I were all delighted. I must say that the research papers I had done under Dr. Lasagna at BCH were in part responsible for the good reception at Michigan.

This brought to an end my career in the pharmaceutical industry. In retrospect, I must say that it was an interesting experience. I gained a much better insight into the way things were done in the health industry in this country and also learned a lot about drugs and drug research. This was the time of the hearings by Senator Estes Kefauver about the drug industry, drug-safety issues and about the pharmacological effects of the marketed drugs. The hearings caused a major upheaval at Parke-Davis. A number of the "drugs" in their catalog were of the "fruit, bark and berry" variety which had no demonstrable beneficial effects other then generating substantial income for the company. When these substances were discussed in lengthy meetings by the company it was the director of the division of pharmacology, a very noted and respected scientist, and I who came out most strongly in favor of eliminating these useless substances from the list. Needless to say this did not endear me with the management. The director of pharmacology was high enough in the company to be safe of any adverse response.

I started my work at the University Hospital on July first and I then remained a faculty member of the University of Michigan Medical School for the next thirty-five years. The department had a good physician staff and an excellent group of residents. There was also a school for nurse anesthetists consisting of six staff nurses and a group of students who were all registered nurses. It was the second oldest of its kind in the United States and had a very good reputation. Although I enjoyed working with nurse anesthetists, having two types of training programs in one department created some problems. Both the student nurse anesthetists and the residents felt that the other group got the best cases. Many years later, when I was in charge of the department, I decided to close the nursing program and after a number of public hearings managed to do it.

In addition to working with the residents in the operating rooms and continuing my clinical research activities with new and experimental analgesic agents, I became heavily involved in what at that time was known as inhalation therapy and is now referred to as respiratory therapy. In the 1960s it was still a fledgling field and the task of the inhalation therapy group, while slowly expanding, was still primarily focusing on providing oxygen for patients. The inhalation therapy personnel were technically under the control of the anesthesiology department but were supervised practically by the head inhalation therapist, Don Gilbert.

When Dr. Sweet asked me if I would be willing to become the director of the section I had a long talk with Mr. Gilbert. I found him to be a highly intelligent person who was very much devoted to providing the best and safest service to the patients and who was very much interested in promoting respiratory therapy and in expanding the field. I believed that we could work well together and therefore I agreed to become the medical director of the respiratory therapy section. The first thing Mr. Gilbert and I did was to design a training course for the staff and, when I found out that there was practically no literature in this field we wrote a simple introductory textbook that was very well received. Soon thereafter I was appointed by the board of the American Society of Anesthesiologists as one of their two representatives on the national accrediting agency, the JRCRTE (Joint Review Committee for Respiratory Therapy Education). The other representatives on the accrediting agency came from the American Thoracic Society and from the American College of Chest Physicians. The six physicians and an equal number of respiratory therapists were charged with the responsibility of inspecting the programs in respiratory therapy and of granting full or partial accreditation on the basis of the findings of the inspection team. After the present chairman of the committee, Dr. Fred

Helmholtz, the distinguished pulmonary medicine specialist at the Mayo Clinic in Rochester, Minnesota retired, I was elected to the chairmanship and served in that capacity for several years. It was an interesting and rewarding position. I met a large number of the professionals in both respiratory therapy and pulmonary medicine and became friends with many of them. With five or six school inspections every year and a considerable number of professional meetings, it was a rare month that I did not have to travel to some part of the country.

During these years respiratory therapy had made enormous strides. Artificial ventilation became a major area of responsibility and for all practical purposes the respiratory therapist functioned as a physician's assistant in this highly important and demanding area. Respiratory therapy education also made significant progress and grew from the two-year associate degree programs to four year, baccalaureate programs. It was my privilege to be closely associated with these developments and to have been working in all areas of respiratory therapy education and practice. I must have been reasonably successful in these activities because I was honored by the national respiratory therapy association with their highest award. During these years I also wrote a number of articles in learned journals and chapters on medical ethics and on medico-legal affairs for the standard major textbook in respiratory care edited by Dr. George Burton who succeeded me as chairman of JRCRTE in which position he served with great distinction.

I also continued my work in anesthesiology and became quite active in several medical school activities. The most ongoing and interesting of these was my membership on the committee to investigate and approve all research programs at the hospital that involved patients in any way. At the organizational meeting of this committee, about half-way through,

I naively asked the question whether somebody should not be taking minutes. Needless to say I was then the secretary of the committee and remained in that position for almost twenty years. We met weekly and discussed the research proposals that were submitted for approval. It was interesting and gratifying to see how the approach to human experimentation changed and improved over the first years of the committee's activities. I was also active on some university-wide committees such as the University Senate and the Presidential Advisory Committee. This latter one was most interesting because it gave me a view of the inner workings of a large university.

The department of anesthesiology underwent a number of changes during my years at Michigan. Dr. Sweet retired and Dr. Peter Cohen became the new chairman with me as associate chairman. When he left several years later I became the interim chairman and served in that capacity for almost eighteen months. It was then that I decided to discontinue the nurse anesthesia program and focus all of our educational efforts on the physician trainees.

During my interim chairmanship the university conducted a careful search for a new chairman and, after a period of about eighteen months, we were successful in getting Kevin Tremper, M.D., Ph.D. to accept the position. I returned to my job as associate chairman. By that time I had turned over my work in respiratory care to a younger associate and focused my activities on clinical anesthesiology. Working mostly in anesthesia for pulmonary surgery, after several years I had the unique distinction of being made an honorary member of the Department of Pulmonary and Cardiac Surgery.

Another area I had become involved in was the field of malpractice litigation. I found this to be an extremely interesting and important area and worked extensively with both defense and plaintiff's attorneys. I testified in a number of cases and also served as a consultant to a large firm of plaintiff's attorneys. It was my responsibility to advise the firm whether the cases brought to it by patients who felt that they had been injured had merit or not. I am pleased to say that the firm followed my recommendations and that I was thus able to prevent a sizeable number of nuisance suits.

There were also two additional very interesting areas I became involved in. The first one was continuing medical education. The chairman of the department of continuing education was a professor of pediatrics who had listened to one of my talks to a group of family physicians and who then asked me if I would be interested in an appointment in his department. I thought that such an appointment would be both interesting and beneficial and therefore I accepted the invitation and was soon thereafter appointed to a professorship in continuing medical education. In this capacity my primary job was to organize a major five-day seminar every June in a northern Michigan resort for a group of seventy to ninety family physicians from Michigan, Ohio and Wisconsin. I also worked with other members of the CME department in designing survey questionnaires. This was an enlightening experience because it made it clear to me how very carefully these questionnaires had to be constructed in order to get valid responses. I suddenly realized how deficient many of the national survey studies were and how some of the conclusions drawn from them had very dubious validity.

Another new area for me opened up by an invitation from the Michigan Board of Medicine to become a part time consultant to the Board, spending three days of the week in Lansing and working with the staff of the Michigan Department of Licensing and Regulation. It was my job to attend the meetings of the board and to assist the members of the board in their review of the issues before the board. I also worked closely with Assistant Attorneys General in investigating physicians who were substance or alcohol abusers.

I was shocked and appalled to learn that approximately fifteen percent of the practicing physicians were either alcoholics or narcotic addicts. When a complaint came to the board or to the AG about such a physician it was my job to take it to the board for study and for a decision to suspend or revoke the physician's license. Another task I had in Lansing was to review malpractice claims against physicians. Under Michigan law every malpractice case filed in Michigan had to be reported to the board in order for the board to review the claim and to decide whether restriction or suspension of the license was indicated.

※

During the years in Ann Arbor our children grew up and for a number of years we had all four at some level in the public schools. The boys were moderately active in sports; both played softball although not with very much enthusiasm. Tom became very active in high school wrestling and participated in all the interscholastic meets with me being in the stands hoping that he would not get hurt. In his senior year he was the captain of the team. An injury to Jim's leg caused him to drop out of wrestling early.

We were struck by the problems of the Ann Arbor K-12 system which had been praised so highly. Tom had spent three years in the Stoneleigh elementary school in Baltimore County. After a couple of weeks in fourth grade in Ann Arbor he told us that they were talking about the same things he had covered the year before at Stoneleigh and also that the discipline in the classroom in Ann Arbor was atrocious. Kids were running around in class and the teacher seemed to ignore it.

When the kids got to high school another problem emerged. Whether for economic or scholastic reasons the curriculum changed between the time Tom graduated and Christine reached her senior year four years later. Tom and

Jim had a number of excellent electives, which were no longer available when Christine went through the program.

We bought a lot on Pearl Lake in Wisconsin about fourteen miles from the little town of Berlin where Helen was born. Having learned to swim in that lake, she had always wanted to have a cottage there. She drew plans for a small and very simple house which was built by a local company. From then on summer was spent at the lake with friends of the kids coming to spend some time there. I am not a water person so that I was not particularly enthusiastic about the place especially when there were six or seven children present with all the noise and commotion that was inevitable. I have never been comfortable in noisy, crowded situations. We bought an aluminum row boat with a 7.5 horsepower outboard and the children started to learn to ski behind it. After a couple of years we bought a Boston Whaler with a forty horsepower engine and Helen and the kids soon became expert skiers. The noise of the boats racing back and forth pulling skiers was unpleasant but fortunately there were, and still are, boating regulations that permit power boating only between the hours of eleven and four o'clock. Because I did not wish to waste my vacation time at the lake I only commuted on alternate week ends, flying from Detroit to Oshkosh on Friday and returning to Ann Arbor on Sunday. About four years after the cottage was built we decided to enlarge it by adding a second story. This was done the next year and was a distinct improvement in the comfort of the place.

Tom earned a bachelor's degree from the University of Michigan and a master's degree from Brown in creative writing. He then joined the Navy, became an officer and served for nineteen years. He and his wife, Nina Fisher, have two daughters. Jim received a bachelor's degree from Michigan State University in Hotel and Restaurant Management. He married Kathryn Deitzer and they have two sons. Later divorced, he married Dawn Penfold. Anne attended the University of Southern California for a year and then married, had four children and lived in California. Christine attended secretarial school and worked as a secretary at the University of Michigan. She married Bildad Hannouche with whom she has three children; they have always lived in South Carolina. When our children were in their early teens, Helen and I took them, first the boys and later the girls, to Europe. We had very enjoyable trips to France, Northern Italy, Switzerland and Austria. Helen, Jim and I also had an interesting trip to England.

With the children grown and gone, Helen and I traveled repeatedly to Europe and also enjoyed two cruises, one in the Mediterranean and one along the east coast of South America. The tours were arranged by the 3M Company and I served as one of the speakers on the tour. This made the trips enjoyable and while I received no honorarium all expenses were paid by the company.

During these years my parents and several other relatives all remained on the east coast. Having made an excellent adjustment to life in the United States, my parents became citizens as soon as they could and truly loved and admired their new country. My father was still active in Hungarian émigré affairs but realized that there was very little, if anything, that could be done to change the situation in Hungary which was then under Communist rule and he resigned himself to the fact that he would not live long enough to see any major changes in Eastern Europe. He died peacefully in 1968 and was buried in Washington very much lamented by all who knew him. My mother survived him by six years. Hanna, Aladár and their children and my sister, Puppa were living with our parents on Patterson Street in Chevy Chase, a suburb of Washington. My sisters visited Hungary several times seeing old friends and some of our former servants. Once they attempted to visit our home on Lendvay utca which had become the French Embassy. They told the receptionist in their fluent French that they had been born in that house and would very much like to see some part of it again. They were summarily dismissed – rudely told to leave at once. My more distant family, uncles, aunts and cousins all lived in New York. Over the years the older generation died and some of my cousins returned to Europe and are now living in Munich, Zurich and Vienna.

All of us thought frequently of the people in Hungary. Mother and Puppa produced on their knitting needles and crochet hooks miles of warm woolen scarves, hats and caps of all kinds, mittens and socks which they packed into boxes to send to friends and the people who formerly served us. Cousin Memi Mauthner devoted her entire life to helping Hungarians in the States.

Although in her seventies, Mother participated in the annual March-of-Dimes campaign every year. Initiated by President Franklin Roosevelt in the 1930's, this was a house-to-house collection of money to combat poliomyelitis which at that time was a major health problem in the United States. Mother, still very active, usually walked through the neighborhood every day. So during the campaign she visited every house, soliciting a contribution. Quite successful, she turned in to the campaign office a considerable amount of money to which she had added her own sizeable donation.

I returned to Budapest for the first time in 1992 to attend the fiftieth anniversary of my graduation from the *gimnázium*. About twenty-five of my former classmates gathered for Mass and a reception at the old Piarist chapel. Luncheon was held at the Hélia hotel where my wife and I were staying. It was a delight to see Tibor Fabinyi, who had organized the reunion, Aurél Dessewffy, Peter de Balogh, Johnny Graham and others after so long a time. It felt strange to be in Budapest again.

The city looked remarkably good and, except for some bullet holes in the walls, there was little evidence of the devastations caused by the siege. Buda was just as lovely as always and the museum and the Széchényi Library, both in the old Royal Palace buildings, were most impressive. We rented a car and drove down to Ireg. I was very pleased to see that the chateau was in surprisingly good condition and that the park was well maintained. It was now a school for problem children. We were not able to get into the building but we walked around and the many precious memories were refreshing for me.

A very dear old friend whom we visited in Buda was Professor Éva Balázs, who had been a student at the university with Puppa and was a frequent visitor in Ireg. She had become one of the most distinguished historians in Hungary.

Later on my wife and I visited Hungary twice. On one of the visits I had been asked to accompany two prominent American real estate experts who were going to Hungary to serve as advisors to the Budapest Board of Realtors. My job was to be their interpreter. It was an interesting experience during which I met several very pleasant Hungarians including József Paulin, a computer expert who became a good friend.

During the summers we returned to Pearl Lake and, in the absence of children, we invited some friends to come and stay for a week or so. We built a garage with a loft above it that served as an office and craft room. It turned out very well and was an important addition to our comfort and activities.

One day in the summer of 1993, very shortly after we had arrived at the cottage, we were preparing to launch our boat and, assisted by Jim and by my colleague from the University of Michigan, Dr. James Sherman, were just hooking it up to the car when Helen, standing by with some towels in her hand, suddenly collapsed. She was unconscious but had reasonable vital signs. We immediately put her into the car and drove her to the hospital in Berlin where she was admitted.

She was seen by an internist and by Dr. Kenneth Viste, a well-known neurologist, who came from Oshkosh where he was the head of the neurology and rehabilitation section of Mercy Hospital. They told us that there was little hope for recovery and that she probably would never regain consciousness.

Jim's family and Christine joined us and on the third day after her collapse Helen suddenly regained consciousness although still unable to speak or engage in any physical activity. When Dr. Viste came by the next day he examined Helen and then told me that much to his surprise she showed marked signs of at least partial recovery and that he would be pleased to have her transferred to the rehabilitation ward at Mercy Hospital. She was there for three weeks undergoing increasingly vigorous physical therapy, occupational therapy and speech therapy sessions. By the end of the third week she could walk quite well with a slight limp, use her right hand well and her left hand to some extent. Unfortunately she was still aphasic (could not speak) and had some difficulty in understanding what was said to her. We managed quite well at the cottage with help from a retired practical nurse who came every morning, helped Helen and fixed lunch. We still went back to Oshkosh three times each week for speech therapy sessions. Helen continued to improve slightly and so in September we were able to go back to Ann Arbor.

I had resigned from the University earlier that year but now they called and asked if I could go back on a part-time basis. I was pleased to do that and we decided that it would be best both for the department and for me if I worked every other week. I would not take call and would not work weekends. This worked out quite well. Initially we had some help for Helen but later she improved sufficiently that I could safely leave her alone during the days when I was working. In the summer of 1994 and 1995 we again stayed at the cottage with friends and family visiting.

In May, 1996, I resigned from the University for the second and last and we decided to go to Hungary with Tom and Nina and our good friends Dr. and Mrs. George Burton. We again stayed at the Hélia hotel. One day we rented a car and drove to Ireg to show the chateau and the park to Tom and Nina and to the Burtons. We had a very nice day and that evening were the Burtons' guests for dinner. The next morning I got up early, dressed quietly and went down to the dining room for some coffee. I took a cup back to the room for Helen but when I pulled the shades up I found that she had died during the night. It obviously was a shock but I must say that I encountered nothing but the greatest courtesy and helpfulness from the hotel, from the Hungarian authorities, including the police and from the United States Embassy. The airlines were also most helpful and allowed us to change our tickets for a date three days later than we planned to go. Five days after Helen died I was able to obtain her ashes in an urn and I returned to the U.S. the next day.

On the flight home a curious thing happened. When I told one of the young flight attendants that I was carrying my wife's ashes in an urn in my carry-on bag and that I wondered what I had to tell the passport and customs officers in Detroit, her eyes became large and round and she said she had no idea. A few minutes later a senior flight attendant came, was asked the same question and reacted in the same way. She said she was going to ask the captain. She also returned a few minutes later and said that the captain did not know either but would radio the main office in Minneapolis and find out. Shortly before landing she came back again and said the Minneapolis people did not know either but that an airline person would be at the gate and would come with me to be of assistance if needed. As it turned out the passport and customs officers could not have cared less and I was cleared without any delay. It is also of interest that the Hungarian police had given me an official document testifying that they had examined the urn and that it contained only ashes. Apparently urns had been used in the past to smuggle narcotics and illegal substances.

We had a service for Helen at the Congregational church in Ann Arbor and then the family went to Berlin where we had another service at the church prior to her burial at the local cemetery. On returning to Ann Arbor I put the house on the market but it took about eight months to sell. I then proceeded to sell the furniture and most of my library. Some of the art works were sold by an auction house in Detroit. I had been planning to rent an apartment in Ann Arbor but then decided that I would move to the lake. The first winter in Wisconsin was an experience. We had very cold weather and heavy snow. I bought my first cellular phone because I felt that if I were to slip on the steps leading to the cottage or to the loft and break a leg I would freeze to death before anybody would find me. Continuing to do the school inspections, I also visited my children in Maryland, Tennessee and South Carolina.

During the early summer of 1998 I was planning to do a school inspection in Morehead, North Carolina. Preparing for the trip I recalled the beautiful letter Helen Hiltabidle had written to me and the children after my wife's death and also how much I had admired her all those years ago in Baltimore. I knew her husband had died and that she was living on the Outer Banks of North Carolina and, after some difficulty, I found her phone number. We had a lovely chat and I explained that I was shortly leaving for a Baltic cruise and would be back in a couple of weeks after which I would be in North Carolina. She graciously welcomed my suggestion that I would like to stop by to see her. We exchanged email addresses and promised to keep in touch. Upon my return from Europe I sent her a message that I was back and asked for directions to her house. I flew to Norfolk, rented a car, and, following her precise directions, found her house in Southern Shores without difficulty. I stayed for a couple of days and the visit was a great success; we picked up as though we had been together regularly rather than not having seen each other for thirty three years.

I had another North Carolina site visit that autumn and I again called Helen and asked if I might stop by. On this visit I became convinced that I wanted to spend the rest of my life with this lady and when I left to drive to the respiratory therapy school I was so euphoric that I was not paying sufficient attention to my driving. A speeding ticked and a hundred dollar fine later I came back down to earth. During the fall I was courting Helen over the internet with daily early morning messages which increased in temperature with the passing weeks. Helen agreed to visit me in Wisconsin in February, 1999. I waited for her at the airport in Milwaukee and when she arrived I asked her to sit down with me for a few minutes in the lobby. When we were settled I asked her to marry me and to my greatest joy she said yes. The wedding took place in May at the Church of Saint Andrew's by the Sea in Nags Head. It was a wonderful affair with both families, her three and three of mine, plus grandchildren in attendance; the younger ones participated in the ceremony.

Our wedding trip included a visit to Hungary and I enjoyed showing Helen all of my favorite places. Travel, both in the U.S. and abroad, became very important to us. Trips to Germany, Italy, Switzerland, Holland and Belgium are favorite memories. We took an automobile tour of France in 2007 and spent a couple of weeks in Paris in 2010. It is our preference to stay at tiny family-owned hotels or Bed and Breakfasts, and we always enjoy learning our way around a European city by metro. Museums and musical performances are for us the most desirable way to spend the days and evenings. In 2004 we traveled by car from Salt Lake City to Seattle. It happened to be our fifth wedding anniversary in Port Angeles, Washington, and we went to St. Andrew's church for the ten o'clock service. The pastor and tiny congregation were very pleased to see us, blessed our marriage and wished us safe journey as we left.

However, it must be said that Hungary remains our favorite destination. Over the years we have visited there many times, enjoying the food, the beautiful city of Budapest and our very good, old friends. Within a year of our marriage we were making an annual fall trip to Budapest, spending at least a couple of weeks each time. On several occasions we rented an apartment from Anna Sándor, a family friend. On Fő utca, about a block from the Batthyány tér, in a nice new building, the apartment was on the fourth floor with a view toward the Danube. We stayed about a month while Helen was studying Hungarian at the *Magyar Iskola* (Hungarian School). We went by the *földalatti* – which was the second oldest metro in Europe and the one I had taken when going to school in the 1930's and 40's. Angéla Kiss was her teacher and we became good friends with her and her husband László Pintér. Six months later we returned, staying in the same apartment. This time Angéla came to us several mornings a week to give the lessons. About a year later we returned to Budapest and again rented an apartment from Anna Sándor. She had sold the Fő utca one and purchased one in an older building in Szász Károly utca, about a block away from Margaret Boulevard. Very comfortable, it was just a few steps away from an excellent grocery store where we did our weekly shopping.

Public transportation is splendid in Budapest and from both apartments we traveled all over the city by the underground, street cars and busses. A monthly travel card allowed us to get on and off wherever we wanted. In the Szász Károly apartment we were close to the Danube and in the evening we walked down to the quay and admired the lights on the Pest side, particularly the Parliament building. We enjoyed visiting the Castle, spending time in the National Gallery in the old Royal Palace. The collection there of carved wooden altars from the eleventh and twelfth centuries is unique in the world and one of the major sights in Budapest. Immediately next to the altars was one of our favorite works of art – an early polychrome statue of the Virgin holding the infant Jesus. I was given permission to take a photograph of it which now hangs in our study. Walking around the Castle, we frequently found ourselves on the beautiful Úri utca and stopped at the patisserie Russwurm which has been in existence for at least two hundred years. It is tiny, but offers the most remarkable pastries of which the *marcipánkrumpli* are the best.

A favorite pastime for us was to take a walk on beautiful Margaret Island beside the Danube. One day as we were heading north to the lovely hotel where we planned to have some coffee, we noticed on one of the many benches a country woman, dressed in rural fashion: voluminous flowered skirt, black sweater, boots, black headscarf and a large black handbag. When we came closer we saw her reach into her bag from which she took a cell phone and made a call. She was not quite the simple country woman we had thought. This was at a time when cell phones were still in somewhat limited use in the United States and therefore it was particularly striking to see an elderly lady in Budapest using such a sophisticated method of communication. When we told this story to a friend in Budapest he laughed and said, "Oh yes, it has become almost impossible to get a land line and many of us have turned to cell phones which we can purchase in fifteen minutes."

While living in Szász Károly utca we also visited Mammut, an enormous, truly mammoth, shopping center. A multi-storey complex it has dozens of very fine shops of all kinds including an excellent bookstore with internet facilities. Behind the shopping center was an open-air market with fruit, vegetable and flower stands and several open meat stalls with cuts of meat and game hanging from hooks. Many housewives with large bags or old-fashioned baskets were going from stand to stand buying their food for the day. We found it thoroughly enjoyable, joined the shoppers and bought beautiful and, by our standards, inexpensive fruit.

We loved exploring restaurants and quickly developed an affection for several. One special place was the Csalogány which was within easy walking distance of our apartment. We became regular patrons and were always given our usual table and had the same dinner consisting of one of the restaurant's excellent soups to be followed by *palacsinta*, the famous Hungarian thin pancakes filled with apricot jam. We became such good friends with the owner that when we went there at the end of our stay to say good-by she presented us with a very good bottle of Hungarian wine as a going away present.

Budapest is a musical city. During our visits we were privileged to hear a number of outstanding performances. We will not forget a spectacular Mozart requiem at the National Academy and an equally outstanding Fauré requiem in a Franciscan church on Margaret Boulevard. With a really great organ and small choir it was a most impressive performance. Another remarkable experience was at the large Franciscan church where we listened, enthralled, to voices singing Gregorian chant. We attended the Opera several times and also heard an open-air concert in the Castle, performed by the Budapest Symphony Orchestra. On another occasion we were visiting the *Mátyás-templom* (Matthias Church) and heard a rehearsal by the choir and orchestra of the University of Szeged. We were rewarded with yet another outstanding performance of classical music.

On several occasions we visited Professor Éva Balázs and on one of these she introduced me to a young Hungarian historian, a former student of hers, Dr. Ágnes Széchenyi. Éva had for many years been talking about the importance of writing a book about my father whom she had held in very high esteem. She felt that Dr. Széchenyi could do this very well and she wanted us to get acquainted. Ágnes became a very dear friend as well as the editor of a book containing a number of my father's writings. Her extensive research about him became the lengthy introductory biography. I also did considerable research about family matters in the National Széchényi Library and in the Hungarian National Archives. In both of these I was received with the greatest courtesy. When the book was finished it was submitted to Corvina Publishers and was accepted for publication. The director of Corvina, Dr. László Kúnos and his charming wife, Gabi, became good friends whom we try to see every time we are in Budapest.

The book was eventually published in 2006 and we were invited for the formal presentation. Unfortunately Helen could not attend because of a severe and very painful back injury. She suggested that I take my grandson Nathan with me which was a marvelous idea. The presentation of the book was a formal occasion attended by a number of distinguished people. There were several speeches including mine. Titled *From Trianon to Trianon*, the book was a success and the first edition sold out promptly. A second edition was then prepared which also did well. I translated the book into English and it was published in the U.S. a year later by our good friend, Professor Peter Pastor, the director of the Center for Hungarian Studies and Publications in Wayne, N.J. For the English edition I added a chapter to the book on my personal recollections of my father.

That autumn Helen and I again returned to Budapest staying at the Pilvax Hotel. We were so pleased with everything about the place that it became our only choice and still is. We especially like the location situated in the middle of town within easy walking distance of shopping and dining. Helen loves the Pilvax because it is old, historic and unfashionable. The poet Sándor Petőfi, prominent revolutionary, was a member of a group of students and intellectuals who met regularly at the Café Pilvax. His poem sparked the Hungarian Fight for Freedom in 1848. Most Americans would not like the place – there is no elevator.

During many of our visits to Hungary we took the train to Vienna to see György's son, Stevie, and his wife, Dorine and cousin Daisy Chorin von Strasser and her husband Rudi.

Our home from 1999 to 2005 was in Southern Shores, North Carolina. Active in community as well as church affairs, we were members of the volunteer fire department medical group which looked after the well-being of the fire fighters during a fire. At the Outer Banks Presbyterian Church I became a Stephen Minister; through St. Andrew's church, Helen worked with women at the county detention center. We were involved in a group working on the problem of substance abuse. As a subset of this group we started an action to establish free clinics in different areas of the Outer Banks with the local clinics providing space, doctors and nurses donating time and drug companies contributing supplies. We were charged to collect contributions from the residents and local businesses to a total of twenty-five thousand dollars in the space of a month. What looked like an impossibility was rewarded with hard work: in four weeks we had collected almost sixty thousand dollars and the program was launched.

Yet another activity that I became engaged in was wood working that I did under Helen's tutelage. She had taken up the hobby in her retirement and had a beautiful, fully equipped shop in the basement of our house. We built a number of rather elaborate pieces for St. Andrew's, including a desk, a storage facility for mail, a large cabinet for the choir music and a number of bulletin boards of various sizes for the classrooms. Helen also started me on wood turning, a hobby I have continued to this day.

In 2003 we started to think of the possibility of moving away from the Outer Banks. The reasons for this very difficult decision were partly the increasing commercialism of the Outer Banks but we also felt that because of our advancing age we would find it increasingly difficult to maintain the house and the garden in first-class condition. We considered various possibilities but eventually came to the conclusion that the best situation for us would probably be a retirement community that could provide continuing health care. This would also make it certain that we would not become a burden on our children. The Baltimore area appealed to us because Helen had two children in the area, one of my sons was living in near-by Annapolis and my sisters were living in Washington. After looking at several such retirement communities we chose Blakehurst, in Towson, just outside Baltimore. Putting our house on the market and making our arrangements with Blakehurst, we waited for a suitable buyer to come along. It took almost a year but in the end we were fortunate in selling the house to a nice couple and getting a good price for it.

Since we could not move into Blakehurst immediately, we stored the furniture and went to Washington to stay in the family home that was empty at the time, Hanna having died and Puppa having moved to an assisted living facility in Arlington, Virginia. The house was large and not in very good shape. Furthermore, Washington in the summer, in a house without air conditioning was uncomfortable and we were glad when we were told that we could move to Blakehurst into a one bedroom apartment until a larger one became available. The remaining time in Washington passed quickly with us taking walks every day and enjoying the many excellent musical performances the town had to offer. The move to Blakehurst went smoothly and we settled down to a new and presumably final way of life. The one-bedroom apartment was nice but confining and we were pleased to move to a two-bedroom apartment when it became available in January, 2006.

Living in an apartment in a retirement community clearly does not measure up to living in your own beautiful home but our life at Blakehurst has many appealing features. We have met a group of interesting people and have formed a surprising number of very real friendships. We are also active in the life of the community, attending lectures and seminars, serving on committees, etc. We became members of the Baltimore Symphony and enjoy the fine performances. As members of the Kennedy Center in Washington, we attend wonderful performances of the world's great ballet companies. We are also still very active physically, going on two to three mile hikes several times each week. The Baltimore area is singularly fortunate in having a number of very good trails within a few miles of where we live. In the summer we return to the cottage in Wisconsin. Helen likes to kayak on the lake and I usually play some golf almost every morning. As the saying goes: we are ancient but not old.

I am continually grateful for the life I experienced before the war. I know full well that everyone in Hungary lost a lot – loved ones, jobs, businesses, careers, homes; far too many lost their very lives. How truly blessed my family and I were to be able to leave and how really extraordinary it has been to come to and live and find happiness in America.

Glossary

Anschluss – Literally "Attachment". The German occupation of Austria in March 1938.

Arrow Cross – The name of the Hungarian Nazi party. Came to power on October fifteenth, 1944. In Hungarian *Nyilaskeresztes*.

Gimnázium – The Hungarian middle and high school of eight years.

Gendarmes – The Hungarian National Police. Stationed in the villages they were responsible for law and order. The leadership was very strongly pro-Nazi and, after March nineteenth, 1944, the gendarmes were responsible for rounding up the Jews in the villages and small towns for deportation.

Gestapo – The Nazi Secret Police.

Green Cross – Rural health service in Hungary staffed by nurses.

Kt. – The abbreviation for Knight.

Lebensraum – Literally "living space". Politically the German drive for areas in the East.

Little Entente – The political association of Czechoslovakia, Romania and Yugoslavia. Primarily an anti-Hungarian organization of the three successor states.

Matura – The final, formal exam at the end of the eighth year of the gimnázium. Both written and oral. A major test and a prerequisite for admission to the university.

Siege – The fight of the Russian troops against the Hungarian and German forces defending Budapest. November, 1944 – January, 1945. Historians tell us that the siege of Budapest was not only ill-conceived, it was unnecessary. Hitler, panicked by the Russian advance from the East, was convinced that he needed the Hungarian oil fields and that he had to protect Vienna. On December first, 1944, he ordered that Budapest would be defended to the last man; house-to-house. The resulting battle destroyed one of the most beautiful cities in the world, killed almost ninety-six thousand people among whom were many of his own troops, damaged or destroyed some thirty thousand buildings and accomplished nothing.

"... the city turned into hell. There were dead horses in the streets and all public parks were turned into temporary cemeteries. Along the Danube the blood-covered quay and the bloody ice-floes gave testimony to the daily massacre of the Jews herded there from the 'safe' houses."

Budapest 1945 by Miklós Tamási and Krisztián Ungváry

SS – Originally the Nazi internal security forces. In charge of the concentration camps responsible for the implementation of the Holocaust. Under Himmler's control. During the war the Waffen SS was established. These were elite army units and fought along the regular Wehrmacht units.

Út – Hungarian word for a large road or avenue.

Utca – Hungarian word for street.

Wehrmacht – The German regular armed forces.

Biographical Sketches

Ady, Endre – The greatest Hungarian poet of the twentieth century. Father supported him during the last year of his life when he was already very seriously ill.

Andorka, General Rudolf – Head of Hungarian Military Intelligence. Friend and coprisoner of Father.

Apponyi, Count György – Hungarian political figure. Friend and coprisoner of Father.

Bakonyi, Pál – Hungarian ministerial official. Family friend. Member of the Thursday luncheon group.

Balog, Ármin – Professor at a Hebrew School. Taught my grandfather Kornfeld Hungarian. A family friend. Spent most summers in Ireg, Taught me to read and write when I was four years old.

Balogh, József – Son of the above. Editor of *Nouvelle Revue* and of *Hungarian Quarterly*. Prepared the catalog of my father's Hungarica collection. A close family friend. Killed by the Nazis.

Balogh, Peter de – No relation to the above. My classmate in elementary and secondary school and a very good friend ever since. He worked for many years for the FAO and now lives with his Dutch wife in Germany.

Baranyai, Jusztin – Cistercian Father. Professor of Theology. Good friend of my parents. Frequently in Ireg.

Bárdossy, László –Hungarian diplomat and politician. Prime Minister 1941–1942. Fervent anti-Semite. Had Hungary declare war on the United States in 1941. Sentenced to death as a war criminal. Executed in 1946.

Becher, Kurt – German SS Standartenführer (Colonel). In charge of the SS Economic Command in Hungary after March nineteenth, 1944. Made the arrangements with the family for a 25-year lease on Csepel in exchange for taking the combined Weiss–Chorin–Kornfeld–Mauthner families to a neutral country. Was accused of war crimes but found innocent. One of his defenders was a member of the family.

Bethlen, Count István – Transylvanian nobleman. Politician. Prime Minister 1921–1931. Remained a powerful political figure until 1944. Arrested by the Russians, died in a Moscow prison. A friend of my father.

Billitz, Vilmos – High official at Csepel. Negotiated the arrangement with the Germans in April–May 1944. Remained in Hungary and died in Vienna in late 1944. One of the hostages.

Böck, Liesl – Teta Liesl was my nanny and dear friend. Married Ferenc Oleár the head gardener in Ireg.

Borbély, Ferenc – Outstanding physician. Director of the Csepel Hospital. After the war lived in Zurich and worked at the Medical School there. Married my cousin Mária (Baby) Mauthner.

Bourbon e Tavora, Maria de Jesus – Young lady we met in Portugal. Related to the former Portuguese royal family.

Carmona, General Oscar – Portuguese military officer and politician. President of Portugal 1928–1949.

Chamberlain, Sir Neville – British politician. Prime Minister 1937–1940. Negotiated the Munich agreement in 1938.

Churchill, Sir Winston – British politician. Prime Minister 1940–1945 and 1951–1955.

Csekonics, Count Iván – Hungarian politician. Friend and coprisoner of Father.

Biographical Sketches

Eissler, Georg – Cousin of my mother. Lived in Vienna until 1938 and then in Hungary. Represented Csepel in Egypt. Eventually he and his family went to Argentina.

Endrédy, Abbot Vendel – Head of the Cistercian monastery in Zirc. Gave refuge to my father and Uncle Feri in 1944.

Gábor family – Father Gábor was a jeweler in Budapest. He and his wife, Jolie, had three lovely daughters, Magda, Zsazsa and Èva. Zsazsa and Èva came to the United States before the war and had a career in Hollywood. Magda and her parents came to Portugal in 1945. After the war Mr. Gábor went back to Hungary and Mrs. Gábor and Magda came to the United States.

Goering, Hermann – Distinguished fighter pilot in the First World War. Became ardent Nazi, appointed Hitler's successor in 1939. Head of the Luftwaffe. Sentenced to death as a war criminal at the Nurnberg trial. Committed suicide in prison.

Gömbös, Gyula – Military officer and politician. Prime Minister 1931–1936. Right winger. Led to Hungary's rapprochement to Italy and, later, to Germany.

Gömöry-Laiml, László – Former official of the Ministry of Foreign Affairs. Taught French to the young diplomats. A voracious eater. Friend of the family and frequent guest at Ireg.

Graham, John – Classmate and good friend. Now lives in Sarasota, Florida.

Grátz, Gusztáv – Hungarian historian and politician. Held several ministerial positions. A friend of my father.

Hatvany-Deutsch, Sándor – Industrialist and patron of the arts. A friend of Grandfather Kornfeld.

Hazai, Samu – Hungarian Minister of War during the First World War. A friend of my father and a member of the Thursday luncheon group.

Himmler, Heinrich – Nazi politician. Reichsführer SS. Head of the German intelligence services and of the Gestapo. Caught by the British. Committed suicide.

Hitler, Adolf – German Chancellor 1933–1945. Head of the Nazi Party. Dictator of Germany. Committed suicide in 1945.

Hohenlohe, Prince Ferenc – Hungarian Military Attaché in St. Petersburg. Frequent hunting visitor in Derekegyháza.

Horthy, Jenő – Brother of Regent Horthy. A friend of my father.

Horthy, Miklós – Austro-Hungarian naval officer. Hero of several battles during the First World War. Head of the Hungarian counter revolution. Regent of Hungary 1920–1944. Tried to take Hungary out of the war. Died in Portugal. Supported for several years there by my Uncle Feri.

Jónás, Ernő – Classmate and very good friend. Spent summers in Ireg. Had a distinguished career in the U.S. as a civil engineer. Lives in Vermont.

Kállay, Miklós – Hungarian politician. Prime Minister 1942–1944. Pro Allies. Tried to get Hungary out of the war. Arrested by the Germans after March nineteenth, 1944.

Kanitz, Felix Philipp – Brother of Manfréd Weiss' mother. A distinguished Balkans explorer and author-illustrator.

Kanitz, Jacques – Cousin of my mother. Lived in Switzerland for many years. Paid for golf lessons for me in St. Moritz.

Károlyi, Counts – Owners of Derekegyháza from whom Manfréd Weiss bought it in 1916.

Keresztes-Fischer, Ferenc – Hungarian politician. Minister of the Interior before and during the Second World War. Strongly anti-Nazi. A friend of my father.

Keresztes-Fischer, Lajos – Brother of the above. Friend and co-prisoner of my father.

Kőnig, Jenő – Hungarian ministerial official. A very good friend of the family known as Uncle King. Frequent guest and hunting companion in Ireg.

Korányi, Baron Sándor – Distinguished Professor of Medicine at the University in Budapest. Distant relative.

Krobatin, Field Marshall Baron Alexander von – Austrian military officer. Monarchy Minister of War during the First World War. Friend of the family. One of the first guests in Ireg.

Kúnos, László – Distinguished Director of the Corvina Publishing Company in Budapest. A good friend and reviewer of this book.

Mansfeld, Géza – Professor of Pharmacology at the University of Pécs. A good friend of the family. Survived a German concentration camp in 1944–45 and returned to Pécs after the war.

Margaretha, Herbert – Scion of a distinguished Viennese family. Married my cousin Krisztina Mauthner.

Meltzer, János – Hungarian attorney. My godfather. A member of the Thursday luncheon group.

Mojzer, Miklós – Director General of the Museum of Fine Arts in Budapest. A good friend.

Montgomery, Field Marshall Bernard – (1987–1976) Distinguished British Military Officer. The victor at El Alamein.

Móricz, Zsigmond – Distinguished Hungarian writer and editor. Friend of my father.

Mussolini, Benito – Prime Minister and Dictator of Italy 1922–1945. Head of the Fascist Party. Killed by partisans at the end of the war.

Oleár, Ferenc – Head gardener at Ireg. Married my Teta Liesl.

Ormódy, Vilmos – Hungarian ministerial official. A friend of my family and a member of the Thursday luncheon group. When I knew him he was 90 years old.

Papen, Franz von – German politician. Chancellor June 1932– November 1932. Hitler's Ambassador in Turkey.

Parragi, György – Hungarian journalist. Coprisoner of Father in Mauthausen.

Pastor, Peter – University Professor of History. A good friend. Editor of the Hungarian History series and reviewer of this volume.

Paulin, József – A young Hungarian friend.

Perczel, Tamás – A very good friend of the family. An official in the Hungarian Ministry of Foreign Affairs. Puppa's steadiest suitor. A frequent visitor in Ireg. Came to the U.S. after the war and lived in Canada.

Petrovich, Elek – Former Director General of the Budapest Museum of Fine Arts. A friend of the family and a member of the Thursday luncheon group.

Peyer, Károly – Distinguished Hungarian politician. Head of the Socialist Labor Party in Parliament. A friend and co-prisoner of my father.

Pilaszanovics, Dódy – Son of the lady in whose apartment I rented a room in Pécs. He was a resident in surgery and a very good friend. Practiced surgery in Hungary after the war.

Popovich Sándor – Hungarian banker, President of the Hungarian National Bank. A friend of my father.

Poprády, Géza – Director General of the National Széchényi Library. A good friend.

Radnóti, József – Hungarian journalist. Wrote the biography of Zsigmond Kornfeld.

Rákosi, Jenő – Coprisoner of my father.

Rassay, Károly – Hungarian politician. Head of the Liberal Party in Parliament. A friend and co-prisoner of Father.

Rothschild, Albert – Head of the Rothschild Banking Group in Vienna. Sent Zsigmond Kornfeld to Budapest to salvage the General Bank of Credit.

Schaffer, János – Our chauffeur who risked his life to become the liaison between the family members in hiding after March nineteenth.

Sombor-Schweinitzer, József – Head of the Hungarian Secret Police. Friend and coprisoner of my father.

Stapenhorst, Major Karl – SS Officer. Adjutant of Colonel Becher.

Széchenyi, Ágnes – Hungarian historian and good friend. Wrote the biography of my father for the *From Trianon to Trianon* book of my father's essays and did all of the editorial work.

Sztehlo, András – A good friend of my sisters. Brother to the distinguished Lutheran Minister Gábor Sztehlo, the savior of hundreds of Jewish children after the German occupation of Hungary.

Szterényi, József – Friend and coprisoner of Father.

Sztójay, Döme – Hungarian diplomat and politician. Ambassador to Germany. Prime Minister May 1944 August – 1944. Executed as a war criminal in 1946.

Szüllő, Géza – Hungarian politician and Parliamentary Representative. Friend of the family and member of the Thursday luncheon group.

Teleki, Count Pál – Distinguished geographer and politician. Prime Minister 1920–1921 and 1939–1941. Strong right-wing sentiments. Committed suicide because of German invasion of Yugoslavia.

Teleszky, János – Former Minister. Friend of Father and member of the Thursday luncheon group.

Terták, Elemér – Classmate and good friend of my brother. Figure-skating champion of Hungary and Olympic skater.

Thaly, Zsiga – High ministerial official. Friend of the family and member of the Thursday luncheon group.

Tóth, Pál – Head forester and hunt master in Derekegyháza. Known as "Baligoma". A good friend of mine.

Varga, Béla – Catholic Monsignor. Politician. Speaker of Parliament in 1945–1947. Friend of my father.

Vuk, Alajos – A good friend of my sisters. Frequent visitor in Ireg.

Wekerle, Sándor – Prime Minister 1892–1895 and 1906–1910. Got the barony for Zsigmond Kornfeld.

Zichy, Count Nándor – Hungarian Parliamentarian. Knew Zsigmond Kornfeld well.

Family trees

WEISS
family tree

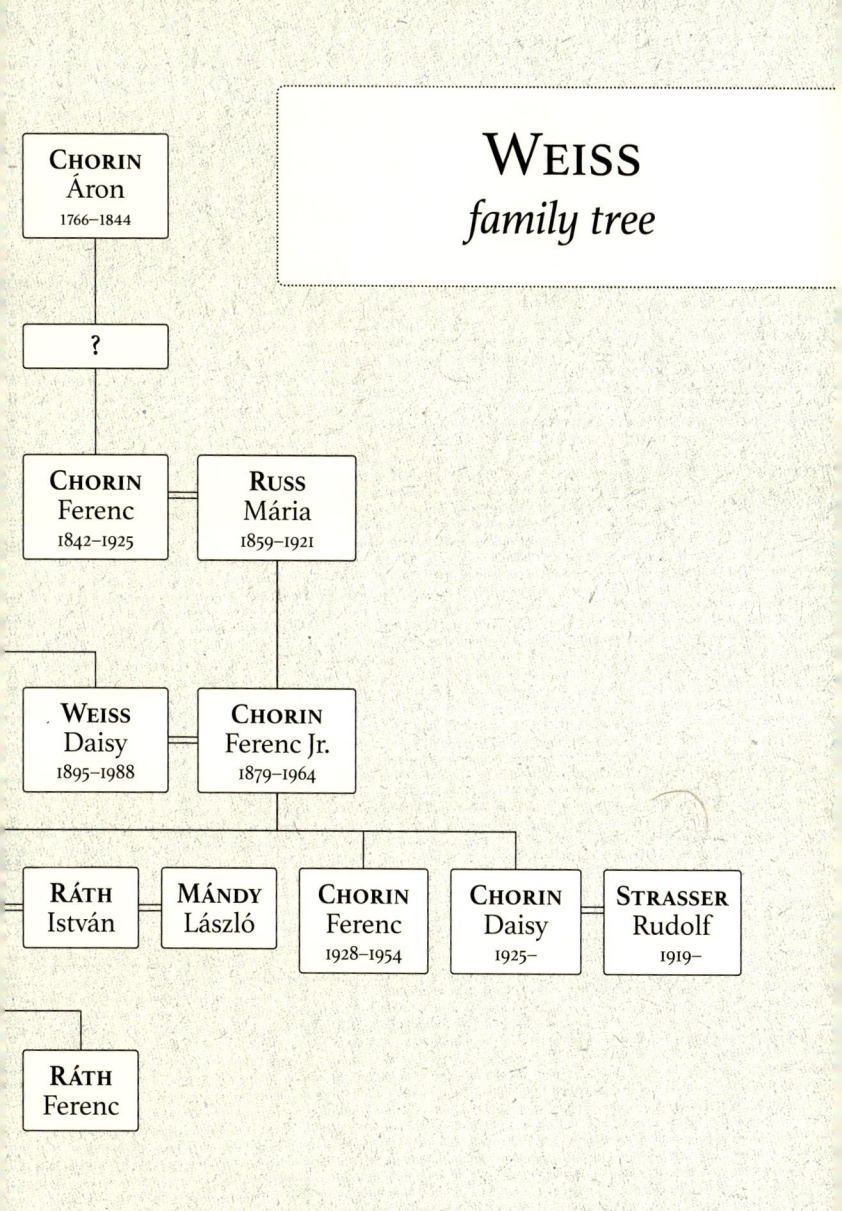

- **Chorin** Áron (1766–1844)
  - ?
    - **Chorin** Ferenc (1842–1925) — **Russ** Mária (1859–1921)
      - **Weiss** Daisy (1895–1988) — **Chorin** Ferenc Jr. (1879–1964)
        - **Ráth** István — **Mándy** László
          - **Ráth** Ferenc
        - **Chorin** Ferenc (1928–1954)
        - **Chorin** Daisy (1925–) — **Strasser** Rudolf (1919–)

Kornfeld
family tree

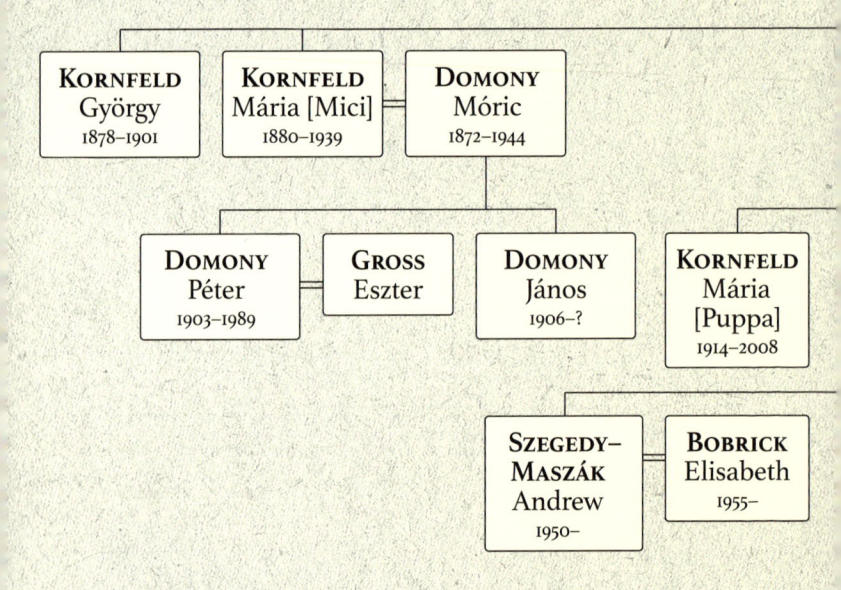

- **Kornfeld György** 1878–1901
- **Kornfeld Mária [Mici]** 1880–1939 — **Domony Móric** 1872–1944
  - **Domony Péter** 1903–1989 — **Gross Eszter**
  - **Domony János** 1906–?
- **Kornfeld Mária [Puppa]** 1914–2008
  - **Szegedy-Maszák Andrew** 1950– — **Bobrick Elisabeth** 1955–

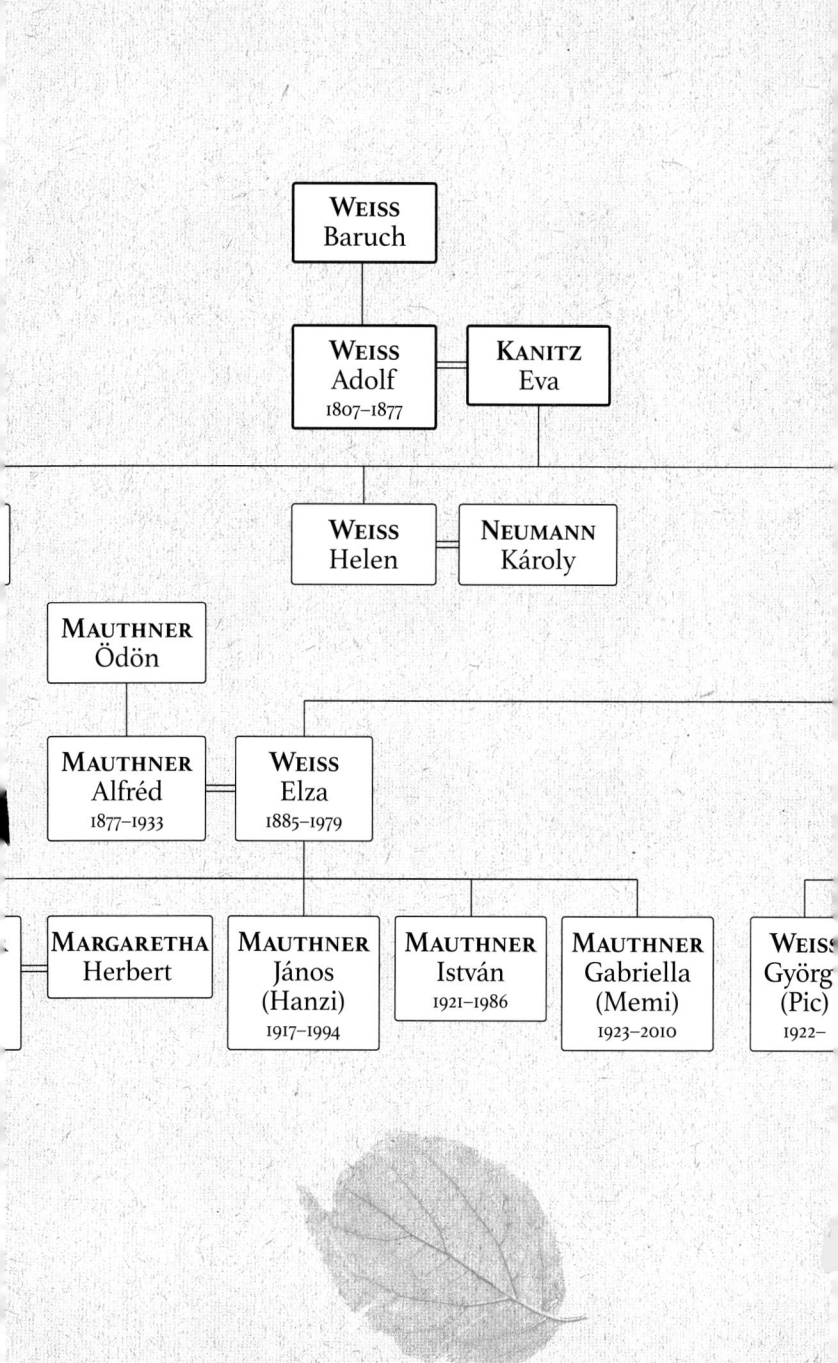

```
                              WEISS
                              Baruch
                                │
                    WEISS ═══ KANITZ
                    Adolf      Eva
                  1807–1877
                                │
                    WEISS ═══ NEUMANN
                    Helen     Károly
```

MAUTHNER
Ödön
│
MAUTHNER ═══ WEISS
Alfréd   Elza
1877–1933   1885–1979

| MARGARETHA | MAUTHNER | MAUTHNER | MAUTHNER | WEISS |
| Herbert | János (Hanzi) 1917–1994 | István 1921–1986 | Gabriella (Memi) 1923–2010 | György (Pic) 1922– |

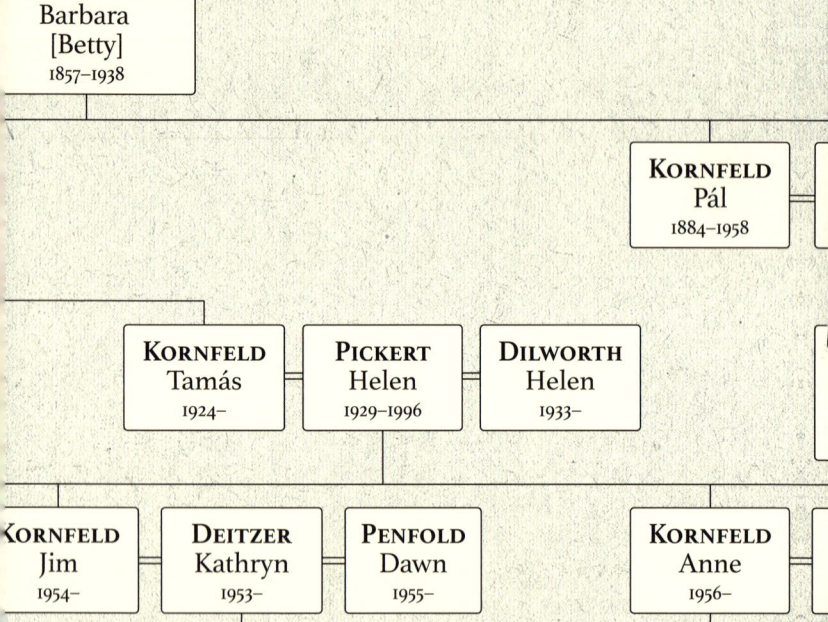

Frankfurter
Barbara
[Betty]
1857–1938

Kornfeld
Pál
1884–1958

Kornfeld
Tamás
1924–

Pickert
Helen
1929–1996

Dilworth
Helen
1933–

Kornfeld
Jim
1954–

Deitzer
Kathryn
1953–

Penfold
Dawn
1955–

Kornfeld
Anne
1956–

Kornfeld
Nathan
1985–

Kornfeld
Jacob
1989–

Smith
Moses

Smith
Sharon

Smith
Daniel

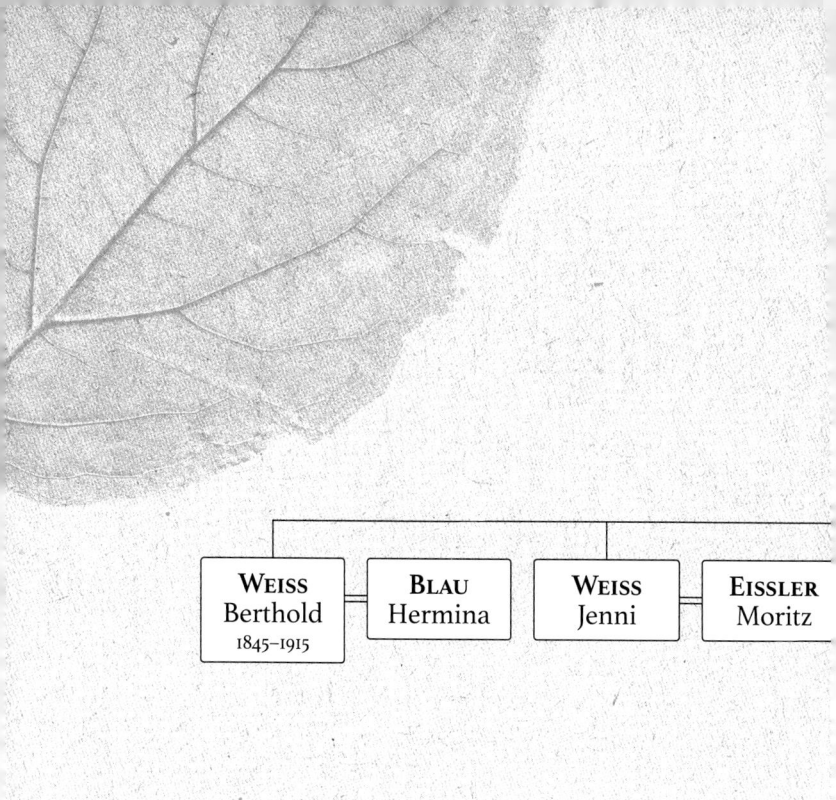

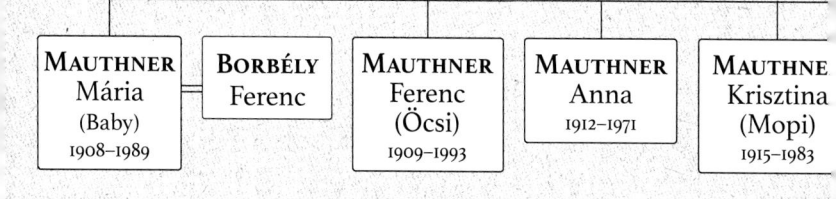

| **WEISS** Berthold 1845–1915 | **BLAU** Hermina | **WEISS** Jenni | **EISSLER** Moritz |

| **MAUTHNER** Mária (Baby) 1908–1989 | **BORBÉLY** Ferenc | **MAUTHNER** Ferenc (Öcsi) 1909–1993 | **MAUTHNER** Anna 1912–1971 | **MAUTHNE[R]** Krisztina (Mopi) 1915–1983 |

The family tree was composed from existing documentary material and secondary sources by Ágnes Széchenyi. The family tree is not complete and in order to make it easier for the reader to follow some of the ancestors and descendants have been omitted.

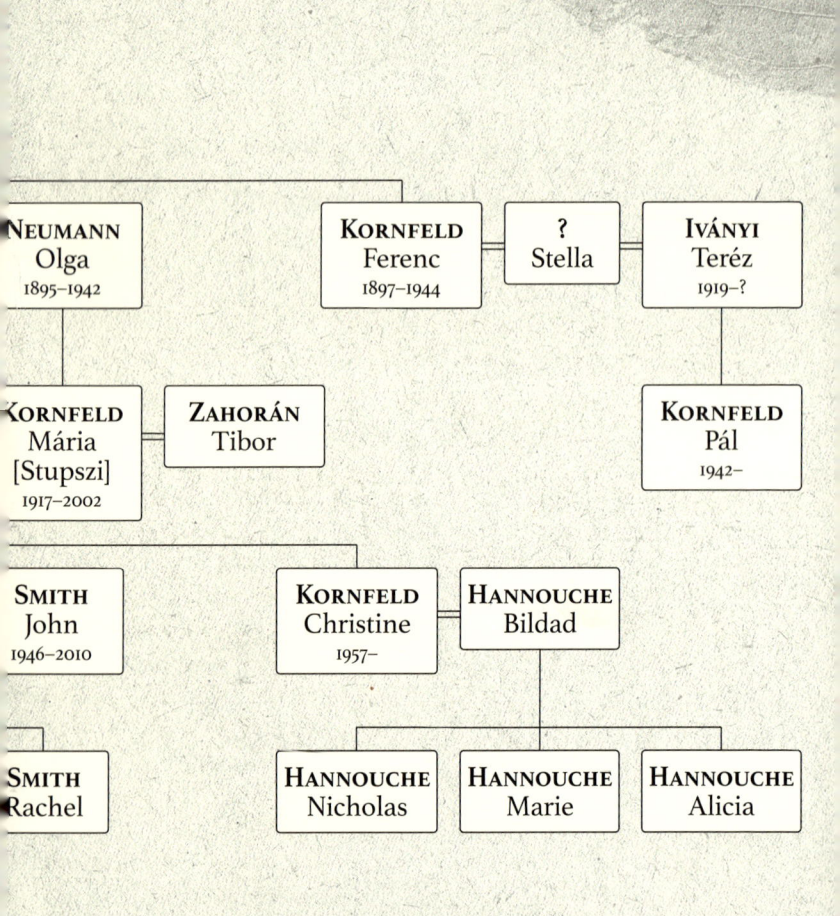

Neumann Olga 1895–1942	**Kornfeld** Ferenc 1897–1944	**?** Stella	**Iványi** Teréz 1919–?	

Kornfeld Mária [Stupszi] 1917–2002 — **Zahorán** Tibor

Kornfeld Pál 1942–

Smith John 1946–2010 — **Kornfeld** Christine 1957– — **Hannouche** Bildad

Smith Rachel

Hannouche Nicholas | **Hannouche** Marie | **Hannouche** Alicia

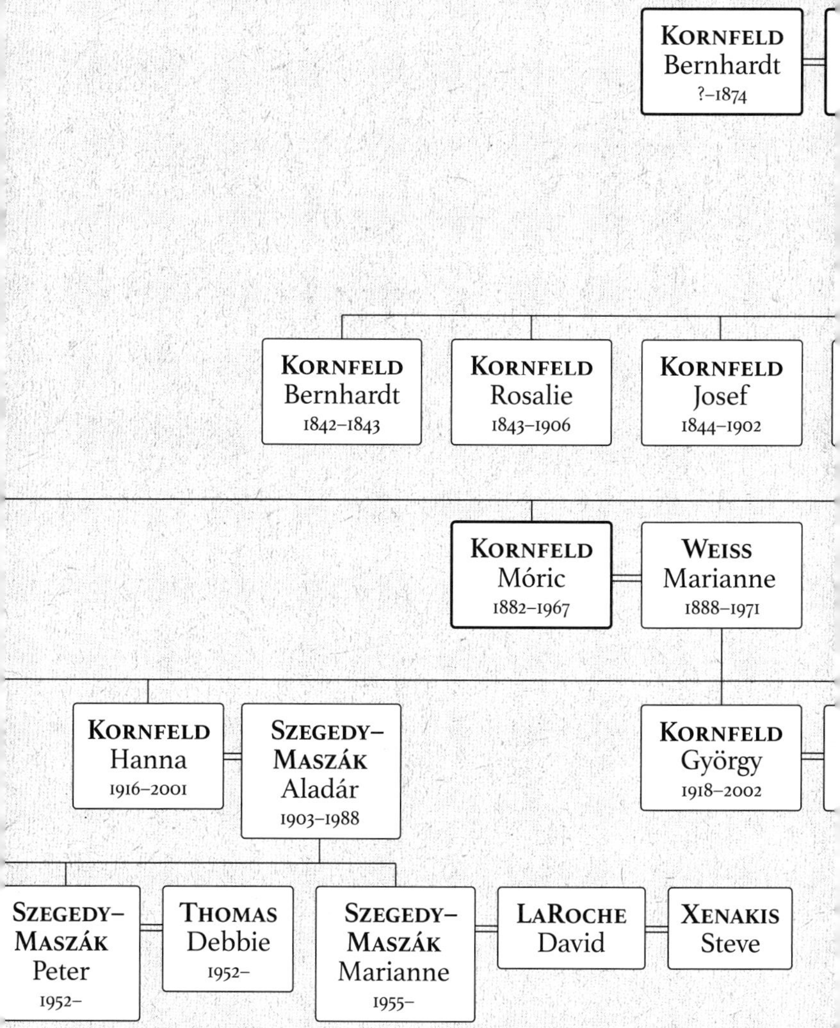
KORNFELD Bernhardt ?–1874
KORNFELD Bernhardt 1842–1843
KORNFELD Rosalie 1843–1906
KORNFELD Josef 1844–1902
KORNFELD Móric 1882–1967
WEISS Marianne 1888–1971
KORNFELD Hanna 1916–2001
SZEGEDY-MASZÁK Aladár 1903–1988
KORNFELD György 1918–2002
SZEGEDY-MASZÁK Peter 1952–
THOMAS Debbie 1952–
SZEGEDY-MASZÁK Marianne 1955–
LAROCHE David
XENAKIS Steve

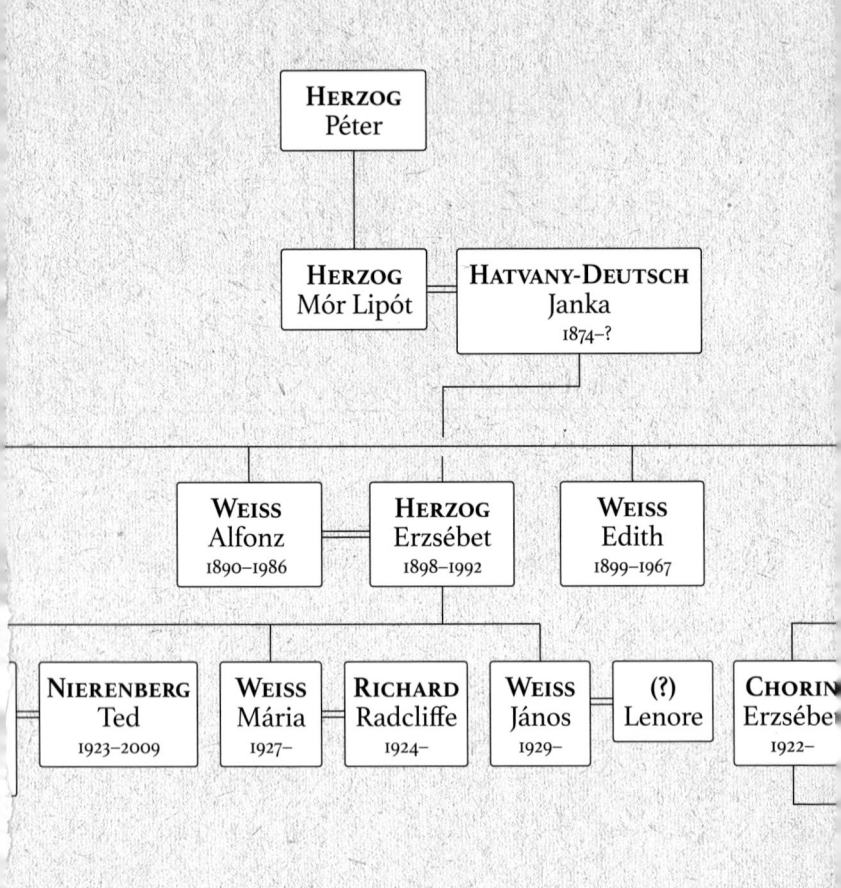

```
HERZOG
Péter
│
HERZOG ══ HATVANY-DEUTSCH
Mór Lipót    Janka
             1874–?
│
├─────────────┬─────────────┐
WEISS ══ HERZOG      WEISS
Alfonz   Erzsébet    Edith
1890–1986 1898–1992  1899–1967
│
├──────────┬──────────┬──────────┬──────────┬──────────┐
NIERENBERG  WEISS    RICHARD    WEISS ══ (?)      CHORIN
Ted         Mária    Radcliffe  János    Lenore   Erzsébet
1923–2009   1927–    1924–      1929–             1922–
```

deWAHL Albert

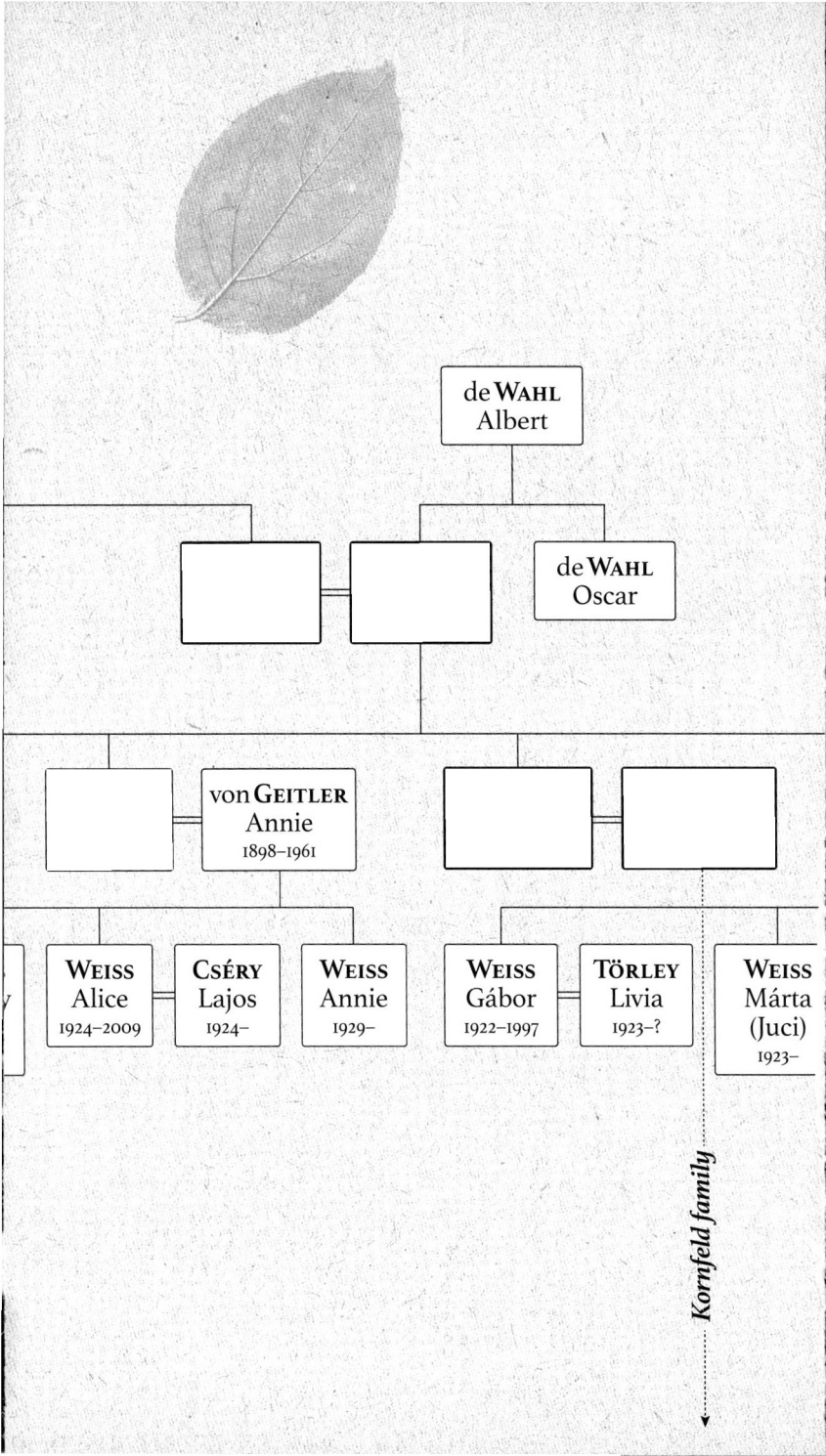

deWAHL Oscar

vonGEITLER Annie
1898–1961

WEISS Alice
1924–2009

CSÉRY Lajos
1924–

WEISS Annie
1929–

WEISS Gábor
1922–1997

TÖRLEY Livia
1923–?

WEISS Márta (Juci)
1923–

Kornfeld family

ROSENBACHER
Theresa
(?–1857)

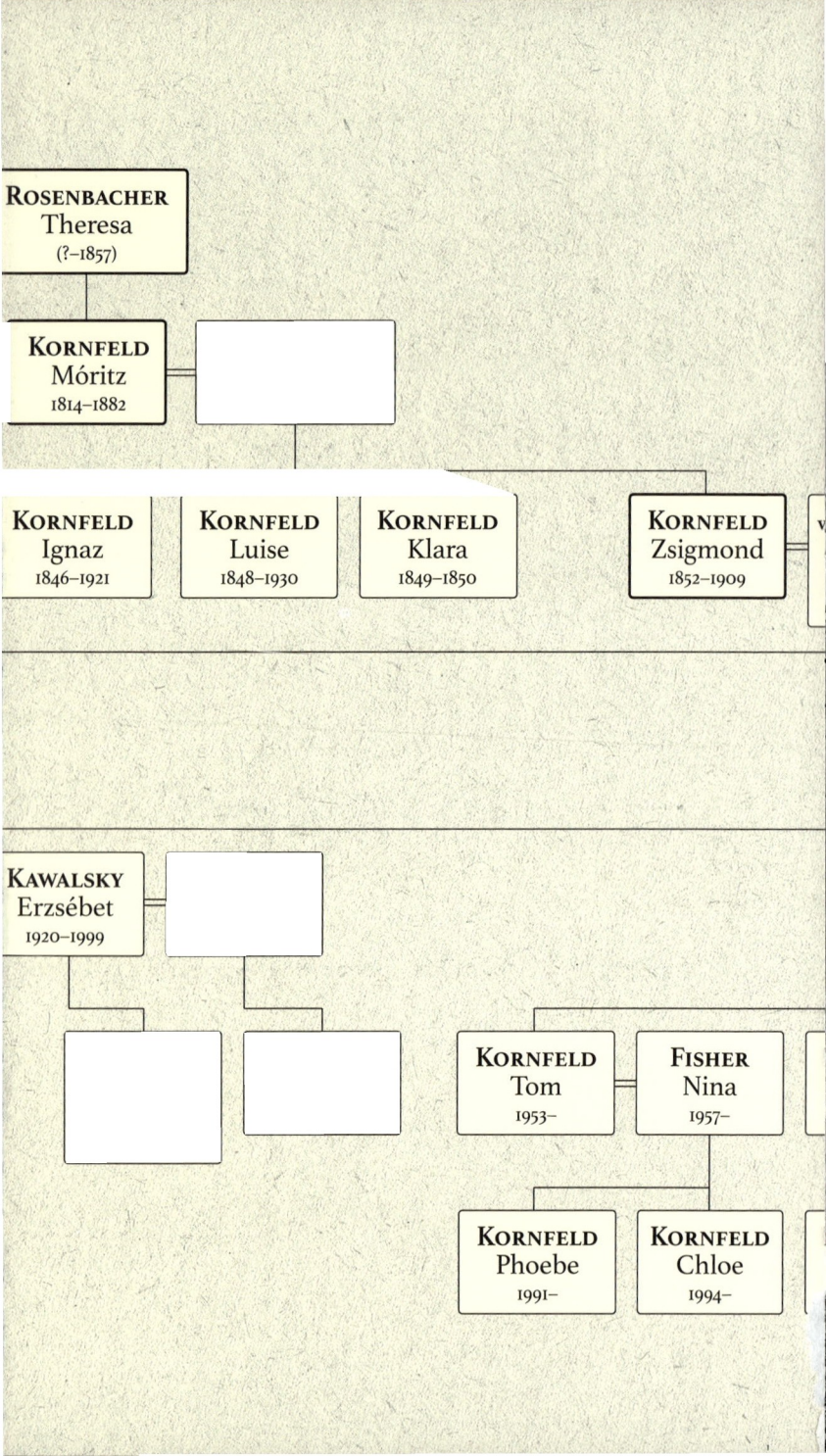

KORNFELD
Móritz
1814–1882

KORNFELD
Ignaz
1846–1921

KORNFELD
Luise
1848–1930

KORNFELD
Klara
1849–1850

KORNFELD
Zsigmond
1852–1909

KAWALSKY
Erzsébet
1920–1999

KORNFELD
Tom
1953–

FISHER
Nina
1957–

KORNFELD
Phoebe
1991–

KORNFELD
Chloe
1994–